Humanitarian Intervention in Contemporary Conflict

A Reconceptualization

To all those who work for the good of humanity
in the appalling conditions of contemporary
conflict

Humanitarian Intervention in Contemporary Conflict

A Reconceptualization

Oliver Ramsbotham
Tom Woodhouse

Polity Press

First published in 1996 by Polity Press in association with Blackwell Publishers Ltd.

2 4 6 8 9 10 7 5 3 1

Editorial office:
Polity Press
65 Bridge Street
Cambridge CB2 1UR, UK

Marketing and production:
Blackwell Publishers Ltd
108 Cowley Road
Oxford OX4 1JF, UK

Blackwell Publishers Inc.
238 Main Street
Cambridge, MA 02142, USA

ISBN 0-7456-1510-4
ISBN 0-7456-1511-2 (pbk)

A CIP catalogue record for this book is available from the British Library and the Library of Congress.

Typeset in 10 on 11.5 pt Sabon
by Best-set Typesetter Ltd, Hong Kong
Printed in Great Britain by Hartnolls Ltd, Bodmin, Cornwall

This book is printed on acid-free paper.

Whatsoever therefore is consequent to a time of war, where every man is enemy to every man; the same is consequent to the time, wherein men live without other security, than what their own strength, and their own invention shall furnish them withall. In such condition, there is no place for industry; because the fruit thereof is uncertain: and consequently no culture of the earth, no navigation, nor use of the commodities that may be imported by sea; no commodious building; no instruments of moving, and removing such things as require much force; no knowledge of the face of the earth; no account of time; no arts; no letters; no society; and which is worst of all, continual fear, and danger of violent death; and the life of man, solitary, poor, nasty, brutish, and short.

It may peradventure be thought that there was never such a time nor condition of war as this; and I believe it was never generally so, over all the world, but there are many places where they live so now.

It may be perceived what manner of life there would be, where there were no common power to fear, by the manner of life which men that have formerly lived under a powerful government, degenerate into in a civil war.

Thomas Hobbes, *Leviathan*

Contents

List of Boxes

List of Diagrams

Preface

This book is about the response of the international community to humanitarian crises. Since the end of the cold war the context for humanitarian intervention has changed. According to Médecins Sans Frontières' *Life, Death and Aid* (Jean (ed.), 1993), the ten most pressing humanitarian crises of the 1990s are all in conflict zones. Unlike the cold war period, when the most debated cases involved oppression by over-strong governments (for example, Indian intervention in East Pakistan in 1971, Vietnamese intervention in Kampuchea in 1978–9, Tanzanian intervention in Uganda in 1978–9), now it is usually a case of over-weak governments (for example, in areas where sovereignty is contested or has collapsed, as in Sudan, Afghanistan, Tajikistan, the Caucasus, Liberia, Angola, Rwanda, Bosnia and Somalia). In these situations the impact is felt in communities where human rights are denied (famine, displacement, etc.) or violated (ethnic cleansing, genocide, etc.).

The terms of the debate about humanitarian intervention have consequently changed. Instead of being a matter of self-help by states, as during the cold war, it is now mainly about collective response through the United Nations. Instead of a primary emphasis on forcible intervention, it is now more a case of trying to understand how what we call non-forcible military options (peacekeeping) and non-military options (broadly, humanitarian assistance) should be brought into play in response to these crises. Although enforcement lies at one end of the scale of possibilities, the main role of military forces in these situations is 'the establishment of a secure environment for non-military operations, such as electoral monitoring, refugee repatriation, and the distribution of humanitarian relief supplies by civilian agencies' (Berdal, 1993, 11). Similarly, the conclusion of William Durch's *The Evolution of UN Peacekeeping* is that 'peacekeeping was devised to untangle warring states but has evolved to assist suffering peoples' (1993, 474). In the wake of disillusionment in Bosnia and the débâcle in Somalia, which prompted a strong reaction, especially in the United States, against UN initiatives in humanitarian intervention – indeed, against humanitarian relief in conflict regions altogether – this option is now in question. However, as subsequent inaction in Rwanda showed, non-intervention is also a questionable option. Nor is there usually a forcible 'quick military fix'. There are no easy answers. This book addresses these issues by means of a reconceptualization of humanitarian intervention, and argues that prevailing, classic, 'narrow' definitions are inadequate in the contemporary context of post-cold war conflict.

The current literature on humanitarian intervention falls into two broad categories. There are books written primarily from the perspective of international relief organizations, and there are those which still focus on the traditional 'narrow' issue of military intervention by states. The burgeoning literature on 'wider peacekeeping' to some extent bridges the two. This book brings both literatures together, thus allowing a more comprehensive – and, it is claimed, a more accurate and realistic – assessment of the nature of the humanitarian challenge and of the range of appropriate responses.

Part I sets the scene for the subsequent reconceptualization in Part II. Chapter 1 offers a more thorough account of humanitarianism than has been usual in the literature about forcible humanitarian intervention during the cold war. This is important in view of the expanded range of humanitarian action now undertaken by humanitarian interveners in the post-cold war world. Chapter 2 reviews the classical debate about humanitarian intervention for comparison with what follows. Chapter 3 describes the contemporary conflict environment, which both makes the question of humanitarian intervention such an urgent one for the international community, and confronts would-be interveners with such severe difficulties when they attempt to respond. In chapter 4 the suggested reconceptualization is outlined and applied, and is compared with application of the traditional concepts of forcible humanitarian intervention described in chapter 2. Chapter 5 maps the key areas of debate which are opened up as a result. The traditional debate on forcible humanitarian intervention is not lost, but is shown to be a special case within a broader range of issues. Part III offers two comparative case-studies, of international humanitarian intervention in Bosnia and Somalia through to the end of 1994. The book was already in production by the time of the critical events in Bosnia in the latter half of 1995, but, in the view of the authors, these do not affect the substance of the reconceptualization offered. Finally, in the Conclusion, the overall argument in Part II is related back to the realist, pluralist and solidarist arguments analysed in chapter 2, and the significance of the whole debate for the evolution of an adequate international response to unacceptable denial or violation of basic human rights and needs is outlined. A set of general framework principles for humanitarian intervention, non-forcible and non-military as well as forcible, is deduced from the sets of criteria proposed by both advocates and critics of various forms of humanitarian intervention.

What follows, then, is an analysis of humanitarian intervention which attempts to clarify the terms of the debate and to modernize the concept in line with experience and practice between the passing of Security Council Resolution 688 in April 1991 and the withdrawal of UNOSOM II from Somalia, completed early in 1995. The book is written primarily for undergraduate and postgraduate students in international relations, security studies, conflict studies, peace studies and related fields.

Bradford, West Yorkshire, March 1995

Acknowledgements

With grateful thanks to Tammy Duffey for expert handling of the manuscript from draft to final form and to Nick Lewer for co-writing the paper from which this book developed and for shared planning, research and criticism thereafter. Thanks also to the members of the Conflict Resolution Research Seminars of the Centre for Conflict Resolution (Department of Peace Studies), who provided a lively and supportive environment in which the ideas that led to this book took shape. Finally, thanks to our families for bearing with and understanding our preoccupation with this task – Meredith, Gill, Edward, Ben, Alexander, Tim, and Jenny.

Part I

The Classical Debate: Forcible Self-Help by States to Protect Human Rights

Introduction: Humanitarian Intervention in Uganda

1 An initial explanation of terms

During the cold war period the term 'humanitarian intervention' was generally understood to refer to the intersection of two discourses. One was conducted mainly in the language of human rights ('humanitarian'), the other in the language of state intervention ('intervention'). The threat to human rights was seen to come chiefly from tyrannical governments, and, in the absence of the possibility of collective intervention by regional organizations or the United Nations, state intervention was usually understood to involve forcible self-help by states (Lillich, 1967). The central question was this: if governments abused their authority by flagrant mass violations of the basic human rights of their citizens, should other governments intervene militarily to remedy the situation?

This definition of humanitarian intervention as forcible self-help by states to protect human rights is still regarded by a number of commentators as the correct usage in international law and state practice. For example, Wil Verwey defines humanitarian intervention as

> [t]he threat or use of force by a state or states abroad, for the sole purpose of preventing or putting a halt to a serious violation of fundamental human rights, in particular the right to life of persons, regardless of their nationality, such protection taking place neither upon authorization by relevant organs of the United Nations nor with permission by the legitimate government of the target state. (Verwey, 1992, 114)

Others, still within what we are calling the 'classical tradition', use a somewhat broader definition. There are two main variants here: first, the inclusion of forcible action by international organizations, as well as action 'by a state or states' (Brownlie, 1974, 217); second, the inclusion of other forms of coercion in addition to the 'threat or use of [military] force' – for example, 'substantial debilitating economic coercion' (Donnelly, 1984, 311). In Part I, in line with the mainstream debate, we follow the restrictionists in confining attention to forcible self-help by states.

2 An example

An example of forcible humanitarian intervention, as defined above, would be the counter-invasion of Uganda by President Julius Nyerere of Tanzania at the end of 1978 and the subsequent ending of the murderous eight-year regime of Ugandan president Idi Amin in April 1979. Strictly speaking, we should call this a *putative* example of forcible humanitarian intervention, because, as in a number of similar cases, whether such an action qualifies as humanitarian intervention is part of what is at issue.

2.1 Provocation

Shortly after his successful *coup* in January 1971, the new president of Uganda, Idi Amin, embarked upon an increasingly vicious course of pogroms and executions against individuals and groups in his country. Some 75,000 Ugandan Asians were expelled in 1972 at 90 days' notice, a third of whom were Ugandan citizens. They were roughly treated, a number were killed, and most of their possessions were seized and distributed among the president's henchmen. In the years that followed, soldiers and civilians belonging to tribal groups other than Amin's, such as the Acholi and Lango, were arbitrarily massacred, political opponents liquidated, and elite and religious leaders annihilated. Whole villages were destroyed. The slaughter became wanton and random, largely perpetrated by army and security forces drawn from the president's own tribal group, the Kakwa, from Nubian Ugandans and from southern Sudanese mercenaries. The fact that the regime was sustained by foreign mercenaries invited comparisons with the worst cases of European imperialism. Estimates of the numbers killed during Amin's reign of terror vary between 100,000 and 500,000 (Amnesty International, 1983), with average figures around 300,000 (Kyemba, 1977). A United Nations report on refugees estimated that by the time Idi Amin was overthrown there were a million widows and orphans of murdered civilians in Uganda, an 'infinitely tragic proof of atrocities perpetrated upon the defenceless population by the armed forces and State Research Bureau' (UN Commission on Human Rights, 1981, quoted by Kuper, 1985, 132–3). Central precepts of international law were being flagrantly and persistently violated on a massive scale.

2.2 Absence of collective response

Between 1971 and 1978 the extravagant and telegenic figure of the Ugandan president was well known through the world's mass media, particularly in the West, where he was often portrayed more as a figure of fun than a vicious dictator. His activities were early brought to the attention of the United Nations Sub-Commission on the Prevention of Discrimination and the Protection of Minorities, which decided with reference to the expulsion of Ugandan Asians in 1972 that it could not even send a telegram of concern to the president. Reports of mounting atrocities multiplied. By 1974 David Martin's graphic description of the regime was published, and the International Commission of Jurists submitted a full report to the United Nations Secretary-General (International Commission of Jurists, 1974). Further complaints followed, and Amnesty International confirmed the charges in a submission to the United Nations Commission on Human Rights in 1977. In response, the United Nations Secretary-General asked President Amin to conduct an investigation himself, while the UN Commission on Human Rights (which included a Ugandan government representative) decided in 1977 to defer consideration to the following year. It was not until March 1978, under pressure particularly from the Nordic countries, that the commission finally decided to implement its ponderous investigation procedures. These had barely begun before Amin was toppled.

Contemplating this catalogue of inaction in the face of what he termed 'political mass murder' akin to genocide (sometimes called 'politicide'), Leo Kuper, writing in 1981, concluded that 'the sovereign territorial state claims, as an integral part of its sovereignty, the right to commit genocide, or engage in genocidal massacres against peoples under its rule, and . . . the United Nations, for all practical purposes, defends this right' (p. 161). He continued:

> The performance of the United Nations Organization in the suppression of the crime of genocide is deeply disillusioning, particularly against the background of the humanitarian ideals which inspired its founding, and which the organization continues to proclaim – ideals in which the suppression of war, of crimes against humanity and of genocide were quite central. But of course the United Nations is not a humanitarian, but a political organization, and its humanitarian goals are at the play of political forces, pressure

groups and blocks, in an area where delegates pursue the divisive interests of the states they represent. Added to this, its ideological commitment to the protection of the sovereignty of the state, with the corollary of non-intervention in its domestic affairs, stands in the way of effective action against 'domestic' (internal) genocide. And above all, it is the rulers of the states of the world who gather together at the United Nations, and it is mainly, though not exclusively, the rulers who engage in genocide. (Kuper, 1981, 175–6)

What was true of the United Nations also applied to the Organization of African Unity (OAU), which met in Kampala, the Ugandan capital, for its twelfth annual summit during Amin's 1975–6 chairmanship, thus adding international respectability to his regime. Three governments boycotted the meeting, including that of Tanzania, which declared that it could not accept 'the responsibility for participating in the mockery of condemning colonialism, apartheid and fascism in the headquarters of a murderer, a black fascist and a self-confessed admirer of fascism' (International Commission of Jurists, 1977, 106–7). When, after the Tanzanian intervention, Nigeria and Morocco expressed concern that the Tanzanian action might set a dangerous precedent, President Nyerere answered that, in the absence of a collective willingness by the OAU to condemn or punish a ruler such as Amin, 'then each country has to look after itself' (Tesón, 1988, 166).

2.3 Recourse to self-help

The stage was thus set for forcible self-help, which was finally triggered by the ill-advised Ugandan occupation of the Kagera salient in Tanzania in October 1978, probably an unpremeditated adventure to cover the fact that Amin loyalists had pursued Ugandan mutineers across the border. There was widespread destruction, and numbers of Tanzanians were killed. The OAU, in deference to the principle of non-interference, did not condemn the Ugandan action. President Nyerere, by contrast, determined not only to expel the invading forces, but to avenge the attack and make sure that it was not repeated. He declared that he had no claim on an inch of Ugandan territory, and in the local language appealed over the radio to the Ugandan people to overthrow the tyrant. On 9 December, Tanzanian Independence Day, he denounced Amin for having killed more black Africans than Southern Rhodesia and South Africa. Despite Soviet military equipment, help from Libya and some Palestinians, and diplomatic support from Kenya and Nigeria, Amin was clearly in a desperate position, and sued for peace. Nyerere was implacable, however, and on 10 April 1979 Kampala fell to a combined force of Ugandan exiles and Tanzanian troops. Amin fled, and a new regime was installed under Jusuf Lule as head of a government of national unity (C. Thomas, 1985, 90–108).

Assessment of the Tanzanian action as an example of forcible humanitarian intervention will be considered in chapter 2. Opponents of forcible humanitarian intervention denied that self-help of this kind was genuinely humanitarian, condemning it as a breach of international law. Proponents of forcible humanitarian intervention, on the other hand, applauded the Tanzanian initiative, and urged that similar action be taken in the far more numerous cases where gross human rights abuse by governments went unchallenged. As we shall see, the ensuing debate went to the heart of the international system.

Before we attempt to come to grips with the question of forcible intervention in these circumstances, however, we must be clear what we mean by 'humanitarian'. This proves to be a more difficult task than we might at first suppose.

1
Humanitarianism, Human Rights and the International Community

1 Humanitarianism

For Wil Verwey, to count as 'humanitarian', a forcible intervention such as that of Tanzania in Uganda in 1978–9 must be 'for the sole purpose of preventing or putting a halt to a serious violation of fundamental human rights, in particular threats to the life of persons, regardless of their nationality' (1992, 114). Setting aside for a moment the strict stipulation that the purpose must be 'solely' humanitarian – a stipulation so strict that Verwey does not think that there have been any examples so far – how helpful is this identification of 'humanitarian' with concern to protect human rights? It is an identification which nearly all commentators on forcible humanitarian intervention during the cold war period made, so we will follow suit. But, before pursuing this line of enquiry, we would do well to look first at the broader language of humanitarianism to which the word 'humanitarian' properly belongs. This will be particularly useful for the reconceptualization undertaken in Part II.

Appeals to humanitarianism have become increasingly common in the post-1945 period. This was already evident in the wording of the UN Charter. For example, included among 'the purposes of the United Nations' is the aim of achieving 'international cooperation in solving international problems of a . . . humanitarian character' (United Nations Charter, 1945, Article 1(3)). Since then, 'considerations of humanity' have been increasingly widely recognized in international law, with references to 'principles or laws of humanity' proliferating in preambles to international conventions, in resolutions of the UN General Assembly, and, more generally, in recent diplomatic practice (Brownlie, 1990, 28). In a well-known ruling in 1949, the International Court of Justice (ICJ) acknowledged 'elementary considerations of humanity even more exacting in peace than in war' as 'general and well-recognised principles' of international law (ICJ Reports, *Corfu Channel* case (Merits), 1949, 22). Similar instances subsequently proliferated, so that by the time of the 1974–7 Diplomatic Conference on the Reaffirmation and Development of International Humanitarian Law it was concluded that 'considerations of humanity' were now grounded not just in 'natural law' or 'general principles of law recognised by civilised nations', as in the past, but more concretely on the foundation of what it called 'the principles of the UN Charter' (Macalister-Smith, 1985, 55).

But, despite all this, there is no general definition of humanitarianism in international law. It has developed piecemeal in a number of distinct but overlapping areas. As Bruce Nicholls remarks, 'a consistent and working definition of humanitarianism has evaded public and private authorities' (1987, 193). The Geneva Conventions, for example, assume, rather than explain, 'principles of humanity', while the International Court of Justice, when determining whether United States aid to the Nicaraguan Contra rebels counted as 'humanitarian' in 1986, did no more than refer vaguely to 'the purposes hallowed in the practice of the Red Cross' (noted in Minear and Weiss, 1993, 7). Such vagueness is clearly a disadvantage from the point of view of those wanting a comprehensive 'general law of humanitarian assistance' which will codify and sanction humanitarian practice, and drives some writers on humanitarian intervention to ask in exasperation, 'What on earth does the word "humanitarian" mean?' (Roberts, 1993b, 13). But it also has advantages. For example, the Independent Commission on International Humanitarian Issues, set up in 1983 in response to the 1981 UN General Assembly resolution on a new international humanitarian order, welcomed the loose generality of the term 'humanitarianism', recognized across different cultures. It was less closely identified with the Western tradition than the relatively more specific terminology of 'human rights', so helping to draw all world traditions 'into a broader and more international definition of humanitarianism' (Aga Khan, 1988, 156; Owen, 1993, 53).

In view of all this, the best strategy for pinning down what 'humanitarian' means is to approach the question obliquely. We will look at three of the main manifestations of humanitarian concern since 1945, and ask in each case how 'humanitarian' is understood by its practitioners. The three areas are (i) the international humanitarian law of armed conflict, (ii) the cluster of enterprises referred to as 'international humanitarian assistance', and (iii) what some call 'international human rights law'. These are also the three aspects of international humanitarian co-operation which are of most significance for the theme of this book, because they all come together in the crucible of humanitarian intervention in contemporary conflict. We begin with the first two, before moving on to focus mainly on the third for the rest of Part I.

1.1 International humanitarian law

The international humanitarian law of armed conflict – in United Nations terminology 'the law of armed conflict', in older just war language *jus in bello*, or war conduct law – is part of public international law, and is defined by the International Committee of the Red Cross as

> [i]nternational rules, established by treaties or custom, which are specifically intended to solve humanitarian problems directly arising from international or non-international armed conflicts, and which, for humanitarian reasons, limit the right of parties to a conflict to use the methods and means of warfare of their choice, or protect persons and property that are, or may be, affected by conflict. (Pictet, 1988, xxi)

A traditional distinction is usually made between (i) the law of the Hague (the law of war), which covers the reciprocal rights and duties of combatants, and (ii) the law of Geneva (humanitarian law properly so called), which aims to protect military personnel *hors de combat* (not fighting), such as prisoners or the wounded, and civilian noncombatants – sometimes called the 'innocent' in the just war tradition (McCoubrey, 1990, 1–2). Although the distinction is controversial and breaks down in detail, it will be taken as significant here. Hague law, initiated by the 1868 St Petersburg Declaration, draws on chivalric traditions of reciprocity among combatants (M. Keen, 1965; Johnson, 1981, 131–50). It emphasizes proportionality, military necessity, and the rights and duties of states. Geneva law, initiated by the 1864 Geneva Convention, is based not on reciprocity but on universal principles of humanity. It is what Karel Vasak calls 'objective law containing rules applicable to all elements of a society' (1988, 298). An exchange of prisoners of war would be an example of reciprocity. A demand that unlawfully imprisoned civilians be released would be an example of the application of universal principles of humanity. In addition to Hague and Geneva law, two further strands of international humanitarian law are sometimes distinguished: (iii) Nuremberg law, which embodies judgements from the Nuremberg and Tokyo international military tribunals of 1946 and 1947, and (iv) law embodied in other sources, including national military field manuals, such as the enlightened Lieber code (1865) in the United States. See box 1 for details of the evolution of Geneva law.

Box 1: The Evolution of International Humanitarian Law

1859 Henry Dunant witnesses destruction at Battle of Solferino.
1863 International Committee for the relief of military wounded formed in Geneva by Henry Dunant and committee of Swiss citizens.
1864 Diplomatic conference held in Geneva leads to 12 European countries signing Geneva Convention. Red cross on white background adopted as symbol.
1867 First International Conference of the Red Cross. Red crescent also adopted as symbol.
1899 Adaptation to maritime warfare of the principles of the Geneva Convention of 1864.
1906 Revision and development of Geneva Convention of 1864.
1907 Adaptation to maritime warfare of the principles of the Geneva Convention of 1906 (Convention no. X of the Hague).
1919 League of Red Cross Societies established.
1928 Statutes of International Red Cross promulgated.
1929 Revision and development of Geneva Conventions of 1906.
1949 Four Geneva Conventions adopted (now ratified by 181 states):
   I: For the amelioration of the condition of the wounded and sick in armed forces in the field.
   II: For the amelioration of the condition of wounded, sick and shipwrecked members of armed forces at sea.
   III: Relative to the treatment of prisoners of war.
   IV: Relative to the protection of civilian persons in time of war.
1952 Revision of the Statutes of the International Red Cross.
1965 Proclamation of the seven fundamental principles of the Red Cross (*humanity, impartiality, neutrality, independence, voluntary service, unity, universality*).
1977 Protocols additional to the Geneva Conventions of 1949 adopted:
   I: Protection of victims of international armed conflicts.
   II: Protection of victims of non-international armed conflicts.
1983 League of Red Cross Societies becomes League of Red Cross and Red Crescent Societies.

At the heart of international humanitarian law lie principles which, in Geoffrey Best's words, embody 'the assertion of values different from those of the warrior' (1994, 374). What are these values? In order to pin them down, we cannot do better than see how they are specified by the organization largely responsible for the existence of Geneva law in the first place – the Red Cross. But first we will expand our field of enquiry to include the second main manifestation of humanitarian concern – the wide and disparate area of activity known as international humanitarian assistance – because, since 1945 (and particularly since the 1967–70 Biafran war), the Red Cross has itself been increasingly active in progressively extending its relief work beyond the original context of inter-state war into humanitarian crisis in general. Red Cross principles are now broadly shared by the wider humanitarian community.

1.2 International humanitarian assistance

International humanitarian relief or assistance is concerned with the immediate needs of victims of natural or political disasters, not necessarily in war zones and not necessarily connected with explicit violations of human rights. Yet the 'three legal pillars of international protection' include international humanitarian law and human rights law as well as refugee law (Tomasevski, 1994, 82). International humanitarian assistance is thus linked to the international law of armed conflict through the work of the Red Cross and to human rights law through Article 25 of the Universal Declaration of Human Rights, which recognizes a right to 'food, clothing, housing and medical care' in crisis situations, although it is at the same time distinct from both. In its classic form, humanitarian assistance is confined to organized refugee, hunger and relief efforts designed to bring immediate aid to those who are suffering in humanitarian crises or emergencies, as against longer-term, more structural concern for development – although this relationship is controversial. A splendid guide to post-war attempts to codify humanitarian practice in this field is Peter Macalister-Smith's *International Humanitarian Assistance – Disaster Relief Actions in International Law and Organization* (1985). As he notes, 'there is at present no international body of law relating specifically and exclusively to humanitarian assistance beyond the context of armed conflict' (p. 52). Whether there should be is beyond the brief of this book. In lieu of formal codification, the effort has been rather to fill out and co-ordinate national and international relief efforts, the setting up of the office of the UN High Commissioner for Refugees (UNHCR) in 1950–1, the UN Disaster Relief Co-ordinator in 1971, and the UN Department of Humanitarian Affairs (DHA) in 1991–2 continuing where the pre-war effort to set up an International Relief Union (1927) under the aegis of the League of Nations had largely failed. See box 2 for details of the development of the machinery of international humanitarian assistance.

The UN High Commissioner for Refugees (UNHCR) was entrusted by the UN General Assembly, via the founding statute, with an explicitly humanitarian, not political, brief. Insistence on this critical conceptual distinction was characteristic of the international humanitarian efforts sponsored through the UN General Assembly and the UN Economic and Social Council (ECOSOC), by contrast with the political dimensions of UN Security Council activity. But, as we will see in Part II, this distinction has been progressively, if problematically, eroded, particularly since Security Council Resolution 688 of 6 April 1991 concerning humanitarian provision in Iraq at the end of the January–February 1991 war. In 1951 the UNHCR had responsibility for some 2 million refugees. It coordinated humanitarian assistance in general up to the time of the severe

---

Box 2: International Refugee Relief and Humanitarian Assistance: Establishment of Instruments and Agents

1914	Committee for Relief in Belgium (CRB)
1921	Fridtjof Nansen appointed High Commissioner for Russian Refugees
1927	International Relief Union
1943–7	UN Relief and Rehabilitation Administration (UNRRA)
1945	Food and Agriculture Organization (FAO)
1946	UN International Children's Emergency Fund (UNICEF)
1946	World Health Organization (WHO)
1947–52	International Refugee Organization (IRO)
1951	UN High Commissioner for Refugees (UNHCR): Statute (1950), Convention (1951)
1963	World Food Programme (WFP)
1965	UN Development Programme (UNDP)
1971	UN General Assembly Resolution 2816: UN Disaster Relief Coordinator
1988	UN General Assembly Resolution 43/131 (see p. 83)
1990	UN General Assembly Resolution 45/100 (see p. 83)
1991	UN General Assembly Resolution 46/182: Emergency Relief Co-ordinator and Department of Humanitarian Affairs (DHA)

1971 East Pakistan crisis, when the sudden influx of 10 million refugees into West Bengal precipitated a radical overhaul. Since 1971, increasingly strenuous efforts have been made to improve relief co-ordination, culminating in the formation of the Department of Humanitarian Affairs (DHA) in 1991, which will be discussed in Part II. It should be remembered that bilateral government–government humanitarian assistance remained the most important channel of aid in many if not most cases. Also important were inter-governmental organizations (IGOs) and, increasingly, non-governmental organizations (NGOs), acting under Article 71 of the UN Charter. (In the United States NGOs are known as private voluntary organizations (PVOs).) NGOs became particularly prominent from the time of the 1967–70 Biafran war, which, being a civil war, proved a severe test for Common Article 3 of the 1949 Geneva Conventions. NGOs, their activities in many cases co-ordinated through Joint Church Aid, were conspicuous in Nigeria despite government obstruction – a harbinger of the kind of intrusive activity which was to become increasingly familiar during the 1970s and 1980s, and which provides much of the substance for the reconceptualization of humanitarian intervention undertaken in Part II.

1.3 Humanitarian principles

What are the core values which underlie international humanitarian law and the diverse enterprises of international humanitarian assistance? What is it that imbues the former with a spirit markedly different from that of Geoffrey Best's warrior, and that serves to mark out the latter as 'humanitarian', not 'political', thereby maximizing international support? For an answer, we turn to the statutes and principles of the Red Cross (see Box 3).

The values which imbue Red Cross humanitarianism are encapsulated in the seven 'fundamental principles' adopted in 1965. They are described as 'an inspiration and a guide for all the movement's humanitarian activities' (*International Review of the Red Cross*, Nov.–Dec. 1984, 328–30). In fact, we will omit three of them, independence, voluntary service and unity (nos 4, 5 and 6), because they apply more narrowly to the inner integrity of the movement itself, and complete this part of our enquiry with reference to the other four: humanity, impartiality, neutrality and universality (nos 1, 2, 3 and 7) (Pictet, 1979).

1.3.1 The principle of humanity.

'The Red Cross, born of a desire to bring assistance without discrimination to the wounded on the battle-

---

Box 3: The Red Cross Movement

The international Red Cross movement is a complex entity, made up, in David Forsythe's phrase, of 'two heads and many arms'. The two 'heads' are the all-Swiss International Committee of the Red Cross (ICRC), responsible for launching the movement in the 1860s, and the League of Red Cross Societies (now Red Cross and Red Crescent Societies), formed after the First World War as a federation of national members. The relationship between the two has at times been acrimonious. The 'arms' are the many national Red Cross and Red Crescent societies. The two heads and all the arms, together with the states which are party to the Geneva Conventions, meet at the International Conference of the Red Cross (Forsythe, 1977, 5). The 600 or so articles which make up the four 1949 Geneva Conventions and the two 1977 Additional Protocols 'incarnate the very ideal of the Red Cross', whose International Committee did so much to bring them about (Pictet, 1988, xxi; Boissier, 1985). In addition, in default of the neutral 'protecting powers' which were supposed to safeguard the interests of those protected under the Conventions, the ICRC was asked to assume these 'humanitarian functions'. It was also mandated to 'work for the faithful application [of international humanitarian law]' by the Red Cross/Red Crescent movement itself (Article 5(2c), Statutes of the International Red Cross and Red Crescent Movement). The ICRC is the only international relief organization apart from UNHCR with a mandate under international law. It has a right to initiate action.

---

field, endeavours . . . to prevent and alleviate human suffering wherever it may be found. Its purpose is to protect life and health and to ensure respect for the human being.'

Here is the heart of humanitarianism – concern for the interests and welfare of human beings, particularly those who are threatened or suffering. This is the spirit of Henry Dunant, founder of the Red Cross, who in 1859 contemplated with horror the unspeakable agony of the battlefield of Solferino, on which 38,000 men lay dead or wounded after 15 hours of fighting, and determined to devote himself to the organization of relief (Dunant, 1986/1862). It was a direct response to the desperate need of victims, which recognized the common humanity that lies beneath political divisions even in war. In the words of the great Swiss jurist Emerich de Vattel, whose monumental *Le Droit des Gens* (The Law of Nations) has inspired humanitarians for more than 200 years: 'Let us never forget that our enemies are men' (1758, bk III, sect. 158). In the same spirit, those who violate the laws of war or of humanity cannot plead politics. Their actions are crimes against humanity itself. As Francis Lieber, inspired creator of the 1865 *General Order No. 100: Instructions for the Government of Armies of the United States in the Field*, put it, unnecessary infliction of suffering on the battlefield 'remains cruelty, as among private individuals', and is to be treated as criminal (Johnson, 1981, 299).

1.3.2 The principle of impartiality.   'The Red Cross makes no discrimination as to nationality, race, religious beliefs, class or political opinions. It endeavours to relieve the suffering of individuals, being guided solely by their needs, and to give priority to the most urgent cases of distress.'

This principle, often confused with the principle of neutrality, emphasizes non-discrimination in responding to need. It is a core value, enshrined in Article 3, common to the four 1949 Geneva Conventions, and in Article 75 of the 1977 Additional Protocol I, which lays down that protection is to be afforded 'without any adverse distinction based upon race, colour, sex, language, religion or belief, political or other opinion, national or social origin, wealth, birth or other status, or any other similar criteria'. To L. C. Green, these articles encapsulate the essence of humanitarian principles, and 'amount to the basic and minimum conditions underlying the rule of law as understood in modern society' (1993, 328). It is human beings as human beings, of equal worth and value, who are the objects of humanitarian concern. We may also note the corollary: that response is to be prioritized in terms of need alone, a stipulation to which we will return in Part II.

1.3.3 The principle of neutrality.   'In order to continue to enjoy the confidence of all, the Red Cross may not take sides in hostilities or engage at any time in controversies of a political, racial, religious or ideological nature.'

This is another principle which will be of critical concern in Part II. The stipulation that humanitarianism must be non-political is seen to be crucial to the effective carrying through of humanitarian activities and, indeed, to their definition as humanitarian: 'the entire body of international humanitarian law is based on the idea that it is possible to separate humanitarian concerns from political concerns and thereby persuade the parties to a conflict to maintain both a modicum of dialogue in the humanitarian sphere and a manner of conduct that serves not only the interests of the victims of the fighting but their own interests as well' (Sandoz, 1993, 2). Neutrality was mentioned in four of the ten articles of the original 1864 Geneva Convention (Best, 1994, 374). Yet the whole idea of separating 'humanitarian' from 'political' action is both conceptually and practically ambivalent. David Forsythe has distinguished between 'realpolitik' (international power politics), 'partisan politics' (national factional politics) and 'humanitarian politics' ('the struggle to implement humanitarian values as official policy in the nations of the world') (1977, 1–2). The ICRC is certainly engaged in the latter. It is as true to say that humanitarian ends can only be achieved through politics as that they can only be achieved by separating them from it. Beyond this, Forsythe further distinguishes three types of humanitarian political engagement: 'impartial humanitarianism' (based on consent from public authorities with little or no overt criticism of their behaviour – the ICRC and UNHCR approach), 'international humanitarianism' (which mixes co-operative and conflictual styles – the approach of most NGOs and UN humanitarian actors) and 'revolutionary humanitarianism' (which disregards the wishes and legal claims of public authorities – the approach of some NGOs and, in extreme form, as armed intervention, some states) (1977, 227). The ICRC's 'non-political' approach (which Forsythe should really have called 'neutral') is itself controversial and in that sense, paradoxically, political. Neutrality means that lines of communication are kept open with all sides in a conflict, thereby preserving humanitarian space, but for that reason may fail to condemn a guilty party. Thus, during the Second World War the ICRC was castigated for effectively condoning Nazi atrocities. It is an unavoidable dilemma, repeated in our own era, for example, in Bosnia. Beyond this again lie all the further dilemmas and controversies which surround 'non-political' humanitarian involvement in conflict situations of the kind which are the subject of Parts II and III.

1.3.4 The principle of universality. 'The Red Cross is a world-wide institution in which all Societies have equal status and share equal responsibilities and duties in helping each other. Our movement's universality stems from the attachment of each of its members to common values.'

This principle, suitably generalized to apply to all humanitarian action, is commented upon further in section 3 of this chapter. In our view, it is fundamental to all activities which aspire to the designation 'humanitarian'. If there are no universally shared humanitarian values, as relativists claim, then the entire humanitarian enterprise collapses. This principle will remain a leitmotif throughout Part II of the book, and will constitute the ultimate, foundational framework principle for humanitarian intervention in the Epilogue. An important corollary here is that humanitarian action must be such as would be internationally endorsed, and, wherever possible, effected through the relevant international bodies.

That these principles imbue humanitarianism in general, not just the activities of the Red Cross movement, can be readily seen. For example, the 1927 Declaration of the abortive International Relief Union laid down that the IRU should operate (a) for the benefit of all those in need (humanity), (b) whatever their nationality and race (impartiality), and (c) irrespective of any political or other affiliation (neutrality). As Bruce Nicholls comments, 'the two principles of nondiscrimination [impartiality] and political neutrality [neutrality] pervade both Geneva law and the public face of modern humanitarianism. Without them, humanitarian practice would be indistinguishable from partisan political activism' (1987, 195). For Peter Macalister-Smith, '[t]o be widely acceptable, humanitarian actions should conform to several basic conditions. As a minimum, humanitarian actions should be free from partisan political objectives [neutrality]; they should be carried out in accordance with appropriate international instruments [universality]; and they should be impartially administered by humanitarian organizations [impartiality]' (1985, 169). Finally, for Jan Eliasson, first UN Under-Secretary-General for Humanitarian Affairs (1992), the new department (DHA) 'will always need to bear in mind' that 'at all times, United Nations humanitarian assistance will be provided in accordance with the principles of humanity, neutrality and impartiality' (1993b, 310–11).

2 Human rights

We turn to the third strand of humanitarianism: the development of an international regime for the protection of human rights. Jean Pictet has suggested that the two legal systems, the international humanitarian law of armed conflict and international human rights law, could be brought together under the heading 'humane law', which he defines as 'all international legal provisions ensuring respect for and full development of the human being' (1988, xxi). In fact, a human rights approach converges with, yet differs from, the approach of the international humanitarian law of armed conflict, covering peace as well as war, and focusing mainly on relations between governments and their own citizens, not governments and the citizens of other states. Whereas human rights law is concerned with the responsibility of the state for the harm suffered by a victim, prosecutions under the law of armed conflict bring criminal proceedings against an accused (Hampson, 1994, 31). Nevertheless, as we will see in Part II, the War Crimes tribunal set up for former Yugo-slavia by the UN Security Council in February 1992 included within its remit violations of the 1948 Genocide Convention and 'crimes against humanity', as well as breaches of the 1949 Geneva Conventions. The same indeterminacy is found in the relationship between human rights and humanitarian assistance. The latter is usually seen to rest on a foundation of response to human needs, rather than human rights. Needs theorists see needs as prior to rights, more objectively quantifiable, and less enmeshed with contentious cultural and political presuppositions (Donnelly, 1985, 27–31). UN Under-Secretary-General for Human-itarian Affairs, Jan Eliasson, for example, is careful to insist that he is not concerned with human rights as he shapes the policy of his new department. But rights add a crucial dimension to needs, as Alexis de Tocqueville noted in a characteristically graphic way with reference to political rights: 'There is nothing which, generally speaking, elevates and sustains the human spirit more than the idea of rights. There is something great and virile in the idea of right which removes from any request its suppliant character, and places the one who claims it on the same level as the one who grants it' (quoted by Vincent, 1986, 17).

Human rights are not liberties, powers or immunities granted by governments or bestowed by condescending humanitarians; they are claims to prior entitlement (Hohfeld, 1919, 38). They are demanded, not pleaded for, and if they are not vouchsafed, the legitimate response is 'not one of disappointment but of indignation' (Vincent, 1986, 17). Shrill insistence on rights may strike some as irksome in certain circumstances, but this is hardly likely to be the case in the kinds of extreme conditions considered in this book. Human rights are a weapon of the weak against the strong, and Jack Donnelly's 'possession paradox' – the fact that rights are typically asserted in situations where they are not already enjoyed – is only an apparent paradox (1985, 15–20). Human rights, by their nature, reach beyond the immediate grasp. They are claimed against powerful oppressors, and are aspirational. That is why, in the end, it is so often the language of human rights that is invoked *in extremis*: the right to protection, to assistance, to democratic governance, to develop-ment, to life itself.

The story of the evolution of natural law into natural rights and natural rights into human rights is too complex to be rehearsed here (Vincent, 1986; Donnelly, 1989). The historical roots go back to the seventeenth century and, on some readings, long before. Landmarks before 1945 include the abolition of slavery, conventions on workers' rights, the political enfranchisement of women and recognition of the one-person, one-vote principle, and acceptance of the principle of self-government for former colonies under the League of Nations mandate system. But it was not until 1945 that, in Lori Fisler Damrosch's phrase, human rights values emerged into full prominence as one of the two main clusters of values around which the new United Nations Charter regime was built (she calls the other cluster 'state system values') (1993, 93). As box 4 shows, the subsequent development of human rights treaty law has, at any rate on paper, been remarkable.

What does all this amount to? We have two aims here: first, to discover what 'humanitarian' means in the human rights field, so as to be able to

---

Box 4: Human Rights Treaties

1926   Covenant to Suppress the Slave Trade and Slavery
1945   United Nations Charter
1948   Convention on the Prevention and Punishment of the Crime of Genocide
Charter of the Organization of American States
1950   European Convention on Human Rights and Fundamental Freedoms
1966   International Convention on the Elimination of All Forms of Racial Discrimination
International Covenant on Civil and Political Rights
Optional Protocol to the above
International Covenant on Economic, Social and Cultural Rights
1969   Vienna Convention on the Law of Treaties
American Convention on Human Rights
1973   International Convention on the Suppression and Punishment of the Crime of Apartheid
1979   Convention on the Elimination of All Forms of Discrimination against Women
1981   African Charter on Human and Peoples' Rights (Banjul Charter)
1984   UN Convention against Torture and Other Cruel, Inhuman or Degrading Treatment
1989   UN Convention on the Rights of the Child

For texts see Brownlie (ed.), 1992. The Universal Declaration of Human Rights (1948) is not listed here because it was not an international treaty.

compare this with our earlier conclusions; second, to look at the kinds of human rights abuse that raised questions about forcible intervention during the cold war period. In considering these issues, we should re- member that we are above all dealing with mass violations of human rights amounting to genocide or politicide. Here are a few examples from the cold war era to set beside the depredations of Idi Amin in Uganda: the estimated 1.7 million casualties in the crushing of the Biafran revolt in Nigeria between May 1967 and January 1970; the mass murders and atrocities perpetrated by the Pakistani Army against the Bengali people of East Pakistan from March to December 1971 leading to an exodus of some 10 million refugees; the systematic slaughter of between 100,000 and 300,000 Hutu by Tutsi authorities in Burundi between April and June 1972; the virtual extermination of the Aché Indians in Paraguay in the 1960s and 1970s; the killing of more than 200,000 East Timorese out of an original population of 650,000 in the 20 years since the Indonesian invasion of 7 December 1975; and the wiping out of some 1 million Cambodians out of a population of 6 million under the Pol Pot regime between 1975 and 1979. Others could be added, of course, such as, ironically, perhaps 200,000 Ugandans killed under Amin's successor, Milton Obote. Many would include the destruction visited by the United States on Vietnam and by the Soviet Union on Afghanistan. This bare recital of statistics does little to convey the unimaginable horror and suffering endured by so many innocent victims of what Alexander Pope called 'man's inhumanity to man'.

2.1 The nature of human rights

To guide us in what, given the limited space available, will have to be a brief survey of a complex field, we will use a well-known analysis of the structure of claim-rights popularized by Alan Gewirth. A claim-right, according to this formula, is held by a subject who asserts a claim to an object against a respondent (who has the correlative duty) on a particular justifying basis or ground (1982, 2). Gewirth adds a fifth element: the nature of the right, but we will take this to be the overall quality which the other four elements serve to define.

Who are the human rights holders? There are deep questions about whether rights holders are individuals or collectivities, but we need not grapple with these here, because our main concern is with gross viola- tions of the rights of large numbers of people in the most blatant form of political mass murder or genocide. Jack Donnelly may be right that these 'should be interpreted merely as the rights of individuals acting as mem- bers of social groups' (1989, 147), and it may be that when it comes to prosecuting for 'systematic' war crimes such as genocide, which need proof of an intention to destroy groups 'as such', this reaches beyond traditional human rights law (which is why the 1948 Genocide Convention is sometimes not included as a human rights treaty), but this is hardly of moment to those who are suffering. Ethnic cleansing threatens groups. It also threatens individuals both in themselves and as members of those groups. The nexus cannot be disentangled. Nor need it be. For our purposes the victims of human rights abuse are human beings threatened by or actually suffering catastrophe on the greatest scale that it is possible to imagine. These are the human rights subjects.

What is it that human rights holders have a right to? Once again, we enter an area of intense controversy: for example, concerning the relationship between 'first-generation' civil and political rights, 'second-generation' economic and social rights, and 'third-generation' solidarity rights, although we can largely sidestep it here (Vasak, 1977). More central to our concerns is the question of whether there are 'fundamental' or 'basic' rights which underlie the others and enjoy some precedence – for example, by being described as 'non-derogable' in human rights treaties, meaning that they cannot be set aside even in national emergency (Meron and Rosas, 1991). Particularly impressive here has been the work of Henry Shue, whose outstanding essay *Basic Rights: Subsistence, Affluence and U.S. Foreign Policy* (1980) has been deservedly influential. Brushing aside debates about 'positive' and 'negative' rights, Shue mounts a powerful argument for recognizing three basic rights: to security, subsistence and liberty. Both the right to security and the right to subsistence are central to the theme of this book, the latter converging with the former in the context of the types of conflict considered in Part II. But in terms of the cold war debate about forcible humanitarian intervention, it is the right to security on its own that is the key – above all, the 'right to life' itself – so we take this as our main human rights object.

Given subjects and objects of human rights, as described above, who bears the correlative duties? It is not true in general that where there is a right there is necessarily a duty, but in the case of a basic right to security of the kind involved here, at least three types of duty do seem to exist. There is the primary duty not to be responsible for the violation in the first place – that is to say, the duty to avoid – and two further secondary duties: to protect and to assist (Shue, 1980). In Part I we are mainly concerned with the secondary duty to protect. This categorization, incidentally, gives the lie to neat attempts to separate 'positive' and 'negative' rights. With reference to the question of humanitarian intervention, John Vincent and Peter Wilson recognize three levels of obligation: (a) the obligation of the subject's own state not to neglect or violate the rights of its subjects; (b) the obligation of other governments within the international society of states; and (c) the obligation of other individuals and groups within the broader community of humankind (Vincent and Wilson, 1993, 123). The third level will be significant in Part II, but plays no part in classical concepts of forcible humanitarian intervention. In chapter 2, therefore, it will be the second level, protection by other states when governments default on their primary responsibilities to their own citizens, which will concern us, so that the respondents in question are other governments.

To sum up, the *rights* of victims call into being, first, the *duties* of their own governments, and second, the *duties* of other governments if host governments fail (the duty of outsiders to act is known in France as the *devoir d'ingérence* (Bettati and Kouchner, 1987)). This in turn raises the further key question for forcible humanitarian intervention: do outsiders have a concomitant *right* to act across borders in response (this is the *droit d'ingérence*)? The key relations are as follows:

> Victim's right to protection and assistance
> Host government's duty to provide it
> Outside governments' duty to act in default
> Outside governments' right to intervene accordingly

What, finally, is the justifying basis for human rights claims such as those made by or on behalf of the victims of gross human rights abuse? A range of possibilities has been suggested, considered by some to be mutually incompatible: religious revelation (Swidler (ed.), 1982), natural law (Finnis, 1980), humanism (Donnelly, 1989, ch. 3), utilitarianism (Singer, 1993). According to the Vienna Declaration and Programme of Action of the World Conference on Human Rights (1993), 'all human rights derive from the dignity and worth inherent in the human person'. Whatever the complications, the ultimate grounding of human rights reaches down beneath the foundations of the justifying system. Using Ronald Dworkin's (1977) terminology, either basic human rights are seen to act as decisive 'trumps' in protecting the weak and those threatened, or they are not, in which case there is little more to be said. Underlying John Rawls's celebrated theory of justice, for example, is the unargued perception that 'the capacity for moral personality' is the basis for equality of consideration, the feature of human beings 'in virtue of which they are to be treated in accordance with the principles of justice' in the first place (1972, 504–5). Henry Shue is right in saying that '[b]asic rights are the morality of the depths. They specify the line beneath which no one is to be allowed to sink' (1980, 18). Whatever it is that constitutes the value of those whose rights are at issue, it is this that thereby at the same time grounds them.

2.2 The realization of human rights

There can be no doubt about the ringing endorsement of human rights values in post-1945 political rhetoric and declaratory international law (D. Jones, 1992). But what does this amount to in practice? Since at least the time of John Austin, sceptical ultra-positivists have concluded that, in the absence of an effective authority with the power to impose sanctions in case of dereliction, so-called declaratory international law amounts to little more than 'positive morality' (Austin, 1954/1832). And states act out of national interest, not morality (Kennan, 1985–6). Many who would like to see an effective human rights regime bewail the fact that, despite earnest protestations and fulsome professions of intent, some late twentieth-century governments, themselves signatories to human rights instruments, have perpetrated human rights abuses as gross as any in history, while other governments have demonstrated a striking indifference to them. The principle of humanity is seen to have counted for little in international affairs. Where there *has* been some attempt to respond, moreover, the principles of impartiality and neutrality have been considered irrelevant. 'Impartiality' in the sense of non-discrimination has been flouted by highly partial selectivity, while 'neutrality' in the sense of non-political response is simply not applicable in relations between states. Those who would like to see proper implementation of treaties like the 1948 Genocide Convention find that the discrepancy between what Leo Kuper calls the 'cliché-ridden and often unctuous' rhetoric indulged in during debate in the UN General Assembly or Commission on Human Rights and the actuality of state action – or rather, inaction – amounts to 'overwhelming hypocrisy' (1985, 89).

The post-1945 international human rights regime is certainly impressive on paper. For example, important contributions have been made under each of the four heads recognized as traditional sources of international law (see box 5) in Article 38 of the 1948 Statute of the International Court of Justice (Davidson, 1993, 47–62).

In terms of (a) treaty law, there are the multilateral conventions listed in box 4. It is significant here that no reneging as a result of individual state reservations (unilateral modifications announced on entry) is allowed in the case of certain so-called non-derogable human rights. Nor, under Article 60(5) of the 1969 Vienna Convention on the Law of Treaties, do normal rules about the termination of treaties apply to 'provisions relating to the protection of the human person contained in treaties of a humanitarian character'. In terms of (b) customary law, usually regarded as consisting of the 'material' element of state practice and the 'psychological' element of acknowledgement of legal obligation (*opinio juris*), the Universal Declaration of Human Rights is now widely

Box 5: Sources of International Law

According to Article 38 of the Statute of the International Court of Justice, the Court, when asked to 'decide in accordance with international law such disputes as are submitted to it', will apply:

(a) international conventions, whether general or particular, establishing rules expressly recognized by the contesting states;
(b) international custom as evidence of a general practice accepted as law;
(c) the general principles of law recognized by civilized nations;
(d) ... judicial decisions and the teachings of the most highly qualified publicists of the various nations, as subsidiary means for the determination of rules of law.

accepted as an authoritative interpretation of the UN Charter human rights provisions (Brownlie, 1990, 570–1). There is also widespread acknowledgement of the existence of 'peremptory norms of general international law' (*jus cogens*) recognized by the 'international community of states', from which 'no derogation is permitted', and which render any treaty that conflicts with them 'void' (Vienna Convention on the Law of Treaties, Article 53). Among the examples of *jus cogens* norms given by the International Law Commission in drafting Article 53 of the Vienna Convention was the prohibition of the criminal act of genocide. In terms of (c) general principles of law, which apply where treaty law and customary law seem to be silent (situations known as *non-liquet*), despite controversy about their nature and status, one example is worth noting with reference to the international humanitarian law of armed conflict. This is the so-called Martens clause (formulated by the Russian jurist F. F. Martens and incorporated in the preamble to the 1899 and 1907 Hague Conventions), which, in the form included in Article 1(2) of the 1977 Additional Protocol I to the 1949 Geneva Conventions, reads: 'In cases not covered by this Protocol or by other international agreements, civilians and combatants remain under the protection and authority of the principles of international law derived from established custom, from the principles of humanity and from the dictates of the public conscience' (Bailey, 1987). Finally, in terms of (d) subsidiary sources of law, innumerable 'publicists' have helped determine the rules of international human rights law, while one example of a significant 'judicial decision' was the Californian court case in which a Paraguayan police inspector (Peña) was sued by the father of a man he had tortured to death in Paraguay (Filártiga) (*Filártiga* v. *Peña Irala*). The US court found that it had jurisdiction under the 1789 Alien Tort Statute, because the crime had been committed in violation of the 'law of nations' (an early term for international law). US Judge Kaufman commented that 'the torturer has become – like the pirate and slave-trader before him – *hostis humani generis*, an enemy of all mankind' (quoted by Vincent, 1986, 104).

But what about the realization of these international aspirations? As Ian Brownlie notes, '[t]here can be little doubt that the main issue is the implementation of the existing stock of standards, and, in that connection, the reduction of the gap between international commitments and the domestic performance of governments' (1990, 577).

It is helpful to consider two levels of application. The first – and in practice the most important – is the realization of human rights in domestic law. Ultimately, the realization of human rights depends upon the willingness of governments to implement them, so that human rights become citizens' rights. Multilateral treaties come into force once they are signed and ratified by a sufficient number of states. International norms are then implemented downwards as they are transmuted into national law, either directly (in monist constitutions) or through separate legislation (in dualist constitutions). Implementation, therefore, depends upon subsequent policy within states. What if things go wrong? Here again, by the 'exhaustion of local remedies rule', recourse moves upwards, beginning with domestic courts. But what happens when governments are themselves the culprits, either by direct violation or through default? What, if anything, is to be done when there is no local remedy? As Shue observes, in the most severe breaches of international human rights norms, the rights at issue have to be asserted *against* governments (1980, 7).

At this point we move up to the second, more contentious level. If particular governments fail in their human rights obligations, what can and should other governments do? There is, first, the question of the place of human rights considerations in the national foreign policy of individual states, and, second, the scope for collective response, mainly through the United Nations, but also through regional bodies or *ad hoc* groupings of states.

The place of human rights in foreign policy is a large subject, which we can only touch on here. Several excellent studies have been made, particularly of United States foreign policy (P. Brown and MacLean (eds), 1979; Luard, 1981; Hoffmann, 1983; Vincent (ed.), 1986; Donnelly, 1993b, ch. 5). Our concern is with one extreme end of the policy options available to governments, forcible intervention, whereas most foreign policy considerations concern a spectrum below that level (Luard, 1981, 26–7).

As to collective realization of human rights through international organizations, this is another large subject beyond the scope of this book. There are several fine studies of the role of regional organizations and the United Nations in standard-setting, promoting and, to a limited extent, policing the nascent international human rights regime (Alston (ed.), 1992; Cassese, 1990; Davidson, 1993; Donnelly, 1989, 1993b; Farer, 1987; Forsythe, 1991). Tolley (1987) has given a splendid account of the work of the UN Commission on Human Rights, while Higgins (1991) has covered the UN Human Rights Committee, set up to monitor the 1966 International Covenant on Civil and Political Rights on behalf of those states which signed up to the Optional Protocol. Theodore Meron offers an acute critique of human rights law-making in the United Nations (1986). We have already noted Leo Kuper's impatience with the empty rhetoric of government spokespersons at the UN who fail to act in the face of massive human rights abuse, mainly by other governments – for example, by making no effort to implement the 1948 Genocide Convention (see box 6). Politics clearly prevails over humanitarianism. On the other hand, others are more sanguine in looking to the slow processes whereby international norms change, as they did in the case of the abolition of slavery and decolonization (Crawford, 1993). In their view, international organizations should not be expected to police these regimes. This can be done only by states. It is the power to legitimate and to castigate that inheres in international organizations, resulting in a gradual leavening of international behaviour as evolving norms are gradually accepted and internalized within the disparate cultures and polities which constitute international society.

3 The question of universality

Are humanitarian principles themselves universal? The principle of universality says that they are, but is this circular? We have seen how particular conceptions of human rights vary in different parts of the world (for Africa, see An-Naim and Deng (eds), 1990; for Asia, see Scoble and Wiseberg (eds), 1985). There is a huge literature here, with increasing interest in non-Western traditions. Recent contributions on Islam, for example, exceed those on Christianity (Renteln, 1990). A well-known argument for relativism can be found in Adamantia Pollis and Peter Schwab (eds), 1980, while Alison Renteln offers a thorough analysis of cultural relativism with a full bibliography (1990). Arguing that 'it is not possible to conclude that all cultures do share the same concept of

Box 6: The Genocide Convention

The 1948 Convention on the Prevention and Punishment of the Crime of Genocide, a term coined by Raphael Lemkin in 1944, represented widespread international revulsion against Nazi extermination policies. It defined acts of genocide (albeit somewhat clumsily) as the destruction of 'national, ethnic, racial or religious groups'; branded them as international crimes, whether committed in peacetime or in war; and held state officials to be punishable. All this represented a normative landmark for the international community. Antonio Cassese (subsequently appointed president of the international tribunal for former Yugoslavia) specifies the weaknesses in the Convention, however (1990, 71–87). Political groups were excluded at the behest of the Soviet Union, as was 'cultural genocide'. This made it easier to evade the Convention. So did the stipulation that 'malice' or the 'intent to destroy a group' is an essential element in genocide. This allowed Paraguay to argue in 1974 that the Aché Indians were not being eliminated 'as such', for example. Above all, the four enforcement mechanisms were almost entirely ineffective:

(a) Trial before the courts of the state on whose territory the offence has been committed is clearly useless, except in cases where there has been a change of regime (as happened after the overthrow of Macias in Equatorial Guinea and of Pol Pot in Kampuchea in 1979).

(b) Trial before an international criminal court is otiose, since such a court has yet to be set up (although the international tribunal established for former Yugoslavia includes breaches of the Genocide Convention among the offences it is competent to try).

(c) Recourse to 'competent organs of the United Nations' to adopt measures provided for in the Charter does not add to what those organs can do in any case, which has been shown to be little.

(d) Unilateral appeal to the International Court of Justice has been neutralized by reservations made by a number of signatories blocking this recourse. When the United States finally ratified the convention in 1989, it lodged similar reservations. In any case the ICJ lacks coercive powers.

International response to some of the worst atrocities during the cold war period will be reviewed in chapter 2. By 1990 there were 96 contracting states, but few would disagree with Cassese's judgement that '[t]he balance-sheet of international action is, sadly, negative' (1990, 85). He concludes:

Faced with inaction by international organs and with the intervention of individual states (moved essentially by political, economic or military aims), there remains only one anchor of salvation: the hope that, if the horrors I have referred to are repeated, public opinion and non-governmental organizations may augment their pressure on governments to leave nationalistic considerations and *Realpolitik* aside in order, finally, to embrace the cause of human dignity. (pp. 86–7)

For the text of the Genocide Convention see Brownlie (ed.), 1992, 31–4.

human rights', she looks for homeomorphic analogues to Western conceptions in other cultures with inconclusive results (p. 88). The story is complicated. For example, some Islamic commentators dismiss the idea of universal human rights as 'Western', whereas others claim priority for Islam and argue that the Universal Declaration of Human Rights of 1948 can be regarded as a reflection of Values laid down in the Qur'an. Nor has the historic relationship between Christianity and human rights been easy. Christians variously maintain that (i) creatures have no inherent rights in relation to the Creator; (ii) a Christian ethic is one of duty, not rights; and (iii) in the spirit of the Sermon on the Mount, Christians should be concerned to waive rights, not assert them (Harries, 1991, 6–7). Other religious traditions are equally ambivalent (Swidler (ed.), 1982). Jack Donnelly (1989) and John Vincent (1986, 1993) offer careful, balanced interpretations.

The Vienna Declaration and Programme of Action of 25 June 1993, adopted after long, testing negotiations at the end of the World Conference on Human Rights, revealed many of these difficulties, and in particular the way in which different concepts of human rights are not only culturally but also politically conditioned. Yet even here, each of the regional declarations which preceded it, including the Tunis Declaration of the Regional Meeting for Africa (clause 8) and the Bangkok Declaration of the Regional Meeting for Asia (clause 11), at one point or another affirmed the universality of the concept of human rights. All this is highly contentious when questions of conditionality, foreign policy pressure and, above all, forcible intervention are raised, as in Part I of this book. As will become evident in Part II, however, this is much less so when humanitarianism is identified more broadly with humanitarian assistance efforts legitimized through the UN General Assembly and Economic and Social Council (ECOSOC), where the influence of the great powers is diluted and respect for state sovereignty is more readily assured. Ephraim Isaac is probably right to argue that if we enquire about 'humanitarianism across religions and cultures', rather than about narrower concepts of traditional political rights, then '[a]ll peoples respect and appreciate humanitarian activities that form part of a common human vocabulary' (1993, 13). Whether this is distinctive or robust enough to ground a regime of humanitarian intervention remains to be seen.

4 Conclusion: the idea of international community

In conclusion, the main thing to take from this chapter for application in the rest of the book is the common core of principles which have been seen to define humanitarianism in its authentic manifestations over the past century. Principles of humanity, impartiality and universality are certainly common to all three humanitarian areas we have looked at. In the human rights field, however, the non-political nature of the principle of neutrality is already deeply compromised, given the characteristically highly politicized environment within which massive human rights abuses are perpetrated. This is a problem that is exacerbated when the question of coercive, and particularly forcible, humanitarian intervention is raised.

Before turning to the question of forcible humanitarian intervention itself, however, we would do well to clarify another term that will be used extensively throughout the book. Following ordinary diplomatic practice, as well as familiar media convention, we call the collectivity which faces the challenge of what to do or not do in the face of human suffering in other countries the 'international community'. Robert Jackson asks, '[i]s there an international community?' (1992). Ken Booth answers that '[i]n G7-speak the phrase "international community" belongs to the platitudes of a "society of states" run by Western governments and a variety of local strongmen which bears an uncomfortable resemblance to a global protection racket' (1994, 57). We intend the phrase in a less determinate way. 'International community' is an informal term which means different things to different people, and for this reason is not employed much in international relations theory. This is an advantage for our purposes. So is the vagueness which surrounds both the word 'international' and the word 'community'. Nevertheless, we owe an explanation, so let us roughly locate the term in relation to others that are more popular with theorists. In diagram 1, we offer a simple model as a basis for what follows.

Here, international community is located in relation to (i) international anarchy, which presupposes little more than bare contact between states within an international system of states; (ii) international society, which includes a spectrum of mutual obligations, reciprocal arrangements and common interests between states (Bull and Watson, 1984, 1); and (iii) world community, or world society, which envisages a global community of humankind. International community is perhaps best identified with the more developed end of international society.

International anarchy	The realm of **power**
International society	The realm of **order**
International Community	
World community	The realm of **justice**

Diagram 1: *International Community I*

Carrying the model one stage further produces a more precise specification of what the concept 'international community' entails (see diagram 2).

Here international community is located at level 3, and constitutes a subset of international society. From the perspective of (1) international anarchy (international system) humanitarianism is seen to be no more than a rather transparent mask for the interests of states, whose governments do (one version) or should (another version) confine their aims to the pursuit of national interest. From a (2) pluralist international society perspective, there is enough commonality to generate rules of association that are generally respected, but not enough to overcome local particularisms. Humanitarianism in its more universalist forms must be subordinated to prudence (one version), or should yield to the pluralist values that inhere in the separate communities which make up the whole (another version). From a (3) solidarist international society perspective, on the other hand (identified with international community), humanitarianism embodies the shared interests and values of the society of states, without which international society itself could not endure (one version) and which provide a springboard for progressively greater convergence and co-operation in future (another version). From a world community (world society) perspective, humanitarianism is one of the main expressions of the unity of humankind, together with economic, environmental, security and cultural interdependencies, which either already do (one version) or should (another version) render particularist loyalties, including loyalties to states, secondary.

As specified here, international community shares certain aspects of international society as described by Alan James: 'to an appreciably greater extent than system, [society] draws attention to the fact that states are made up of human beings. Thereby it refers to the ultimate components of the international collectivity, suggesting the coming together of humankind' (1993b, 282). It also assumes levels of interdependence and common regime-building of the kind analysed by Robert

International anarchy

1 *Natura*	The realm of **power**	Realist

International society

2 *Societas*	The realm of **order**	Pluralist/statist
3 *Communitas*	The realm of **legitimacy**	Solidarist/internationalist

World community

4 *Universitas*	The realm of **justice**	Universalist

Diagram 2: *International Community II*

Keohane and Joseph Nye and by Stephen Krasner (Keohane and Nye, 1977; Krasner (ed.), 1983). It coincides, moreover, with what Fred Halliday calls the 'stronger variant' of international society, which he terms 'homogeneity' – 'the need for societies to share common internal norms' (1995, 49–51). As Halliday points out, this part of the spectrum of international society 'has been inadequately studied in international relations', which has tended to concentrate on the relationship between level 2 and level 1 (p. 49).

In brief, international community is most simply defined as that subset of international society which embodies the minimum solidarity needed for the question of humanitarian intervention to be raised in the first place.

Suggested reading

On the international humanitarian law of armed conflict, see McCoubrey, 1990, and two books by Geoffrey Best (1983, 1994), both written for the non-specialist reader. On international humanitarian assistance, Macalister-Smith, 1985, gives an excellent account. Forsythe, 1977, 1988, provide careful, sophisticated analyses of the ICRC. On international human rights, from a vast literature, Vincent, 1986, and two books by Jack Donnelly (1989, 1993b), offer thorough, well-balanced introductions. A reliable and up-to-date overall appraisal of the United Nations human rights regime can be found in Alston (ed.), 1992, while Claude and Weston (eds), 1992, includes a well-chosen, wide-ranging selection from the literature with linking editorial comment. Brownlie (ed.), 1992, contains an authoritative set of basic human rights documents. Shue, 1980, is justly famous, while Kuper, 1985, gives a powerful criticism of the failure of the international community to respond adequately to some of the most outrageous violations of basic human rights. On international community, Booth and Smith (eds), 1995, offers excellent introductory essays on what we here refer to as 'international anarchy', 'international society' and 'world community'.

2
Forcible Self-Help in Defence of Human Rights: 1945–1990

1 Sovereignty, non-intervention and intervention

In order to approach the classical debate about forcible humanitarian intervention, the natural place to begin is with the core concept of state sovereignty. We move on to consider the principle of non-intervention closely associated with it, and, in light of this, come on to define the concept of intervention. These concepts are interrelated in a more complex way than is often acknowledged. This provides the necessary background for understanding the traditional concept of forcible humanitarian intervention and the cold war debate about it.

1.1 Sovereignty and international anarchy

The modern state system is usually said to have emerged in recognizable form in Europe some time between the Treaty of Cateau-Cambrésis (1559) and the series of treaties which made up the Peace of Westphalia at the end of the Thirty Years War (1648). Its evolution was a slow, untidy process, still far from complete in many parts of Europe for at least two more centuries. Yet, as early as the second half of the sixteenth century, with remarkable prescience, the Frenchman Jean Bodin and the Italian Alberico Gentili were among the first to perceive the significance of the central organizing element, the sovereign state, and to articulate clearly the main features of its internal and external character.

With regard to its internal nature, Bodin did not tire of stressing the

qualitative difference between the loose amalgamation of semi-independent liberties, corporations and orders making up earlier types of polity
and the fully sovereign power, owing no outside allegiance, which,
by asserting unchallenged authority within its borders, transformed
itself into an internally coherent unity, a *magna persona* (1967/1576).
The idea of the sovereign state was from the start something of a fiction,
more aspiration than actuality. Its early prophets, such as Machiavelli,
Bodin and Hobbes, writing at times of disruption and civil war, proclaimed what they dearly wanted to see, rather than what they experienced. Nevertheless, slowly and unevenly, in a process continuing into
the nineteenth century in Europe, ecclesiastical liberties were reduced,
baronial castles were converted into stately homes, and town fortifi-
cations into tourist attractions. Borders were tidied into reasonably
clear frontier demarcations, and territorial integrity was achieved.
Eventually, for the keeping of internal order, armed forces were replaced
by police.

Meanwhile, as a complement to the internal dimensions of sovereignty, the external aspect was also being worked out. If peace was the
hallmark of the internal aspect of sovereignty, war was its characteristic
external aspect. Alberico Gentili, writing a generation after Bodin, was
one of the first to discern the implications: 'The sovereign has no earthly
judge, for one over whom another holds a superior position is not a
sovereign. . . . Therefore it was inevitable that the decision between sovereigns should be made by arms' (1964/1598, 15). Thomas Hobbes's
sovereign Leviathan may have reduced internal anarchy to some kind of
order, but, in relation to other sovereigns, was itself still living in a 'state
of nature'. This was the international anarchy. And, just as individuals'
rights in a state of nature were for Hobbes no more than whatever those
individuals had the power to do, so in the international anarchy, states'
rights clearly included a right to go to war. Indeed, this was the most
jealously guarded right of all. Gentili was typical of others who followed
him in beginning his treatise with an assumption of the primary right to
wage war, hence the title of his book: *De Jure Belli*. For Grotius, too,
peace came second: *De Jure Belli ac Pacis* (1925/1625).

1.2 Non-intervention and international society

The non-intervention norm, which prohibits states from intervening in
each other's domestic affairs, is often described as the other side of the
coin of sovereignty. This is somewhat misleading, as can be seen by
comparing the right to wage war, long regarded as constitutive of sovereignty (its outward manifestation) with the principle of non-intervention,

also seen as constitutive of sovereignty, only this time a manifestation of its inner integrity. If the former gives rise to the image of Hobbes's anarchy, the latter suggests an entirely different image antithetical to it. This is usefully illustrated by the 'egg-box' model, in which the value contained in each sovereign 'egg' is preserved only by virtue of the inviolability of its shell, itself protected only by the existence of the egg-box (Hoffmann, 1978, 117; Vincent, 1986, 173, citing Suganami as co-inventor of the model). The egg-box is the strange structure of voluntarily observed norms, practices and restraints, underpinned by more or less stable balance-of-power relations, which go to make up the non-intervention tradition. In other words, the non-intervention norm is in this sense a *constraint on* sovereignty.

1.2.1 The outer aspect of non-intervention: reciprocity and the juridical equality of states.   Instead of the unbridled exercise of power in pursuit of interest characteristic of the free-for-all of international anarchy, the non-intervention norm introduces the concept of mutually respected order characteristic of international society. In the tradition of the 'English school' of international relations, this is seen as a qualitative change, from an anarchical international *system* of states, constituted by the bare fact that 'the behaviour of each is a necessary factor in the calculations of the others', to an international *society* in which states have 'established by dialogue and consent common rules and institutions for the conduct of their relations, and recognise their common interest in maintaining those arrangements' (Bull and Watson, 1984, 1). This international society of states is seen to have expanded progressively from the original small club of so-called civilized nations (most of them European) to include the ever-growing number of members of the United Nations. The essential point is that whereas the right to wage war *inheres in each state individually* within the international anarchy, the non-intervention norm is *constitutive of the collectivity* of the international society of states. That is, without a non-intervention norm, there could not be such an international society. As John Vincent shows in his classic study of 'nonintervention and international order', this was first clearly articulated in the eighteenth and nineteenth centuries. Hugo Grotius in the seventeenth century had no conception of non-intervention, because he did not see an intermediate condition between peace and war, and because the 'Grotian conception of international society' was 'solidarist'; that is to say, he envisaged a universal community of humankind in which natural law applied to individuals as well as to states (Bull et al. (eds), 1990). It was in the writings of Christian Wolff and Emerich de Vattel in the eighteenth century that '[t]he principle of nonintervention finds its first explicit manifestation', although not its technical definition (Vincent, 1974, 26). From then on, within the classic tradition, international law (as it soon came to be called) was seen to apply solely to states, not individuals, and, as Vattel put it, 'the natural society of states cannot continue unless the rights which belong to each by nature are respected' (Vattel, 1964/1758, introduction).

The paradoxical nature of the resulting non-intervention norm is well brought out by Caroline Thomas: 'What sovereignty really connotes in inter-state relations today is a claim to independence which is theoretically tempered by the recognition of an equal claim to this by all states, and by a duty and obligation not to intervene in the domestic affairs of other states' (1985, 15). The reference to 'duty' and 'obligation' shows that the norm is aspirational, if not fictional, resting as it does on the abstract notion of the juridical equality of states. In Christian Wolff's words, 'since the moral equality of men has no relation to the size of their bodies, the moral equality of nations has no relation to the number of men of which they are composed' (quoted in Vincent, 1974, 27). Do states in fact behave like this? Do they respect each other's autonomy and independence even when they are larger and more powerful than their neighbours? Why should they? The legal 'positivists' of the nineteenth century, who tried to get away from the 'naturalist' tradition of deducing the 'law of nations' from abstract principles of reason and nature and to ground a science of international law in the agreements and behaviour of states, were in the end unable to answer these questions in the way they wanted: 'Where practice provided but an equivocal guide to principle, refuge was found either in borrowing from the naturalist international lawyers or in the assumptions or first principles upon which the system of international law was supposedly based' (Vincent, 1974, 37). In short, the right to wage war and the non-intervention norm, both integral aspects of sovereignty, pulled in opposite directions, leading by the end of the nineteenth century to the apparently paradoxical outcome that the greater threat to the integrity of states (waging war) was widely regarded as legitimate, but the lesser (intervention) was not.

1.2.2 The inner aspect of non-intervention: popular sovereignty and self-determination.   So far we have distinguished two conceptual aspects of the state as seen from the perspective of the sovereign: (a) Bodin's 'internal' supremacy of the sovereign within the state and (b) Gentili's 'external' right to wage war (see diagram 3). We have contrasted (b) with (c), a perspective which views the state 'from outside' in the form of the reciprocal non-intervention norm. It remains to contrast (a) with (d), a final aspect of the modern state which sees it as if 'from inside'. This is the

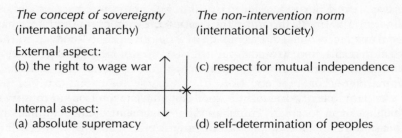

| The concept of sovereignty | The non-intervention norm |
| (international anarchy) | (international society) |

Diagram 3: *Sovereignty and Non-Intervention*

other half of the non-intervention norm, constituted by the key concepts of popular sovereignty and self-determination.

Since the time of the American and French revolutions, the idea of princely sovereignty has given way to the idea of popular sovereignty, and James Mayall is right to argue that the resulting principle of national self-determination, however problematic, is now globally unassailable, and has been the most important modification to the idea of international society since its inception (1990, 149). This underpins the non-intervention norm by constituting the 'value' inside the eggshell of sovereignty which the egg-box is there to protect, but at the same time compromises it. If particular governments lose inner legitimacy (aspect (d)) because they are not popularly based, do they by the same token lose their outer legitimacy within the society of states (aspect (c))? This question lies at the heart of much of the debate about humanitarian intervention to be outlined later in this chapter. It leads to further profound questions about what the principle of the 'self-determination' of peoples or nations means (Hannum, 1990; Moynihan, 1993). And it raises the issue, so lucidly analysed by Robert Jackson, of the 'gap' between juridical and empirical statehood in the case of many of the newer members of the United Nations:

> The ex-colonial states have been internationally enfranchised and possess the same external rights and responsibilities as all other sovereign states: juridical statehood. At the same time, however, many have not yet been authorised and empowered democratically and consequently lack the institutional features of sovereign states as also defined by classical international law. . . . [E]mpirical statehood in large measure remains to be built. (Jackson, 1990, 21)

These have been christened 'quasi-states' (Bull and Watson, 1984, 430), because they possess 'negative' but not 'positive' sovereignty. The crucial point for our purposes is that the two aspects of the non-intervention norm, the outer aspect (c) and the inner aspect (d), can be seen to be in tension here. The roots of the classical debate about forcible humanitarian intervention thus lie *within* the non-intervention norm – a somewhat surprising fact which explains much of its elusiveness. Moreover, to the extent that these two aspects represent two poles of international society, as suggested in the conclusion to this chapter, the core debate is located *within* international society. As Antonio Cassese points out, many of the gravest massacres and genocides since 1945 have taken place in countries which lack the social structures and government machinery to mediate inner conflict, as more settled polities on the whole manage to do (1990, 85–6). Yet the elites perpetrating such outrages, who thereby entirely forfeit the domestic legitimacy which constitutes the inner aspect of non-intervention, are nevertheless protected and often materially bolstered by its outer aspect, through external recognition within the international society of states. The question is: should they be?

This critical tension at the heart of the non-intervention norm is well illustrated in the post-1945 United Nations Charter. Building on earlier attempts to ban inter-state aggression, such as the 1928 Kellogg–Briand Pact, Article 2(4), astonishingly, outlawed war under the guise of the 'threat or use of force': 'All members shall refrain in their international relations from the threat or use of force against the territorial integrity or political independence of any state, or in any manner inconsistent with the purposes of the United Nations.' What had traditionally been assumed to be a primary sovereign right of states, the right to wage war, was thereby abruptly abrogated; whereas what had been widely seen to be illegitimate – namely, intervention in the domestic affairs of other states – was not specifically condemned. Instead, it was the United Nations itself which was banned from unauthorized intervention in Article 2(7): 'Nothing contained in the present Charter shall authorise the United Nations to intervene in matters which are essentially within the domestic jurisdiction of any State or shall require the members to submit such matters to settlement under the present Charter; but this principle shall not prejudice the application of enforcement measures under Chapter VII.'

In what way did the non-intervention norm, therefore, apply to individual states? It could only be deduced by implication from other Charter articles: in particular, Article 1(2), which enjoins 'respect for the principle of equal rights and self-determination of peoples'; Article 2(1), which emphasizes 'the principle of the sovereign equality' of member states; and Article 55, which also stresses respect for the principle of equal rights and self-determination of peoples (C. Thomas, 1985, 36). The concept of non-intervention was subsequently elaborated in a series of UN General Assembly resolutions, notably the Declaration on the Inadmissibility of Intervention in the Domestic Affairs of States and Protection of their

Independence and Sovereignty of 21 December 1965 (Resolution 2131 (XX)) and the Declaration on Principles of International Law Concerning Friendly Relations and Co-operation among States in Accordance with the Charter of the United Nations of 24 October 1970 (Resolution 2625 (XXV)). The former reproduced a crucial passage (Article 15(2)) from the earlier Charter of the Organization of American States: 'No state has the right to intervene, for any reason whatever, in the internal or external affairs of any other state. Consequently armed intervention and all forms of interference or attempted threats against the personality of the state or against its political, economic and cultural elements, are condemned.'

Reference to the 'personality' of the state recalls Jean Bodin, while mention of 'political, economic and cultural elements' shows how it is the 'inner' integrity of the state (aspect (d)) which underpins and justifies the non-intervention norm. Some of the complexities in the further reaches of the humanitarian intervention debate can be glimpsed when it is seen that the UN Charter articles on self-determination, appealed to in support of the non-intervention norm between states in the absence of an explicit Charter article condemning intervention, are the same articles appealed to by many of those who advocated humanitarian intervention during the cold war. Self-determination is used both to justify and to condemn humanitarian intervention.

1.3 Intervention and the UN Charter regime

1.3.1 Definition.   One of the reasons for the absence of an article in the UN Charter specifically condemning intervention by individual states or groups of states in each other's domestic affairs was the difficulty of determining just what would constitute intervention. A special committee set up by the UN General Assembly in 1963 to formulate the principle of non-intervention as a legal principle failed: 'debate in the Special Committee brought practising international lawyers [and state representatives] no nearer a consensus on such questions as the definition of intervention . . . than the debate among their academic counterparts' (Vincent, 1974, 247). Broad interpretations according to which intervention was 'treated as synonymous with influence' virtually equated intervention with international affairs in general (Rosenau, 1969, 166). Even inaction was seen by some as intervention 'where action would have resulted in a different outcome' (C. Thomas, 1985, 18). More persuasive were those who saw 'the essence of intervention' as 'the attempt to compel' (A. Thomas and Thomas, 1956, 72). For Hans Lauterpacht, intervention 'signifies dictatorial interference in the sense of action amounting to a denial of the independence of the state' (1955/1906, 19). John Vincent followed James Rosenau in arguing that intervention (i) interrupts the conventional pattern of international relations, having a clear-cut beginning and end (for example, the intrusion and withdrawal of military forces), and (ii) is aimed at the authority structure of the target state. He summed up by specifying intervention as 'that activity undertaken by a state, a group within a state, a group of states or an international organization, which interferes coercively in the domestic affairs of another state' (1974, 8). This conclusion coincides with the 1986 International Court of Justice ruling in the *Nicaragua* case that it is '[t]he element of coercion, which defines, and indeed forms the very essence of, prohibited intervention' (ICJ Reports, 1986, 108). We should note the use of 'prohibited' here, which suggests that there is such a thing as 'legitimate' intervention.

For our purposes, however difficult it may be to pin down what intervention implies in practice, we can define the classic concept quite clearly in relation to the ideas of sovereignty and the non-intervention norm as described above. Intervention is the abrogation of sovereignty. It occurs when one or more external powers exercise sovereign functions within the domestic jurisdiction of a state. In terms of the egg-box analogy, intervention is whatever breaches the eggshell.

1.3.2 Empirical and normative analysis.   Detailed empirical analysis and normative assessment of the practice of state intervention is beyond the scope of this book (see Bull (ed.), 1984; Little, 1975, 1993). We will accept Marc Trachtenberg's acute suggestion that, historically, there have been two normative traditions of state intervention: (a) intervention to preserve the balance of power and (b) intervention to assert internationally accepted values, which in the nineteenth century were European values. The former tends to be a matter of the foreign policy interests of great powers like Britain in the nineteenth and the United States in the twentieth century. The latter is regularly invoked as an overall justification for foreign adventures, as with American President McKinley, whose rationale for intervention in Cuba in 1898 was 'to put an end to the barbarities, bloodshed, starvation, and horrible miseries now existing there, and which the parties to the conflict are either unable or unwilling to stop or mitigate'. He disarmingly added that 'the right to intervene' might also be justified by the 'very serious injury to the commerce, trade and business of our people' (Trachtenberg, 1993, 25). So far as forcible humanitarian intervention is concerned, little seems to have changed in this respect during the succeeding century.

In view of the often repeated assertion that Third World countries are uniformly opposed to intervention by the powerful states, it is well to note that, although there is truth in this, there has at times been widespread support for both of Trachtenberg's forms of intervention. Intervention to uphold the non-intervention norm, however paradoxical, is often welcomed by Third World states, the ending of the cold war and the withdrawal of great power interest in a number of regions being viewed as much with dismay as with relief. Moreover, as exemplified in section 4.2 below, whereas on a number of other issues it was the states of the Communist world and the Third World which defended the non-intervention principle against erosion by the Western powers, as regards the assault on colonialist regimes and apartheid in South Africa, it was the other way round. From the 1950s, Third World countries invoked 'human rights' values in the UN Charter to urge intervention, including if necessary military intervention, in South Africa and Southern Rhodesia, while Western governments demurred (Vincent, 1974, 261–74; C. Thomas, 1985).

1.3.3 The question of legitimacy.   Detailed consideration of the cold war debate about the legitimacy of forcible humanitarian intervention is given below. The context as regards international law is provided by what William V. O'Brien calls the UN Charter 'war decision' regime (1990). Restrictionists who wanted to eliminate the scope for arguments in favour of legitimate intervention adopted two main strategies. The first was to invoke a 'broad' interpretation of Charter Article 2(4), in order to rule out not only aggression but also intervention. The second was to adopt a 'narrow' definition of intervention itself as forcible self-help by states, so that it would come under the article thus specified. This is further developed in section 4.4. On a broad interpretation of Charter Article 2(4) there are only two surviving legal exceptions to the ban on 'the threat or use of force'.

The first is collective action 'with respect to threats to the peace, breaches of the peace and acts of aggression', under Chapter VII of the Charter. If, under Article 39, the Security Council determines that there is such a threat, it may decide upon coercive measures short of the use of armed force, such as economic sanctions, under Article 41. Or, by Article 42, '[s]hould the Security Council consider that measures provided for in Article 41 would be inadequate or have proved to be inadequate, it may take such action by air, sea or land forces as may be necessary to maintain or restore international peace and security'. The original intention was for decisions about the use of force under Article 42 to be as binding on members as are decisions under Article 41. To this end, Articles 43–7 set out mechanisms whereby members would contribute to a Security Council operation run by a UN Military Staff Committee. So far this has not happened, however, so the Security Council has done no more than 'authorize' members to act voluntarily under Article 42, and, more controversially, has even delegated responsibility almost entirely, as in the 1990–1 Gulf War. Article 42 decisions are, therefore, not binding on members, although they remain binding for the target state, which is thereby barred from invoking self-defence under Article 51.

The second exception to the ban on the use of force by states comes in Charter Article 51: 'Nothing in the present Charter shall impair the inherent right of individual or collective self-defence if an armed attack occurs against a Member of the United Nations, until the Security Council has taken measures necessary to maintain international peace and security.' Article 51 comes after Article 42, thereby emphasizing that in the original conception even self-defence was considered an interim recourse until collective mechanisms could be activated. Those invoking self-defence still had to report immediately to the Security Council.

Finally, we should note the unequivocal judgement of the International Court of Justice on forcible intervention in 1949 in the *Corfu Channel* case:

> The court can only regard the alleged right of intervention as the manifestation of a policy of force, such as has, in the past, given rise to the most serious abuses and such as cannot, whatever the present defects in international organization, find a place in international law. Intervention is perhaps still less admissible in the particular form it would take here [Britain sweeping the territorial waters of Albania to remove mines]; for, from the nature of things, it would be reserved for the most powerful states, and might easily lead to perverting the administration of international justice itself. (ICJ Reports, *Corfu Channel* case (Merits), 1949, 39)

This encapsulates the powerful 'argument from abuse' against all forms of forcible intervention, including humanitarian intervention.

2 Forcible humanitarian intervention: the classic concept

Many, if not most, analysts during the cold war period adopted severely restrictionist definitions of the 'intervention' component of the concept of humanitarian intervention, with attendant ambiguities and contentiousness (see box 7). Here the tendency was to relapse into formalism and beg substantial questions. In addition, a further twist was applied by equally restrictionist interpretations of the 'humanitarian' component. Here the

Box 7: The Restrictionist Definition of Humanitarian Intervention

In order to clarify some of these conceptual problems, we will take Wil Verwey's own restrictionist definition cited at the beginning of this book, which he claims is the only correct usage in accordance with international law and state practice. Humanitarian intervention is:

> The threat or use of force by a state or states abroad, for the sole purpose of preventing or putting a halt to a serious violation of fundamental human rights, in particular the right to life of persons, regardless of their nationality, such protection taking place neither upon authorization by relevant organs of the United Nations nor with permission by the legitimate government of the target state. (Verwey, 1992, 114)

This is an expansion of Richard Lillich's celebrated 'forcible self-help by states to protect human rights' (1967).

John Vincent suggests that there are six major features of intervention: the actors, the target, the activity, the types of intervention, the purpose and the context (1974, 4–13). We will reorder and adapt these to clarify the successive restrictionist moves which make up Verwey's definition.

(a) Purpose: 'humanitarian' is identified with the protection of fundamental human rights threatened by the host government. 'Fundamental human rights' are undefined. The key restrictionist stipulation is that the purpose of the intervention must be 'solely' humanitarian. The only criterion that is considered is that of motive. Humanitarian motives must be pure, or at any rate paramount. State interest must not be significant. Given the political interests inevitably involved in forcible cross-border action, this is enough on its own to rule out the possibility that forcible intervention can be humanitarian. If an action is not disinterested, it is not humanitarian.

(b) Agency: restrictionist definitions are careful to rule out intervention by the UN itself, although there is no unanimity here (e.g., a restrictionist like Ian Brownlie does not rule it out). Verwey sees UN Security Council action, even if for humanitarian ends (including authorization of others), as a species of the genus 'UN enforcement action' and, since the Security Council has the authority to 'auto-interpret' all Charter provisions relating to its own function, not covered by Article 2(7) which specifically excepts 'the application of enforcement measures under Chapter VII' (Verwey, 1992, 114). If an action is authorized by the Security Council under Chapter VII of the UN Charter, then it is not intervention.

(c) Target: restrictionists stipulate that the action must be non-consensual to count as intervention. This again is controversial (e.g., Wight, 1979, disagrees). It assumes that it is clear when 'permission' is given and who the 'legitimate government' is. If consent is not withheld, then the action is not intervention. Also important here is the 'threshold' debate about whether the intervention amounts to an infringement of 'the territorial integrity or political independence' of the target state, thus

Box 7 (*continued*)

transgressing UN Charter Article 2(4). As we will see in section 4.4.1, restrictionists argue that, by definition, it does. In this way they make sure that humanitarian intervention comes under the Article 2(4) ban, which thus rules it out as illegitimate from the start. If an action does not breach the Article 2(4) threshold, then it is not intervention.

(d) Force level: restrictionists adopt a broad definition of UN Charter Article 2(4) which rules out the 'threat or use of force' except for (a) collective action under Article 42 and (b) self-defence under Article 51. They then adopt a narrow definition of intervention to make sure that it comes under the Article 2(4) prohibition. They do this (a) by equating intervention 'upwards' with 'the threat or use of force', as Verwey does, against the tradition which distinguishes intervention from war, and (b) by separating it 'downwards' from non-forcible action, against the tradition which cites coercion rather than force as the defining criterion (ICJ Reports, *Nicaragua* case (Merits), 1986, 108). If an action is not a 'threat or use of force', then it is not intervention.

(e) Context: the context assumed by classic definitions of humanitarian intervention was one in which the threat to human rights was seen to come chiefly from tyrannical governments, and the question consequently posed was whether other governments, in the absence of collective resort to self-help, should intervene militarily to remedy the situation. If an action is not aimed at preventing governmental violation of its citizens' rights, then it is not humanitarian intervention.

(f) Legitimacy: the sum total of these legalist-restrictionist stipulations amounts to a tendency to rule out humanitarian intervention as illegitimate by definition. Substantive questions which cannot be ruled out in this way are dismissed as not having to do with humanitarian intervention at all. Not all debate was constrained in this way, but a surprising proportion of the academic debate in the English-speaking world was. In Vincent's words:

At this point, the notion of intervention has become confused in legal thought by the reluctance to call a lawful act 'intervention'. . . . This is the core of the confusion between the use of the word intervention as a description of an event in international relations and its use as a normative expression by international lawyers. If intervention by right is held not to violate the independence of a target state, a violation which features in most definitions as the thing which above all differentiates intervention from other phenomena, then is it to be understood that intervention by right is not intervention? (1974, 11–12)

That is to say, substantial debate about whether an act of intervention is legitimate, becomes side-tracked by the reluctance of restrictionists to call a possibly legitimate act 'intervention'.

tendency was to adopt a reading which made the composite concept of humanitarian intervention a contradiction in terms. The sole test of humanitarianism was taken to be the 'motive' of the intervening government, and this was interpreted so strictly that no state intervention could qualify. Beyond that, the humanitarian element was left unanalysed. Each of these aspects was disputed, and there was no generally accepted definition of humanitarian intervention. As Wil Verwey puts it, 'there may be few concepts in international law today which are as conceptually obscure and legally controversial'. Others agree (Malanczuk, 1993, 39).

3 Forcible humanitarian intervention: the classic concept applied

What happens when the restrictionist definition (see box 7) is applied? It is immediately apparent that there are problems in specifying what instances should be cited as examples of forcible humanitarian intervention in the first place. A comparison of some of the most acute analyses from the cold war period shows how definitional difficulties are encountered at the outset. Comparing Akehurst, 1984, 95–9; Ronzitti, 1985, 93–106; Verwey, 1985 and 1986, 60–5 (a shorter version of the former); and Tesón, 1988, 155–200, the number of instances is found to vary from four (Tesón) to nine (Verwey). A recent review by Anthony Arend and Robert Beck lists eleven putative examples of forcible humanitarian intervention (1993, 112–37):

The interventions of six Arab states and Israel in Palestine (1948)
Belgian intervention in the Congo (1960)
Belgian and US intervention in the Congo (1964)
US intervention in the Dominican Republic (1965)
Indian intervention in East Pakistan (1971)
Indonesian intervention in East Timor (1975)
South African intervention in Angola (1975)
Vietnamese intervention in Kampuchea (1978–9)
Tanzanian intervention in Uganda (1979)
French intervention in Central Africa (1979)
US intervention in Grenada (1983)

Others have included interventions in Ethiopia (Bazyler, 1987), the Falklands in 1982 (Levitin, 1986), Sri Lanka in 1987 (Ispahani, 1992), and Panama in 1989 (Nanda et al., 1990). Questions have been asked about why there was no humanitarian intervention in Nigeria during the

Biafran war (Reisman and McDougal, 1973) or in Northern Ireland during the troubles (Quigley, 1983).

There are a number of discrepancies here. In only three instances did the interventions take place, belatedly, where the most severe cases of mass violation of human rights occurred as listed by Leo Kuper (1985) and by Frank Chalk and Kurt Jonassohn (1990) and described in chapter 1. The three cases are the interventions in East Pakistan, Kampuchea and Uganda. The habit of concentrating on putative examples of forcible humanitarian intervention, instead of approaching the problem from the wider perspective to be suggested in Part II, leads to extraordinary results, such as inclusion of Indonesian intervention in East Timor in 1975 as a possible candidate for benign humanitarian intervention, while ignoring the subsequent Indonesian massacres of the Timorese people and the earlier Indonesian government slaughter of Communists. Uncertainty about the criteria for forcible humanitarian intervention leads to similar inconsistency. For Natalino Ronzitti, of all the cases cited, it was the Vietnamese intervention in Kampuchea which was 'probably the one which throws most light on the relation between the use of force and the protection of human rights' (1985, 98), yet neither Fernando Tesón nor Wil Verwey include this example. Conversely, whereas Tesón sees the Tanzanian intervention in Uganda as 'perhaps the clearest in a series of cases which have carved out an important exception to the prohibition of article 2(4)' (1988, 167–8), Ronzitti denies that it is a relevant case (1985, 102–6). A striking example of the way in which substantive judgement becomes confused with legalistic definition in this field is seen in the application of Arend and Beck's four-criteria test. In their view, to count as forcible humanitarian intervention, an action must (a) be a response to an immediate, widespread threat to fundamental rights, (b) be essentially limited to protecting fundamental human rights, (c) not be undertaken with the consent of the target government, and (d) not be authorized by the UN Security Council. Not one of the eleven cases they study passes the test. In other words, in their view, there have been no examples of forcible humanitarian intervention during the cold war period. A similar result obtains in the case of putative examples of forcible humanitarian intervention before the cold war. A restrictionist like Ian Brownlie was prepared to acknowledge only one possibly genuine example in the nineteenth century: the 1860 intervention by French forces to protect Christian Maronites in Lebanon (1963, 338–9). More recent analysis casts doubt on this also (Pogany, 1986).

There are two ways of regarding this negative outcome. One is to see it as the result of careful case-by-case empirical analysis which yields cumulatively negative results, such as Farooq Hassan's judgement with reference to the Tanzanian intervention in Uganda that ' "Humanitarian intervention" is nothing more than the entry of the *realpolitik* into international law' (1981, 862). The other is to conclude that even the possibility of a positive judgement is ruled out from the start by definition. In our view, both apply, although restrictionist definitions, which have evolved with the explicit aim of ruling out the possibility of forcible intervention in international law, tend towards the latter. This may be a normatively useful result, but it short-circuits substantial debate. Instead of beginning by removing the ground for discussion in this way, therefore, we will look at some of the political and ethical dimensions of forcible humanitarian intervention before returning to the legal aspects at the end.

4 Forcible humanitarian intervention: the cold war debate

A survey of the academic literature on forcible humanitarian intervention during the cold war period suggests that much of the debate in the English-speaking world was characterized by preoccupation with questions of international law at the expense of broader political, social and cultural considerations and by concentration on a rather narrow, military-political definition of humanitarian intervention to the exclusion of other dimensions of international action and concern.

However, a more careful analysis shows that the cold war debate was richer and more nuanced than a restrictionist approach would suggest.

4.1 The debate within political and ethical traditions

As Martin Wight observed some years ago, the issue of intervention 'raises questions of the utmost moral complexity: adherents of every political belief will regard intervention as justified under certain circumstances' (1979, 191). More than that, as box 8 suggests with reference to attitudes to forcible humanitarian intervention in the West, every major political and ethical tradition can be seen to have been deeply divided on the issue.

The same is true when it comes to political persuasions. Both conservatives and liberals in the West have been divided on the issue, depending upon circumstance. Michael Smith divides conservatives into 'prudential non-interventionists' and 'ideological interventionists' (1989, 9). The former, using the 'argument for stability', warned that interventionism undermines the *status quo* by encouraging others, less reliable, to behave likewise. For Hans Morgenthau (1967), intervention on 'ideological' grounds in defence of humanitarian values is in any case not as effective

Box 8: Western Ethical Traditions and Humanitarian Intervention

Within the main Western ethical traditions this ambivalence has afflicted utilitarians, Kantians and Rawlsians (Lewer and Ramsbotham, 1993, 59–64). Many utilitarians equate the principle of equal consideration of interests with the conviction that as citizens of the world our basic duty is to the welfare of humankind (Singer, 1993). Jeremy Bentham himself envisaged a world 'Common Court of Judicature', and supported the idea that armed forces 'furnished by the several states' should be used as a last resort 'for enforcing the decrees of the Court' (Bentham, 1786–9, quoted by Luard (ed.), 1992, 417). J. S. Mill was generally opposed to intervention on the grounds that it undermined the inherent value of autonomous political community, but was prepared to allow it in cases (a) where a political community within existing state borders is struggling for independence (secession or national liberation) and (b) where a foreign power has already intervened (counter-intervention) (Mill, 1875/1959). He also included cases of protracted civil war in which there seemed to be no prospect of a restoration of order. In addition, Mill held that 'civilised nations' could intervene in the affairs of 'barbarians' because normal reciprocity did not apply. Michael Walzer, not himself a utilitarian, who generally upholds the 'legalist paradigm' of non-intervention, adds a third exception, (c), in cases where 'the violation of human rights . . . is so terrible that it makes talk of community and self-determination . . . seem cynical and irrelevant' (1992/1977, 90). Kantians are equally ambivalent. Immanuel Kant himself, cited by Martin Wight as the archetypical 'universalist', upheld the principle of non-intervention in the fifth preliminary article of his 'Thoughts on a Perpetual Peace': 'No state shall forcibly interfere in the constitution and government of another state' (Kant, 1991/1793, 96). There is no simple equation between universalist conceptions and the advocacy of forcible intervention. On the other hand, what Alan Donagan (1977) calls the 'common morality' of the natural law tradition, often associated with Kantianism, does imply 'positive concern for the welfare of people outside one's own community', and can thus be seen to provide the normative ground for a justified 'humanitarian' use of force (Boyle, 1992, 123). Meanwhile, attempts to apply Rawlsian concepts, notably John Rawls's theory of justice, to the international sphere has produced discrepant results, Charles Beitz on this basis advocating a cosmopolitanism which overrides the statist 'priority principle' and justifies humanitarian intervention (1975, 309), John Rawls himself coming out in support of pluralistic values and the principle of non-intervention (1972, 378).

as creating an exemplary society at home 'as a model for other nations to emulate'. Ideological interventionists, on the other hand, have been concerned above all with the 'moral legitimacy' of US policy. The 'Reagan doctrine', for example, 'rests on the traditional American doctrine, stated in the Declaration of Independence, that the legitimacy of a government depends on its respect for individual rights and on the consent of the governed' (Kirkpatrick and Gerson, 1991, 22). Here is an example from the political 'right' of the argument that the external aspect of non-intervention is valid only if underpinned by its internal aspect, usually identified with the political 'left'. What could be more solidarist than President Reagan's 5 May 1985 clarion call from Bitburg air base which launched the doctrine? 'Today freedom-loving people around the world must say: I am a Berliner, I am a Jew in a world still threatened by anti-semitism. I am an Afghan and I am a prisoner in the Gulag. I am a refugee in a crowded boat foundering off the coast of Vietnam' (Kirkpatrick and Gerson, 1991, 22).

Nor were liberals immune from mutual inconsistency. Just as Gladstone swung from stern non-interventionism to the impassioned advocacy of humanitarian intervention to stop the Armenian massacres in the nineteenth century, so, as Richard Falk points out, late twentieth-century liberals have been torn between the moralistic rhetoric of 'liberal interventionism' (our term) and a reluctance to pay the price. Since at least the time of the Vietnam War, moreover, liberal non-interventionists have been highly suspicious of militarized foreign policy adventures in which support for often unscrupulous political allies was masked by a spurious ideological veneer (Falk, 1993, 756). It is characteristic of this paradoxical situation that it is not Jimmy Carter, the president whose foreign policy is identified with human rights advocacy, whose actions are most closely associated with the issue of forcible humanitarian intervention, but Ronald Reagan.

Academics have struggled as helplessly as politicians. Two of the most thoughtful writers on the subject, Hedley Bull and John Vincent, 'implicitly recognise that humanitarian intervention poses the conflict between order and justice in its starkest form for the society of states. In their discussions of the issue, they both exhibit . . . realist and pluralist considerations which coexist uneasily with the solidarist elements in their thought' (Wheeler, 1992, 486).

Nor, finally, were Western traditions alone in finding the issue of forcible humanitarian intervention a difficult one to accommodate consistently. The Marxist socialist bloc was equally riven, as attempts were made to square peaceful coexistence and non-intervention with proletarian internationalism and socialist solidarity. As for the Third World, we have already acknowledged the universal roots of cosmopolitan humanitarianism (as distinct from 'Westernized' human rights), exemplified, for example, in the Tao of Lao Tzu, the Islamic Sunna, Hindu and Buddhist dharma, Confucian 'style of life' and Japanese giri (Chopra and Weiss, 1992, 109). On the question of forcible intervention on human-itarian grounds, the general antipathy to anything that might revive colonial domination by the powerful has been generally emphasized, but the three most prominent and frequently discussed examples of forcible humanitarian intervention in the cold war period were all interventions by Third World countries: India into East Pakistan, Tanzania into Uganda, and Vietnam into Kampuchea. Perhaps the only generalization that can be made is that within political and ethical traditions world-wide, whether humanitarian intervention has been advocated or opposed has depended less upon clearly formulated principles or law and more upon circumstance, including political interest, but also normative commitment.

4.2 The debate in international politics

The 1945–90 period was a momentous one in world history. At the geopolitical level, the dominant dynamic was the titanic struggle between the two superpowers with their attendant alliances, blocs and ideologies. But even more significant was the complex mix of shifting power relations, interests and norms referred to by the blanket term 'decolonization', together with a near quadrupling of the number of states in the United Nations (Crawford, 1993). All at once, the non-intervention norm was to be applied to a host of new members, many of whom lacked the inner resources of 'positive' sovereignty to underpin external acceptance within the society of states. Many (but by no means all) of the worst cases of mass atrocity during the cold war period were perpetrated by fragile, vicious regimes in relatively new states. The per-petrators were more often than not protected, albeit in client status, by one or other of their superpower patrons, and were propped up by the non-competitive norms of international society. Subsidized and armed from outside, they had less need to struggle to raise taxation and con-scription from inside, which would have provided opportunities for the development of civil society (Jackson, 1990, 187). Meanwhile, the rulers of neighbouring weak or marginal states feared repercussions in their own countries if they rocked the boat. Grounds for forcible humanitarian intervention coexisted with systemic inhibitions upon it. Great power rivalry, local self-interest and the non-intervention norm all protected injustice.

A regional survey confirms that not only were there few examples of forcible humanitarian intervention coinciding with the greatest outrages, but that even in those few, the overwhelming response of the international community was indifference or disapproval.

4.2.1 Europe.   Here, although there was massive human rights abuse, in particular the colossal violations of Stalinist Russia, the great NATO–WTO confrontation across the central German plain scotched any thought of forcible humanitarian intervention – for example, in response to Soviet-led repression in Hungary in 1956. Meanwhile, European countries were engaged in the protracted, often bloody process of withdrawal from empire. It is striking that the list of putative forcible humanitarian interventions in this period includes only three examples involving European powers: Belgian intervention in the Congo in 1960 and 1964 and French intervention in the Central African Empire in 1979, none of which is a strong candidate.

Meanwhile, as part of the 'Helsinki' compromise formalized in 1975, the West recognized existing borders (non-intervention), while the Socialist bloc accepted the concept of common human rights standards (in some eyes, intervention). By the end of the period, in November 1990 at the Paris summit, the members of the Conference on Security and Co-operation in Europe (CSCE), which included all European countries except Albania, together with the United States and Canada, agreed to a complex array of principles and standards, including human rights measures, while upholding the norm of the non-use of force.

4.2.2 Middle East.   From the perspective of Arab states in the Middle East, the overwhelming example of fundamental human rights abuse was that perpetrated on Palestinians by the forced creation of the state of Israel. The ensuing conflict in 1948 has been proposed as an example of forcible humanitarian intervention, albeit a questionable one. Apart from this, no other instances come from the region, despite many examples of oppression and human rights abuse. It is worth noting that this is notwithstanding the fact that most UN peacekeeping operations at the time were located there. By contrast with the post-1990 period, peacekeeping and humanitarian intervention were not closely associated. Thus, Lebanon, which in the post-cold war world would surely have been a strong candidate, does not feature on any list (Zimbler, 1984).

4.2.3 Africa.   A number of suggested instances of forcible humanitarian intervention were in Africa (Congo/Zaire, Uganda, Central African

Empire, Ethiopia), as were various cases in which, in the eyes of many, there should have been intervention but was not (Burundi, Biafra/ Nigeria). The Organization of African Unity (OAU), despite its endorsement of the Banjul Charter on Human and Peoples' Rights in 1981, scrupulously adhered to the non-intervention convention. In response to the 1972 Tutsi massacres of Hutu in Burundi, for example, the OAU Secretary-General visited President Micombero at the height of the slaughter, and expressed total solidarity with him. The OAU summit at Rabat the following month did the same. As for the United Nations, when the Sub-Commission on Prevention of Discrimination and Protection of Minorities forwarded an account to the Commission on Human Rights, the latter, meeting in 1974, shelved the matter by appointing a working party to communicate with the Burundi government and report back the following year (Kuper, 1981, 163).

What were the reactions to the Tanzanian intervention in Uganda, leading to the flight of Idi Amin in March 1979, described at the beginning of chapter 1? At the sixteenth OAU summit in Monrovia in July 1979, most states 'remained silent, thereby indicating a tacit approval of Tanzanian action' (C. Thomas, 1985, 109). Sudan and Nigeria objected strongly, the latter no doubt in pique at Tanzanian recognition of Biafra during the Nigerian civil war. President Binaisa of Uganda urged African leaders to raise human rights issues openly, in order not to be accused of double standards, and denounced violations in the Central African Empire and Equatorial Guinea. The chairman of the OAU, however, ordered that President Binaisa's remarks be deleted from the record. As for the wider international community, most countries soon recognized the new regime in Uganda, and criticisms of Tanzanian action were muted. Caroline Thomas suggests that the reasons for this were (a) that the region was of little strategic significance, (b) that the conflict was not part of a broader pattern of hostilities, and (c) that Tanzania was a roughly equal power, not a regional hegemon (1985, 117). President Nyerere's declared aims in intervening included (a) humanitarian considerations, but his main concerns were (b) punitive action, (c) the prevention of future Ugandan claims, (d) support for legitimate Ugandan opposition, and (e) counter-intervention to match the presence of some 1,000 troops from Libya aiding Amin (C. Thomas, 1985, 92–108).

To balance this picture of regional endorsement of the non-intervention principle, we should remember the very different sentiments voiced over many years by a number of black African governments when it came to action, including military action, against human rights abuses in South Africa. This is well chronicled by John Vincent (1974, 261–77). It was the Tunisian representative to the United Nations who in 1961 declared that protection of human rights and fundamental freedoms was the essential purpose of the UN, and that the organization would dig its own grave if it tolerated abuses and failed to intervene (Vincent, 1974, 275). It was the South African representative who referred to 'dictatorial interference', questioned the General Assembly's competence, complained that to allow the UN to intervene 'was tantamount to denying the principle and attributes of sovereignty', and said that South Africa would never have joined the UN in 1945 had Charter Article 2(7) not been included (Vincent, 1974, 271).

4.2.4 South Asia.   This region exemplifies in microcosm the power politics of forcible humanitarian intervention on the global scale. Given Indian hegemony, there was only one possible serious intervener. Weak powers are not generally in a position to intervene against the strong. Hindu–Muslim violence in India is unlikely to invite Pakistani intrusion. The long-standing conflict in Kashmir sucked in UN observers and peacekeepers, but is not mentioned in connection with humanitarian intervention. The main examples of forcible humanitarian intervention in the region that have been put forward are Indian involvement in East Pakistan in 1971 and Indian action in Sri Lanka in 1987.

In East Pakistan the massacres of Bengalis in what became Bangladesh, beginning in March 1971, were, from the beginning, widely reported in the world's media. Yet, in August 1971, the UN Sub-Commission on Prevention of Discrimination and Protection of Minorities dismissed a written request for action by 22 international non-governmental organizations and a plea from the International Commission of Jurists. Only one member appears to have argued that silence should be broken. Leo Kuper comments: 'I find it almost unbearable to read this discussion by a United Nations body of one of the major genocides of the twentieth century; it was so procedural and so devoid of human compassion' (1981, 172). The UN Security Council and General Assembly did not become formally involved until December 1971, prompted by Indian intervention. Prior to this, the only effective action taken by the United Nations was to mount a large programme of humanitarian relief, which continued after the Indian intervention. Here is a case, far from unique, in which 'humanitarian assistance', although no doubt welcome, seems to have been resorted to as a substitute for coming to grips with the political dimensions of the problem, and as a way of shelving the question of protecting threatened people. Behind this lay the superpower line-up, with the United States and China supporting Pakistan and the Soviet Union supporting India.

In the event, India invaded East Pakistan on 5 December, and the next day recognized Bangladesh as an independent state. By 16 December the

West Pakistan army had surrendered at Dacca. Michael Akehurst points out that, although to begin with India offered some justification in terms of humanitarian intervention in the Security Council, when the proceedings were published these passages were deleted. He concludes that India 'realised that humanitarian intervention was an insufficient justification for the use of force'. Instead, India argued that Pakistan had attacked first (Akehurst, 1984, 96). Fernando Tesón responds:

> Contrary to what some commentators assert, India *did* articulate humanitarian reasons as justification for her military action. However, whether she did it or not . . . are matters of little importance. The important point here is not so much whether the Indian leaders harboured selfish purposes along with humanitarian ones, or in what proportion did those purposes blend as an efficient cause of the intervention (how could anyone establish that anyway?), but rather that the whole picture of the situation was one that warranted foreign intervention on grounds of humanity. Humanitarian intervention is the best interpretation we can provide for the Bangladesh war. (1988, 186)

Underlying this exchange is a semi-philosophical debate about the weight that should be assigned to declared motives when interpreting state practice in the light of international law, a point we return to at the end of the chapter.

Thomas Franck's and Nigel Rodley's judgement in the wake of the Bangladesh disaster, based on a comparison of the Indian response with that of other countries, was that 'in a surprising number of instances where the humanitarian factor was great but no threat existed to the political or economic concerns of foreign powers, states have evinced little interest in forceful surgical intervention' (1973, 279).

4.2.5 East Asia.   In this large region a number of post-colonial governments emerged and struggled to contain insurgency and build national cohesion. The most dramatic events were the Maoist seizure of power in China and a series of ferocious colonial and post-colonial wars culminating in American intervention in Vietnam. Massive human rights violations were perpetrated, particularly in China, Indonesia, Cambodia and latterly Myanmar (Burma). Characteristic of regional response has been the attitude of members of the Association of Southeast Asian Nations (ASEAN) since the formation of the organization in 1967, founded on adherence to the 'Asian way', whereby member governments support each other – for example against Communist insurgents – but on no account meddle in each other's domestic affairs, observing the 'rule of silence' when disagreement threatens (M. Haas, 1989). Western attempts to link aid to human rights or to orchestrate protest against China for repression in Tibet or for the Tiananmen square massacre, or against Indonesia for the Dili massacre in East Timor are branded 'cultural imperialism'. Emphasis is placed on the different traditions of mutual respect indigenous to local culture, while human rights linkage to trade and investment is seen as 'protectionism by other means', part of a global campaign 'to make us permanent developing countries' (Prime Minister of Malaysia, quoted by Klintworth, 1991).

At first sight this behaviour contrasts with UN Commission on Human Rights resolutions in March 1978 and March 1979 noting gross human rights abuse in Kampuchea and proposing to keep the situation under review. In submitting the 1978 draft, the United Kingdom representative referred to the Commission's examination of human rights abuse in Chile and South Africa, and warned that to turn a blind eye to what was going on in Kampuchea for political reasons would discredit the whole organization. After the Vietnamese invasion of 25 December 1978 and the subsequent overthrow of Pol Pot, however, the new Kampuchean government was not recognized, and, despite all the evidence of mass graves and heaps of bones, the General Assembly voted in September 1979 by a majority of 71 to continue assigning the Kampuchean seat to the ousted government. Pol Pot was tried *in absentia* by the new regime, in itself a rare event, but international society rewarded the perpetrators of one of the most grotesque atrocities in recorded history with immunity and the continuing formal respect due to a fellow club member. The West did not want to recognize a puppet government installed by a client of the Soviet Union. For their part, Vietnam and the Soviet Union defended the intervention, not on humanitarian grounds, but mainly as a double action, made up of (a) Vietnamese self-defence in response to Kampuchean cross-border aggression and (b) independent action by Kampuchean opposition forces who overthrew the Pol Pot regime. Michael Akehurst notes that in Security Council discussions not a single state spoke in favour of a right of humanitarian intervention (1984, 97). See also Gary Klintworth's analysis of the Vietnamese intervention, which includes consideration of the issue of humanitarian intervention in general (1989, 41–58).

4.2.6 Western Hemisphere.   In this region, as in South Asia, there was a single hegemon, in this case an overwhelmingly strong one. It is not surprising, therefore, that the relevant instances involved intervention by the United States, in the Dominican Republic (1965), Grenada (1983) and Panama (1989). The Monroe doctrine prohibited intervention in the region by outside powers, but not, evidently, intervention from within by the United States. All three seem questionable instances of humanitarian intervention.

In 1965, in preparing for intervention in the Dominican Republic, the United States took care to secure the backing of the Organization of American States (OAS) (Bogen, 1966). Justifying the action initially on the grounds of rescuing US and other nationals, President Johnson subsequently explained it as an action to prevent another Communist government in the region. Michael Akehurst questions its status as humanitarian intervention because, in theory, it was undertaken with the consent of the Dominican factions. In Grenada President Reagan's 'Operation Urgent Fury' launched on 25 October 1983 was also presented as 'humanitarian' in its early stages (Schachter, 1984; Levitin, 1986). But the State Department legal adviser later offered three different rationales: (a) protection of nationals, (b) collective action under the UN Charter, and (c) response to a request from the lawful authority (Arend and Beck, 1993, 127). The US aimed to extinguish Cuban influence on the island. Despite the fig-leaf of endorsement by the Organization of East Caribbean States, the action was immediately repudiated by 79 governments, and condemned as a violation of international law by a 108 to 9 vote in the UN General Assembly. The United States invasion of Panama on 20 December 1989 with 10,000 troops, aimed at seizing General Noriega ('Operation Just Cause'), was only obliquely presented as a humanitarian operation (Nanda et al., 1990). President Bush gave four objectives for the mission: (a) protection of US nationals, (b) defence of democracy, (c) elimination of drug-trafficking, and (d) upholding the Panama Canal Treaty. Strictly, none of these count as 'humanitarian'. The Organization of American States strongly criticized the United States, and only British, French and US vetoes prevented a condemnatory Security Council resolution.

A general conclusion on state reaction to massive human rights violations during the cold war era would have to be that the normal response was to do nothing. Not only were instances of forcible intervention rare, but even formal protest and the initiation of collective measures through recognized human rights procedures were seldom and, even then, only reluctantly invoked. It is striking that instances where mitigation of suffering was greatest as a result of the intervention, as in Kampuchea, received least international endorsement (Morris, 1991, quoted in Wheeler, 1992, 472). More usual was the practice of 'humanitarian aid' as a substitute for effective political engagement. The stipulation that to count as forcible humanitarian intervention, an action must be 'purely' or 'essentially' humanitarian in the sense of non-political seems quite

inappropriate in a situation in which the original violations were politically motivated, and in which the projection of armed force across a
border against the will of the target government in response was, by its
nature, political through and through. No wonder analysts who employ
such criteria conclude that there have been no examples of forcible
humanitarian intervention at all.

4.3 The debate in international ethics

In what follows, ethics will be understood to refer to 'a wide range of
considerations to do with choice and action' (Nardin and Mapel (eds),
1992, 3), not the narrower sphere defined by conventional rules of
proper conduct – what Bernard Williams calls 'the peculiar institution of
morality' (1985, 6). It is common, particularly for opponents of forcible
humanitarian intervention, to brand those they disagree with as moralists
who do not engage with tough practicalities, as Michael Stedman does in
his criticism of 'the new interventionists' (1993, 1–2). In our view, all
those who evaluate policy options and defend recommendations by
appeal to general principles which apply in comparable situations are
engaged in ethical debate. They are making judgements about what *is* the
case in order to advocate what *should be* the case. This applies as much
to those opposed to humanitarian intervention as to those in favour. In
a heated public issue such as this, where very high values are at stake, all
positions at critical points take on an ethical dimension, including those
of 'realists' and 'pragmatists'.

The core of the ethical debate lies in the tension between the two
clusters of values reflected in the UN Charter, which 'intersect with each
other and which may sometimes work at cross-purposes' (Damrosch
1993, 93). These are state system values and human rights values. The
two main components of the non-intervention norm can be recognized
here: reciprocity and mutual recognition of juridical equality representing the first cluster, popular sovereignty and the self-determination of
peoples the second. In other words, the ethical debate about forcible
humanitarian intervention is a debate *within* ethics. It is also, in its
furthest reaches, a debate *about* ethics. In what Robert Jackson calls
'classical' international ethics, it is the first cluster of values which takes
priority (1993, 582). Here the burden of proof lies with would-be
interveners. For cosmopolitans, on the other hand, the roles are reversed,
and the burden of proof shifts accordingly. To hold on to both sets of
values is to be confronted by a dilemma, which has been well described
by Fernando Tesón:

The first horn of the dilemma [intervention] opens the door for unpredictable and serious undermining of world order. The second horn of the dilemma [non-intervention] entails the seemingly morally intolerable proposition that the international community, in the name of the non-intervention rule, is impotent to combat massacres, acts of genocide, mass murder and widespread torture. (1988, 4)

This can be further clarified by reference to the model of the international collectivity developed in the conclusion to chapter 1 (see diagram 4).

Associated with (1) international anarchy (international system) is intervention by the powerful in pursuit of national interest (intervention (A)). Here, on most readings, there is no room for humanitarian intervention. Associated with (2) the pluralist/statist end of the international society spectrum is the non-intervention norm, which precludes intervention altogether. It is a bridle on international anarchy. Associated with (3) the solidarist/internationalist end of the international society spectrum (international community), we find the locus where forcible humanitarian intervention is most likely to emerge as a possibility (intervention (B)). At the level of world community or world society (although there is ambiguity here between Kant's federalist and universalist models), the separation of states, upon which the whole notion of intervention is predicated, has disappeared. The central dilemma, therefore, is this: if we *are not* allowed to move from non-intervention to intervention (B), then victims are abandoned to their fate, and the most appalling crimes go unchecked and unpunished; on the other hand, if we *are* allowed to move from non-intervention to intervention (B), then the breach thus made is likely to encourage an upsurge in intervention (A) (this is the 'argument from abuse').

We cannot go through all the arguments in detail, but it is important to recognize that each position is complex and includes an important normative component. Taking the realist/pluralist/statist argument against forcible humanitarian intervention first, the *realist* element is

1 International anarchy   Intervention (A): interest and power
   Realist
2 International society (i)   Non-intervention: the value of order
   Pluralist/statist
3 International society (ii)   Intervention (B): humanitarianism
   Solidarist/internationalist
   (International/community)
4 World community   Intervention no longer defined
   Cosmopolitan/universalist

Diagram 4: *Two Types of Intervention*

both descriptive (governments do not in fact behave like that) and normative (governments should not behave like that). Hans Morgenthau argues that states both intervene and oppose intervention when it is in their interest to do so: moral and legal arguments serve no other function than 'to discredit the intervention of the other side and to justify one's own' (1967, 425). On the other hand, when 18 US Rangers were killed in Somalia, outraged senators thundered that this was an ethical impera-tive: governments *should* not risk their soldiers' lives except 'for the safety and security of this nation' (McCain, 1994, 67). An example of the *pluralist* element is Michael Walzer's (1983) argument that there are overlapping 'spheres of justice', not just a single universal sphere. But he does concede that genocide, such as that perpetrated by Pol Pot in Kampuchea, breaches a universal minimal code and is intolerable, re-gardless of whether it reflects genuine local cultural practice and enjoys widespread popular support (which this did not). This is linked to an important normative component which locates value in the variety of political community. For communitarians it is what is inside the eggshell (community) that explains why it is worth preserving the egg-box (non-intervention). For intricate debate here, see the interchange between the communitarian Michael Walzer and his 'four critics' (Walzer, 1992/1977, 1980; Wasserstrom, 1978; Doppelt, 1978; Beitz, 1980a,b; Luban, 1980a,b. See also Elfstrom, 1983, and McMahon, 1986). David Luban argued that loss of inner legitimacy through gross human rights abuse thereby forfeited outer immunity: 'in such a case intervention is justified' (1980a, 180). Walzer's final position was that even though the 'fit' between government and the 'political life of its people' may be bad, this is no justification for humanitarian intervention. We must act *as if* governments are internally legitimate, because to do otherwise threatens the autonomy necessary for the natural, if painful, emergence of free, civilized polities. This is the argument of John Stuart Mill. On the other hand, as we have seen, Walzer (1980) conceded that if the 'fit' is very bad – that is to say, if there is genocide or its equivalent – then forcible intervention may be justified after all, other things being equal. Finally, the *statist* element brings the realist and pluralist positions together by combining (i) the continuing threat from predatory states of far greater power and (ii) the absence of international consensus on human rights norms, in order to argue against the human-itarian intervention option in case it thereby opens the door to abuse by the powerful and jeopardizes the precarious order of the international society of states (Bull, 1995/1977, 92–4). Here it is 'state system values' which are seen to prevail.

    What of the solidarist/internationalist/universalist position? *Contra* the realists and statists, *internationalists* emphasize the role of international law, not only as representing the interests of states, but also as the embodiment of aspirations towards the creation of a more civilized international community. Human rights values are given as much weight as state system values, and individuals and peoples are recognized as subjects for whom international society as a whole has responsibility. Such responsibility also carries concomitant rights to act in appropriate ways and through appropriate channels as legitimized through international law. In the words of UN Secretary-General Pérez de Cuéllar, 'the principle of non-interference with the essential domestic jurisdiction of states cannot be regarded as a protective barrier behind which human rights could be massively and systematically violated with impunity' (1991, 5). The principle of the territorial integrity and political independence of states embodied in the non-intervention rule would itself be undermined if it were taken to imply that sovereignty included the right to commit massacre and genocide. Pluralist communitarian arguments are met by the *solidarist* sentiment eloquently articulated 400 years ago by Alberico Gentili when arguing in favour of humanitarian intervention in a chapter entitled 'Of an honourable reason for waging war': 'the subjects of others do not seem to me to be outside that kinship of nature and society formed by the whole world. And, if you abolish that society, you will destroy the unity of the human race' (1964/1598, 122). The argument is underpinned by rejection of cultural relativism and vigorous *universalist* espousal of the cross-cultural humanitarian norms recognized in international humanitarian law. Earlier in the chapter we suggested that at its core the debate was one within the international society paradigm, focused on the two components of the non-intervention norm. Fernando Tesón shows this clearly in his unequivocal assertion of the interventionist case:

> My main argument is that because the ultimate justification of the existence of states is the protection and enforcement of the natural rights of the citizens, a government that engages in substantial violations of human rights betrays the very purpose for which it exists and so forfeits not only its domestic legitimacy, but its international legitimacy as well. (1988, 15)

As a corrective to the idea that the ethical debate about forcible humanitarian intervention was a simple line-up between realists, pluralists and statists on the one hand and internationalists, solidarists and universalists on the other, it is as well to remember how ready interventionist 'political realists' were to breach the non-intervention norm on broad humanitarian grounds of solidarity, as in the case of the Atlanticist values espoused by President Reagan and Prime Minister Thatcher. The same was true, as we will see below, of 'legal realists'. Conversely, thoughtful commentators such as Jack Donnelly, who calls himself an 'internationalist', and Richard Falk, whose support for the concept of a 'global civil society' suggests strong universalist or cosmopolitan sympathies, although they both insist on the primacy of human rights values, are at the same time both opposed to forcible humanitarian intervention (Donnelly, 1984; Falk, 1992, 227).

4.4 The debate in international law

The debate about forcible humanitarian intervention in international law was technical and elaborate. We will follow Anthony Arend and Robert Beck in comparing restrictionist interpretations of the UN regime, which were mainly used to rule out forcible humanitarian intervention, with counter-restrictionist interpretations, which were mainly used to rule it in (Arend and Beck, 1993, 112–37). Restrictionists and counter-restrictionists disagreed under four main heads: (a) interpretation of the UN Charter; (b) interpretation of UN General Assembly resolutions and International Court of Justice judgements; (c) interpretation of customary international law; and (d) assessment of likely consequence (for the relevant literature, see box 9).

4.4.1 Interpretation of the UN Charter.   Restrictionist readings of the UN Charter were constructed from two main elements. First is the assertion that other UN aims were clearly subordinate to the overarching purpose of maintaining international peace and security. This was

---

Box 9: Restrictionists and Counter-Restrictionists

Although lumping commentators together into two rival camps is somewhat crude and overlooks nuances, the restrictionist case may broadly be said to have been supported by Akehurst (1984); Bowett (1986); Brownlie (1963, 1973); Chatterjee (1981); Chimni (1980); Fairley (1980); Farer (1973); Franck and Rodley (1973); Hassan (1981); Higgins (1984); Jhabvala (1981); Ronzitti (1985); Schachter (1984); Verwey (1985). Counter-restrictionists included Bazyler (1987); Behuniak (1978); Chilstrom (1974); D'Amato (1987); Fonteyne (1973, 1974); Lauterpacht (1955); Levitin (1986); Lillich (1967; (ed.), 1973); Moore (1974); Reisman (1990); Reisman and McDougal (1973); Sornarajah (1981); Tesón (1988); Umozurike (1982); Wright (1989).

argued, in part, by reference to the *travaux préparatoires* (preparatory work) at the time the Charter was being produced and to subsequent state practice. Counter-restrictionists insisted that equally important was the purpose of protecting human rights. They pointed to Articles 1(3), 55 and 56 of the Charter:

> The purposes of the United Nations are . . . [t]o achieve international co-operation in . . . encouraging respect for human rights and for fundamental freedoms for all without distinction as to race, sex, language or religion. (Article 1(3))

> [T]he United Nations shall promote . . . (c) universal respect for, and observance of, human rights and fundamental freedoms for all. (Article 55)

> All members pledge themselves to take joint and separate action in co-operation with the Organization for the achievement of the purposes set forth in article 55. (Article 56)

With reference to the 1948 Universal Declaration of Human Rights, Michael Reisman and Myres McDougal commented: '[t]he Preamble to this Declaration, a luminous and moving expression of human dignity, emphasized the Charter's conception of the inseparability of human rights and international peace' (1973, 173; see also Tesón, 1988, 131).

Second, restrictionists adopted a broad interpretation of Article 2(4) of the UN Charter, which increased its scope for restricting the use of force. Article 2(4) reads:

> All members shall refrain in their international relations from the threat or use of force against the territorial integrity or political independence of any state, or in any manner inconsistent with the purposes of the United Nations.

It was seen to impose a strict prohibition on the unilateral use of cross-border force, except in self-defence against armed attack (Article 51). General Assembly Resolution 3314 (1974) on the definition of aggression was held to confirm a strict definition of 'self-defence'. Even self-defence was now under UN control, intended as an interim measure while collective response was being prepared. In short, there was seen to be no room for forcible humanitarian intervention under the UN *jus ad bellum* regime. Counter-restrictionists offered a different interpretation. They argued that forcible humanitarian intervention was below the 'threshold' of Article 2(4), because it was strictly limited and temporary, and did not threaten the 'territorial integrity or political independence' of the target state (Reisman and McDougal, 1973, 177; Tesón, 1988, 131). They further claimed that since, as noted above, protection of human rights *was* one of the two main *raisons d'être* of the United Nations, humanitarian intervention was not 'inconsistent' with its purposes. Restrictionists denied that forcible humanitarian intervention as normally envisaged was below the threshold, pointing out that the clauses in Article 2(4) were disjunctive, linked by 'or', so they applied severally. Article 51 was more significant in the debate about intervention to protect nationals than in the debate about humanitarian intervention, because including intervention to protect the citizens of another country as 'self-defence' would be too far-fetched.

4.4.2 Interpretation of UN General Assembly resolutions and International Court of Justice judgements.

With specific reference to intervention, as against general prohibition on the threat or use of force, further weight was placed by restrictionists on General Assembly Resolutions 2131 (1965) on the Inadmissibility of Intervention in the Domestic Affairs of States, and 2625 (1970) on Principles of International Law Concerning Friendly Relations and Co-operation Among States (see section 1.2). In the *Nicaragua* case (1986) the ICJ treated the 1965 resolution as not only elucidatory of the UN Charter, but as declaratory of customary norms of international law. Counter-restrictionists noted that General Assembly resolutions were not binding, pointed to the inconclusive results of attempts to define intervention, and, as elaborated below, denied that forcible humanitarian intervention was proscribed by customary international law. On the specific issue of interpreting the 1986 *Nicaragua* judgement, compare Nigel Rodley's restrictionist interpretation (1989, 327–32) with Fernando Tesón's counter-restrictionist interpretation (1988, 201–44).

4.4.3 Interpretation of customary international law.

This was one of the centre-pieces of the counter-restrictionist case. Having denied that the UN Charter imposed absolute restrictions on forcible humanitarian intervention, they further pointed to the fact that the collective measures envisaged in the UN Charter for enforcing UN purposes had in the event failed. As a result, customary law was revived, and forcible self-help to protect human rights re-emerged as legitimate action, just as it had been before 1945 (Lillich, 1967, 335; Lillich (ed.), 1973, 61; Reisman and McDougal, 1973, 178; Tesón, 1988, 137–42). This is sometimes referred to as the 'link' argument. The debate about whether there actually *was* a pre-1945 customary right of forcible humanitarian intervention was extensive, counter-restrictionists relying on judgements such as that of Sir Hersch Lauterpacht that a 'considerable body of opinion and practice' supported such a customary right (1955/1906, 312). The evidence cited by Jean-Pierre Fonteyne for a pre-1914 customary right was influential (1974, 232–6; see also Bazyler, 1987, 573), but has been recently challenged (Grewe, 1984, cited in Malanczuk, 1993, 9). On the whole, as often happens in such arguing, those who thought that there *should* be such a customary right also thought that there *was*, whereas those who thought that there *should not be* maintained that there *was not*. In response to the 'link' argument, restrictionists point to the ICJ ruling in the *Corfu Channel* case (1949), that intervention is prohibited 'whatever the present defects in international organisation' (ICJ Reports, 1949, 35).

4.4.4 Assessment of likely consequence.   Here the technical debate within international law connects with the broader political and ethical debates described above. The anti-intervention case is clearly presented by Ian Brownlie, a leading restrictionist:

> My position is that humanitarian intervention, on the basis of all available definitions, would be an instrument wide open to abuse. . . . [T]here is a great deal of useful circumstantial evidence which suggests both that the law does not recognise humanitarian intervention and also that the prognosis for such action as a genuine instrument for the benefit of mankind is not good. . . . [W]hatever special cases one can point to, a rule allowing humanitarian intervention, as opposed to a discretion in the United Nations to act through the appropriate organs, is a general license to vigilantes and opportunists to resort to hegemonial intervention. (1973, 146–8)

Arguing the other way is Richard Lillich, to the effect that, whatever the state of law as it is (*lex lata*), what is important is to develop law as it should be (*lex ferenda*): 'Surely to require a state to sit back and watch the slaughter of innocent people in order to avoid blanket prohibitions against the use of force is to stress blackletter [law] at the expense of far more fundamental values' (1967, 344). Behind this again lay differing interpretations of the meaning of the word 'legitimacy' and different understandings of the nature of international law itself.

5 Conclusion: international community revisited

In a pure international anarchy there would, as John Austin argued in the last century, be no room for international law (see diagram 5), but only for the municipal law of separate states (1954/1832). In a world community with an effective world government, international law would become global-domestic law, and humanitarian protection would thus be a matter for 'internal' police action. International law lies somewhere

1 International anarchy   State-domestic law
2 International society (i)   International law (i)
3 International society (ii)/ International law (ii)
   International community
4 World community   Global-domestic law
                               (Natural law?)

Diagram 5: *International Society, International*
Community and International Law

between the two, identified in particular with the broad spectrum of the international society of states. But it presides precariously in this position. Is international law to be seen as 'a progressive instrument of change, as a means of furthering the interests of peoples rather than governments, as something antithetical to the Hobbesian world of brute force'? (Roberts, 1990, 84). On this reading (level 3), it aspires 'upwards' towards international community and beyond. Or is it, rather, to be seen as 'a practical means of devising modest and limited adjustments between conflicting interests of great powers, who are the principal agents of its creation'? (Roberts, 1990, 84). On this view (level 2), it looks 'downwards' into the international anarchy, where, without world government or a central court, international law is auto-interpreted by the states that have created it, with the powerful states calling the shots. Our model suggests that international law is both of these.

This ambivalent position of international law can lead to some odd results. For example, in the debate about the nature of international law, advocates of the legitimacy (in both the broad and the narrow senses) of forcible humanitarian intervention try to overcome the non-intervention prohibition from 'above' as well as 'below'. Fernando Tesón (1988) argues mainly from above, affirming the ethical foundations of international law, *contra* the legal positivists. This could be called a 'natural law' approach. Anthony D'Amato and the so-called realists of the Yale school of international law, on the other hand, argue from below, as the name 'realist' implies. Like most political realists, they argue, *contra* the 'classical' school, that '[t]he truly operative rules generated by the customary practice of states . . . are the rules that in reality accommodate the most deeply felt interests of the community of states' (1987, 231). In other words, if there are deeply held common state interests, then these will prevail in emergent customary law, even if they are at variance with the 'received wisdom' of inherited constraints. States can, in the end, do what they want. In Tom Farer's phrase, the legal realists thereby 'skip lightly over the wall between law and normative preference' (1991, 195). The unusual twist is that among the 'deeply felt interests' of the community of states some legal realists include concern for universal human dignity ('the inherent and equal value of every human being'), not usually seen as a 'realist' value. In this way they square the circle. Such are some of the paradoxes inherent in the ambivalent position of non-intervention and international law, perched uncomfortably between a realist world of interest and power and a cosmopolitan world of shared values and justice.

The cold war debate about humanitarian intervention, richer and more complex than restrictionist definitions suggest, is, therefore, a debate within international society – indeed, within the two main aspects of the non-intervention norm. In its developed form it is a global debate within international politics, international ethics and international law, which, at its deepest level, reaches down to questions about the very nature of the international collectivity itself. Since the end of the cold war, it has become a critical debate about how the international community should respond to the escalating impact of armed conflict on civilian populations. This issue, the contemporary context for humanitarian intervention, is the subject for chapter 3.

Suggested reading

On state sovereignty see C. Thomas, 1985, and Jackson, 1990. On non-intervention, the classic recent text is Vincent, 1974. On intervention, a well-known collection of essays edited and contributed to by Hedley Bull (1984) can be recommended. For up-to-date brief surveys, see Little, 1993, and Trachtenberg, 1993. Useful introductions to humanitarian intervention are offered in Rodley (ed.), 1992, and Arend and Beck, 1993, ch. 8. An excellent idea of the nature of informed scholarly debate in the 1960s and 1970s can be gained from Lillich (ed.), 1973, which has contributions by Brownlie, Falk, Farer, Fonteyne, Lillich and Reisman among others. Moore, 1974, is another classic text by a writer who is sympathetic to the concept. The debate is summarized in Beyerlin, 1982. For debate in the 1980s, compare Tesón's (1988) advocacy of humanitarian intervention with Akehurst's (1984) restrictionist account. On the debate in international politics, see references for the various relevant interventions given in the text. On the debate in international ethics it is a good idea to begin with Walzer's argument in 1992/1977, then move on to the debate it stimulated in the pages of the journal *Philosophy and Public Affairs*, much of it usefully collected in Beitz et al. (eds), 1985, 165–246.

Part II

Reconceptualization: Humanitarian Intervention in Contemporary Conflict

Introduction: Humanitarian Intervention in Iraq

In Part II we turn to the period 1991–4 to see how much of the cold war debate about forcible humanitarian intervention has survived the end of the cold war. It is dangerous to reach hasty conclusions about world politics so soon after the collapse of an old order. After each of the upheavals of 1815, 1871, 1918, and 1945, it took several years for the nature of new geopolitical configurations to emerge clearly, and there is no reason why the situation should be any different in the post-cold war world. The fact that there were no UN Security Council vetoes between June 1990 and May 1993 (when Russia vetoed a resolution about financing the peacekeeping operation in Cyprus) does not mean that new hard-line governments in Russia or China may not revert to confrontation and once again emasculate the machinery for collective action. Nor may the United States government be prepared to continue to underwrite UN operations. Conflict patterns may shift again. Nevertheless, the literature on post-cold war forcible humanitarian intervention is already extensive, and comparison with (i) the cold war literature on forcible humanitarian intervention and (ii) the post-cold war literature on nonforcible humanitarian intervention shows that a fundamental transformation has already taken place. This was presaged as early as April 1991, when, in the immediate aftermath of the 1990–1 Gulf conflict, the 'new world order', proclaimed by President Bush somewhat hastily in September 1990 (Bush, 1990), received an unexpected challenge in the form of the humanitarian crisis that threatened to overwhelm Kurds and Shi'a in the north and south of Iraq. UN Security Council Resolution 688 of

5 April 1991 ushered in a new phase of the humanitarian intervention debate.

1 Security Council Resolution 688 and forcible humanitarian intervention: 'Operation Provide Comfort' and 'Operation Southern Watch'

On 27 February 1991 President Bush declared an end to 'Desert Storm', the six-week campaign to expel Iraqi forces from Kuwait. In so doing, he abandoned Kurdish and Shi'ite insurgents in the north and south of Iraq whom he had earlier encouraged to 'take matters into their own hands to force Saddam Hussein the dictator to step aside and to comply with the United Nations resolutions' (*International Herald Tribune*, 16 February 1991, cited in Freedman and Boren, 1992). The dictator, far from stepping aside, immediately began to wreak terrible vengeance on the rebels. Some 400,000 Kurds fled to the frozen mountains bordering Turkey, destitute and vulnerable. By the end of March, television pictures were reaching the West showing 1,000 dying daily. By early April, pressure was mounting on the victorious allies to act.

Did those who were suffering have a right to assistance and protection? If so, who had a duty to provide it in the absence of proper conduct by the government of Iraq? What means could and should be adopted? With what authority?

What happened next was unexpected, and has been much debated since (see Adelman, 1992a,b; Freedman and Boren, 1992; Gallant, 1992; Stromseth, 1993). At first the United States was reluctant to do anything substantial, not wanting to contravene the principle of non-intervention which had just been upheld in the war, fearing involvement in a Vietnam-style quagmire, and reluctant to trigger a breakup of Iraq which might be to Iran's advantage. Media pressure mounted, however, and France and Turkey convened a meeting of the UN Security Council. Both Turkey and Iran insisted that the flood of refugees, as well as Iraqi cross-border incursions, made this a matter fit for Security Council consideration. The result was the promulgation of Security Council Resolution 688 on 5 April 1991, which, under the usual rubric of 'removing the threat to international peace and security in the region', made the demands set out in box 10.

During the next few days, 'Operation Provide Comfort' was launched to protect the Kurds. (i) Airdrops of food, blankets and clothes were made (crates dropped on 18 April inadvertently killing some of the refugees); (ii) an air exclusion zone was imposed north of the 36th parallel; and (iii) 'safe havens' were set up for the Kurds in northern Iraq (as suggested by a number of leaders, notably John Major on 8 April, and

Box 10: Security Council Resolution 688

Adopted by the Security Council at its 2982nd meeting on 5 April 1991

The Security Council,

Mindful of its duties and its responsibilities under the Charter of the United Nations for the maintenance of international peace and security,

Recalling Article 2, paragraph 7, of the Charter of the United Nations,

Gravely concerned by the repression of the Iraqi civilian population in many parts of Iraq, including most recently in Kurdish populated areas, which led to a massive flow of refugees towards and across international frontiers and to cross-border incursions, which threaten international peace and security in the region,

Deeply disturbed by the magnitude of the human suffering involved,

Taking note of the letters sent by the representatives of Turkey and France to the United Nations dated 2 April 1991 and 4 April 1991, respectively (S/22435 and S/22442),

Taking note also of the letters sent by the Permanent Representative of the Islamic Republic of Iran to the United Nations dated 3 and 4 April 1991, respectively (S/22436 and S/22447),

Reaffirming the commitment of all Member States to the sovereignty, territorial integrity and political independence of Iraq and of all States in the area,

Bearing in mind the Secretary-General's report of 20 March 1991 (S/22366),

1. Condemns the repression of the Iraqi civilian population in many parts of Iraq, including most recently in Kurdish populated areas, the consequences of which threaten international peace and security in the region;

2. Demands that Iraq, as a contribution to remove the threat to international peace and security in the region, immediately end this repression and express the hope in the same context that an open dialogue will take place to ensure that the human and political rights of all Iraqi citizens are respected;

3. Insists that Iraq allow immediate access by international humanitarian organizations to all those in need of assistance in all parts of Iraq and to make available all necessary facilities for their operations;

4. Requests the Secretary-General to pursue his humanitarian efforts in Iraq and to report forthwith, if appropriate on the basis of a further mission to the region, on the plight of the Iraqi civilian population, and in particular the Kurdish population, suffering from the repression in all its forms inflicted by the Iraqi authorities;

5. Requests further the Secretary-General to use all the resources at his disposal, including those of the relevant United Nations agencies, to address urgently the critical needs of the refugees and displaced Iraqi population;

6. Appeals to all Member States and to all humanitarian organizations to contribute to these humanitarian relief efforts;

7. Demands that Iraq co-operate with the Secretary-General to these ends;

8. Decides to remain seized of the matter.

at first resisted by the United States, which finally acquiesced on 16 April). Six protection zones were established by US, British, French and Dutch troops. Saddam Hussein's attacks on Kurdish towns and villages were halted, and most of the surviving refugees eventually returned to their homes. On 26 August 1991 a second no-fly zone was imposed south of the 32nd parallel to protect the Shi'a. This was 'Operation Southern Watch'. Good accounts of these events can be found in Freedman and Boren, 1992, and Stromseth, 1993.

1.1 Was the action humanitarian?

It was immediately clear that the humanitarian aspect of the intervention had expanded beyond the cold war norm. In so far as the military action was entailed in Security Council Resolution 688 (to be discussed below), the humanitarian brief went beyond ensuring that 'the human and political rights of all Iraqi citizens are respected' to include demands that the Iraqi authorities 'allow immediate access by humanitarian organizations to all those in need of assistance in all parts of Iraq'. Member states were asked to contribute to these 'humanitarian relief efforts'. If military action was justified under this rubric, its function was not only to protect threatened populations but to help create the space within which humanitarian assistance could be provided. In other words, the identification of 'humanitarian' solely with protection of human rights, as in the classic definitions of humanitarian intervention, was no longer adequate. In addition, as we argued in chapter 2, in the cold war debate the 'humanitarian' dimension was in any case neglected and was in need of more careful conceptualization. This strongly suggests two adjustments.

First, we use the outcome of the enquiry into the nature of humanitarianism in chapter 1 to specify what 'humanitarianism' entails. There we drew not only on human rights discourse, but also on international humanitarian law and humanitarian assistance in general, to conclude that humanitarianism is best defined in terms of the four principles of humanity, impartiality, neutrality and universality.

Second, with this in mind, in determining whether a particular cross-border action counts as humanitarian, we move beyond the one-dimensional criterion of 'motive' and 'relative disinterest' characteristic of the earlier debate. Asked whether the motive of an intervening state is 'purely' or 'essentially' humanitarian, the only sensible answer is that motives are no doubt mixed, that they vary within the complex decision-making body of government, shift over time, are difficult if not impossible to impute, and in any case will be differently interpreted, no doubt in contradictory ways, by others involved, their judgements being similarly conditioned. Imputation of purpose or motive cannot on its own sustain such a load. We propose, therefore, to expand the list of criteria to include five questions: (i) was there a *humanitarian cause*? (ii) was there a declared *humanitarian end* in view? (iii) was there an appropriate *humanitarian approach*? – in other words, was the action carried out impartially, and were the interests of the interveners at any rate not incompatible with the humanitarian purpose? (iv) were *humanitarian means* employed? (v) was there a *humanitarian outcome*? It would be nice if these questions could be answered objectively. Unfortunately, they cannot be. They are matters of judgement and interpretation, and are therefore bound to be controversial. The criterion of humanitarian outcome in particular is very difficult to apply.

1.1.1 Humanitarian cause. The prima facie case for there being a humanitarian cause is strong, because the human suffering was so great. But questions arise when it is remembered that similar situations in other countries did not produce comparable efforts; nor, more to the point, had similar suffering by the Kurds in the past occasioned more than lukewarm protest. Again and again, the great powers had supported then abandoned the Kurds, as when promises of independence made in the 1920 Treaty of Sèvres were laid aside in the 1923 Treaty of Lausanne, or when former backing was removed for geopolitical reasons in 1975 (Adelman, 1992b, 6). Encouraged by Iran during the 1980–8 Iran–Iraq war, incipient Iraqi Kurdish opposition was subsequently crushed in the 'Anfal', a brutal campaign in which some 100,000 were killed and whole villages destroyed, and in which the notorious chemical weapon attack on Halabja was made in March 1988. Refugees poured across the Turkish border. Protests were eventually made by France and the United States, but no sanctions were imposed. The Soviet Union and France continued to supply arms to the Iraqi regime. The United States supported Saddam Hussein as a counter to Iran. Turkey was preoccupied with its own Kurdish problem. Even Iran played a double game. When, in 1991, the Iraqi Kurds at last received serious attention, it was the turn of the Shi'a in the south to be relatively neglected. Western press bias virtually ignored the much greater numbers of Shi'a refugees in Iran. Although Security Council Resolution 688 covered 'those in need of assistance in all parts of Iraq', and the official report from UN special rapporteur Max van der Stoel later confirmed massive human rights abuse among the Shi'a and other minorities in the region, humanitarian assistance of the kind negotiated in the north was not allowed in the south, and no safe havens were set up.

1.1.2 Humanitarian end.   As to the declared ends being humanitarian, this was certainly how the operation was described by President Bush in announcing 'Operation Provide Comfort' on 16 April (USIA, 18 April, quoted by Freedman and Boren, 1992, 55). But when states are sending troops across borders, it is, to say the least, unlikely that humanitarian ends can be separated from political ends, as the humanitarian principle of neutrality implies. John Major's original proposal of 'safe enclaves' was altered by the British Foreign Office to 'safe havens' because of the political connotations of 'enclaves'. State intervention in volatile international-social conflicts (a term explained in chapter 3) is bound to have political connotations, no matter what the declared ends, as in this case where the allies had to damp down the Kurdish political expectations raised by the intervention and urge limited autonomy within Iraq rather than secession. Beyond this lies the question of whether humanitarian ends should be separated from political ends in the first place. As Jane Stromseth notes, an overtly non-political 'humanitarian' approach may command greater normative agreement, and even turn out to be the first step on the way to an eventual settlement, but, by the same token, it is unlikely on its own to address the underlying political problems which caused the suffering in the first place, and may be used as a pretext for not doing so (1993, 100).

1.1.3 Humanitarian approach.   Were motives humanitarian, and were the political interests of the interveners compatible with the declared humanitarian ends? This is what has traditionally been taken to be the critical criterion. No doubt genuine humanitarian concern on the part of the main actors was mixed with prudent calculations of military capability and political interest. James Mayall, in a judgement widely endorsed elsewhere in the literature, sees the reason for the belated allied response to Kurdish and Shi'a suffering as 'not because of a reassessment of international obligations towards those who have had their rights systematically abused, but because the attention devoted by the Western media to the plight of the Kurds along the Turkish border threatened the political dividends that Western governments had secured from the conduct of the war itself' (1991, 426). The role of Turkey is also worth commenting on as an example of regional considerations. The whole of 'Operation Provide Comfort' (as also the Gulf War itself and further Western policies throughout the wider region) was dependent upon Turkish co-operation. Turkey for its part was a member of NATO, had just signed the Conference on Security and Co-operation in Europe (CSCE) Treaty of Paris, with its stipulations about minority rights, and was keen to associate itself with the prospective European Union. On the other hand, it was locked in vicious repression of its own large Kurdish minority, according to some accounts as brutal as that of Saddam Hussein (letter from Turkish Kurdish MP Leyla Zana, *The Times*, 14 September 1994). The separatist Turkish Kurdish Workers' Party (PKK) had been strengthened by the earlier 1988 Iraqi Kurdish influx, and was trying to stir up support in Iraq for an independent Kurdistan. Turkish motives for convening the Security Council meeting were therefore mixed. The same was true of its own independent military intervention in Iraq in August 1991 in response to a PKK attack. This is a good example of the tangled political web of international-social conflict in which interventions are inevitably caught up. At various times the Turkish government aligned itself with Saddam Hussein against the Iraqi Kurds, with the moderate Iraqi Kurdish leadership against the PKK, or, as at the time of the August incursion, found itself opposed by a reconciled Iraqi government–Iraqi Kurd front.

1.1.4 Humanitarian means. This is an important dimension which is generally ignored in classic discussions. Were the means employed compatible with a humanitarian mission? In this instance, because allied military preponderance was so great in the aftermath of the Gulf War, apart from the occasional shooting down of an Iraqi plane and bombing of anti-aircraft emplacements, threats were usually enough, so the issue of humanitarian interveners themselves contravening humanitarian standards in this sense hardly arose. But this has not been the case elsewhere. Moreover, as Max van der Stoel noted in his 1993 report to the UN, suffering induced by continuing economic sanctions which affected the whole of Iraq (which on our reconceptualization also counts as intervention) ironically added to Saddam Hussein's 'internal blockade' of the Kurdish region to impose a double embargo on those who were supposed to be receiving UN aid (Commission on Human Rights, *Report on the Situation of Human Rights in Iraq*, UN Doc. E/CN4/1993/45).

1.1.5 Humanitarian outcome. This is notoriously difficult to assess, but let us agree that as far as the Kurdish population was concerned, the result was indeed a marked diminution in human suffering, at least in the immediate aftermath. Whether a failure to address the underlying political conditions which stimulated the humanitarian concern in the first place means, paradoxically, that the situation in the end is worse than it would have been without the intervention remains to be seen. The situation was soon complicated by political in-fighting among the Kurdish groups. The debate about outcome is further bedevilled by problems of counter-factuality: we cannot rewind the tape, remove an ingredient, and replay it to see what difference it would have made. Nor can those who intervene know at the outset what the overall future outcome will be. They have to estimate as best they can. In this case, Massoud Barzani, president of one of the two main Iraqi Kurdish political parties, the Kurdistan Democratic Party (DPK) describes the tears and flowers when allied coalition forces began to pull out in July 1991 and hand over to the much smaller numbers of UN guards (1993, 63). This may vindicate the action in terms of Michael Walzer's test: does the outcome converge with the wishes of those in whose name it is carried out? The fate of the Shi'a and other peoples living in the marshlands to the south, however, was very different. The allied air exclusion zone did not prevent devastating attacks by land.

How well do the humanitarian credentials of 'Operation Provide Comfort' and 'Operation Southern Watch' survive this scrutiny? Unsurprisingly, the balance sheet is patchy and inconclusive. Nevertheless, despite severe criticism of previous neglect and dubious political motivation, we conclude that they should not be dismissed out of hand. It is worth adding that of the 10 states which voted for SCR 688, most justified it mainly, if not exclusively, in terms of the threat to international peace and security from trans-border flows of refugees. France added UN responsibility in the aftermath of war. Only a few states, notably Britain and France, stressed internal human rights. For France, in a striking departure from statist orthodoxy, human rights violations 'become a matter of international interest when they take on such proportions that they assume the dimension of a crime against humanity', whether or not there are direct cross-border implications (UN Doc. P/SV. 2982, 53; see Stromseth, 1993, 86–8, for a fuller account).

1.2 Was the action forcible intervention?

Two key questions were raised here. The first concerned agency, the second consent. On both counts, what was at issue was whether the action counted as forcible humanitarian intervention in the restrictionist sense.

On the question of agency, the critical question was: were operations 'Provide Comfort' and 'Southern Watch' authorized by the United Nations Security Council under SCR 688? If so, then here, perhaps, was a remarkable precedent whereby, for the first time, forcible humanitarian intervention was carried out, if not by the United Nations, then under the aegis of the United Nations. But would this count as forcible humanitarian intervention? According to the classical tradition, as we have seen, by definition it would not. First, collective enforcement action by the Security Council under Chapter VII of the UN Charter can only be in response to threats to international peace and security. Second, even if humanitarian concerns were smuggled in under the rubric 'threats to international peace and security', for restrictionists this would still not count as humanitarian intervention. Intervention by the United Nations itself is covered in UN Charter Article 2(7), but this specifically excepts 'the application of enforcement measures under Chapter VII'. And the Security Council, on most readings, can itself interpret the Charter provisions pertaining to its own function. In addition, the trouble in this case was that, despite its peremptory language and incantation of threats to international peace and security, SCR 688 in fact made no mention either of Chapter VI or of Chapter VII, but was kept deliberately vague (Rodley (ed.), 1992). Certainly, US and British spokespersons, particularly in the first fortnight after the resolution had been promulgated and before the Iraqi president came to a separate understanding with the UN, claimed that enforcement action was sanctioned under SCR 688. Most commentators agree with the view of then UN Secretary-General Pérez de Cuéllar, however, who strenuously denied that this was the case, insisting that foreign military presence in Iraq required *either* Iraqi consent *or* separate Security Council authorization. Verbal consent was never granted, nor authorization given. Indeed, the main reason why the wording of SCR 688 was kept vague was to secure its passage, despite the grave reservations of a number of Security Council members, including some who voted for it. The resolution was passed by a much narrower margin than earlier resolutions during the Gulf crisis. Zimbabwe, Yemen and Cuba voted against it, the Yemeni representative arguing that it set a 'dangerous precedent that could open the way to diverting the Council away from its basic functions and responsibilities for safeguarding international peace and security and towards addressing the internal affairs of countries', that most states will encounter 'internal difficulties and trans-border problems', and that it would be a step towards an ominous new world order that might change 'the rules that have contributed to stability over the past four decades' (UN Doc. S/PV. 2982, 28–30). India and China abstained, the latter's Li Daoyu acknowledging the trans-border effects of the Iraqi crisis, but expressing reservations on the grounds that

this is a question of great complexity, because the internal affairs of a country are also involved. According to Paragraph 7 to Article 2 of the Charter, the Security Council should not consider or take action on questions concerning the internal affairs of any State. As for the international aspects involved in the question, we are of the view that they should be settled through the appropriate channels. We support the Secretary-General in rendering humanitarian assistance to the refugees through the relevant organisations. (UN Doc. S/PV. 2982, 55–6)

Even a state like Ecuador, which voted for the resolution, thought that the Security Council might have no authority to act 'if we were dealing solely with a case of violation of human rights by a country within its own frontiers' (UN Doc. S/PV. 2982, 36). In fact, Western leaders themselves at other times offered different rationales for their forcible actions, such as British Foreign Secretary Douglas Hurd, who, in a remarkable reinterpretation of traditional norms, justified 'Operation Southern Watch' in the more conventional 'self-help' terms of customary international law:

[W]e operate under international law. Not every action that a British government or an American government or a French government takes has to be underwritten by a specific provision in a UN resolution provided we comply with international law. International law recognises extreme humanitarian need . . . We are on strong legal as well as humanitarian ground in setting up this 'no fly zone'. (Interview, BBC Radio 4, *Today*, 19 August 1991, quoted in Greenwood, 1993, 36)

A variant of this was the appeal to justified self-defence, as when Hurd explained the 13 January 1992 air strikes against Iraqi anti-aircraft missiles on those grounds.

As to the question of consent, classical definitions of forcible humanitarian intervention rule out actions carried out at the invitation of the target government or with permission. There were two difficulties here. First, the Iraqi president himself 'was ambivalent, formally protesting at the infringement of [Iraqi] sovereignty, but not resisting the action and in substance acquiescing' (Jennings and Watts (eds), 1992, 443). But this was only under duress, as a defeated power ever mindful that behind the velvet glove of 'Operation Provide Comfort' loomed the iron fist of 'Operation Poised Hammer' (see below). The second point is that within a fortnight of SCR 688 being passed, as detailed below, Saddam Hussein reached an understanding with UN representatives about the 'voluntary' arrangements to succeed the allied military action.

In short, before discussion of the significance of the operation began, unresolved ambiguities had already clouded the prior question of what its nature was. This was a foretaste of the kinds of conceptual, definitional and classificatory difficulties that would beset attempts to apply traditional restrictionist notions of forcible humanitarian intervention to the confusion of post-cold war conflict.

1.3 What precedent was set?

Bedevilled by these and other difficulties, a flood of comment followed about whether a significant precedent had been set and, if so, for what. To simplify, some observers saw SCR 688 and the action that followed as a global turning-point in forcible humanitarian intervention, in which, at last, statist non-intervention norms were giving way before a new international consensus that minimum humanitarian standards within states would be enforced by the international community (Chopra and Weiss, 1992; Garigue, 1993). This new area of activity might need (a) proper codification and (b) a restructuring of UN decision-making and capacities for collective implementation (Chopra and Weiss, 1992, 113); or perhaps the UN Charter should be adjusted to include a new chapter on human rights (Kartashkin, 1991, 203–4). Others, more cautiously, were at least prepared to conclude that international law 'no longer forbids military intervention altogether' when a government massacres its own people (Greenwood, 1993, 40; see also Klintworth, 1991). Others, even more cautiously, warned that 'it would be unwise to build on the safe havens case' (Freedman and Boren, 1992, 83), and that SCR 688 'is a fragile straw in the wind for future action' (Rodley (ed.), 1992, 33). James Mayall (1991) doubted whether action following on the special conditions of the aftermath of the Gulf War created significant precedents at all, while Adam Roberts, sceptical about the way in which the United States, Britain and France had created the safe havens by 'stretching the elastic of Security Council resolutions [not just 688] to breaking point', suggested setting aside the question of humanitarian intervention altogether, and interpreting the action in terms of allied responsibility after the war as a customary law variant on the rights of victors (1993a, 438). From this perspective, SCR 688 should be seen as a subset of the truly innovative and intrusive SCR 687 which had imposed the peace terms.

Whatever view was taken, the events of 1991 had materially shifted the terms of the forcible humanitarian intervention debate. First, the humanitarian component was widened to include the full range of humanitarian activity. Second, the intervention component was transformed by the substitution of UN Charter Article 2(7) for 2(4) as the main focus of discussion. The issue was no longer primarily about self-help by states. The key question was: should the international community move towards the development of collective mechanisms for responding to large-scale human suffering within states (Damrosch and Scheffer (eds), 1991, 215)?

2 Security Council Resolution 688 and non-forcible humanitarian intervention: the Memorandum of Understanding and General Assembly Resolution 46/182

But a second precedent was set in these events, one that in our view was just as significant as the first and that from now on would have to be considered alongside it. Indeed, a strong case can be made for the claim that this second precedent was what was truly significant about SCR 688. Exclusive preoccupation with classical definitions of forcible human-itarian intervention, which (a) linked SCR 688 to 'Operation Provide Comfort' and 'Operation Southern Watch', and (b) focused on human rights violations only, has obscured this. SCR 688 is probably best understood, not in connection with these two operations, but in connec-tion with the Memorandum of Understanding (MOU) of 18 April 1991 and with General Assembly Resolution 46/182 of 19 December 1991. From this perspective, SCR 688 was only ambiguously – and perhaps not at all – to do with precedents for forcible international response to humanitarian crises. What it *did* constitute was 'an attempt to respond collectively to . . . urgent humanitarian needs . . . through diplomatic pressure and the involvement of humanitarian relief agencies under UN coordination' (Stromseth, 1993, 88). In David Scheffer's words, it 'estab-lished an unprecedented set of rights and obligations for aid agencies and the host government', particularly where the 'target' government resists such intervention (1992, 267). We follow Scheffer in calling this 'non-forcible humanitarian intervention', a term that will be justified more fully in chapter 4. Katerina Tomasevski sees SCR 688 as a significant precedent in the same way, because 'until that point the Council prim-arily concerned itself with issues of international security, rather than those of human rights and humanitarian affairs' (1994, 84). In addition to demands for an end to Iraqi government suppression of Iraqi citizens' human and political rights came explicit injunctions to 'allow immediate access by international humanitarian organizations to all those in need of assistance in all parts of Iraq'. The UN Secretary-General was enjoined to pursue humanitarian efforts with all the resources available, and member states of the United Nations were asked to contribute accordingly. This was to be a co-ordinated international enterprise, carried out in Iraq, with which the Iraqi authorities were peremptorily told to co-operate.

2.1 The Memorandum of Understanding

To understand this interpretation of SCR 688, it is helpful to look at the Memorandum of Understanding which flowed from it. This was an agreement between the Iraqi government and the United Nations, reached by Saddam Hussein, Eric Suy (personal representative of the Secretary-General) and Prince Sadruddin Aga Khan (executive delegate for the UN Humanitarian Programme). It applied throughout the whole of Iraq, like SCR 688 and unlike 'Operation Provide Comfort' and 'Operation Southern Watch' which applied only in restricted areas. Among other things, it included the setting up of 100 UN civilian-run camps, involving not only the International Committee of the Red Cross (ICRC) but also regional Red Crescent and Iraqi Red Crescent societies. Here was another significant precedent, it being asserted in the memorandum 'that humanitarian assistance is impartial and that all civilians in need, wherever they are located, are entitled to receive it'. This was the authentic voice of humanitarianism, with a 'right to assistance affirmed for the first time' (Tomasevski, 1994, 84). It was this that caused such enthusiasm among supporters of a 'devoir d'ingérence' (duty to intervene on humanitarian grounds), as a complement to the right of assistance which was seen to belong to those in need. It completed the equation by acknowledging a 'droit d'ingérence' (right to intervene) endorsed by the United Nations. Once again, the term 'humanitarian intervention' is being used freely in what in the view of international law is a non-traditional way, to include 'non-forcible' (albeit constrained) cross-border humanitarian action by governmental and non-governmental agents. From this perspective the significance of SCR 688 was that it created 'a fundamental precedent by linking the right to intervene on humanitarian grounds with the internal policies of nation states' (Garigue, 1993, 676). Governments, UN agencies, the ICRC and a number of NGOs were involved in implementing the Memorandum. Disaster Assistance Response teams from the US Office of Foreign Disaster Assistance (OFDA) sent daily situation reports from the field via satellite to the US Secretary of State – the only on-site information at first available. Relief programmes in northern Iraq were co-ordinated through the UN, with some 20 NGOs in the field. Despite continuing military action in certain areas and persistent economic sanctions, the United Nations International Children's Emergency Fund (UNICEF) was to conduct a vaccination programme, the World Health Organization (WHO) was to distribute medicine, and the World Food Programme (WFP) was to deliver food throughout the country.

Already several problematic features of collective non-forcible humanitarian intervention in international-social conflicts were evident. These will occupy us in the remainder of the book. They are not problems which featured in the narrower cold war forcible humanitarian intervention debate. For example, there were tensions between official UN 'humanitarian diplomacy' and NGOs not party to the MOU or who subsequently withdrew from it, refusing to engage in the politics of harassment practised by Saddam Hussein and preferring to work directly with Kurdish authorities without reference to Baghdad (a clear example of the appropriateness of the term 'intervention'). Criticisms were levelled at the lack of skilled personnel on the ground and of poor inter-agency co-ordination, as well as bad co-ordination between agencies and Kurdish and other authorities (M. Griffiths et al., 1993, 60–1). Particularly crucial, and central to the theme of this book, was the relationship between all this and the use of military force. Saddam Hussein's agreement to the MOU, his subsequent acceptance of the 18 May annex detailing the hand-over from allied troops in the 'safe havens' to some 500 UN guards, and his general acquiescence in the UN programme were elicited under duress. Behind his compliance, even after the withdrawal of most of the allied troops and the hand-over to the UN High Commissioner for Refugees in July 1991, lay the threat of 'Operation Poised Hammer', the strong continuing allied military presence at Diyarbakir and Incirlik air base in Turkey (Freedman and Boren, 1992, 55). The problem of the enforcement of UN Security Council resolutions of this kind, as also of the safety of non-forcible interveners, would not in future be so easily met when conflicts were less clearly militarily resolved at the outset in the interveners' favour. Even so, it was striking that the Iraqi president, despite catastrophic military defeat a few weeks before, was still able to bargain toughly on the implementation of SCR 688. He refused to accept armed UN police, settling eventually for 'guards' who were allowed to carry 'personal weapons' (Freedman and Boren, 1992, 65). Very few humanitarian agencies were allowed in the south, and there was continual play with renewing agreements, withholding visas and searching vehicles – harbingers of the experience of future humanitarian interventions in comparable international-social conflicts.

2.2 UN General Assembly Resolution 46/182

All this should be viewed in light of the remarkable developments taking place in the UN General Assembly during the same months, the culmination of a complex process in the field of humanitarian assistance which came to a head in the late 1980s. By that time the idea that humanitarian relief and emergency assistance were 'above politics' had gradually come to be accepted by the governments of a number of donor nations, urged on by media pressure such as that applied by Michael Buerk's famous BBC documentary on the 1984–5 Ethiopian famine (Jansson et al., 1987). This created political space for the United States and other Western donors to disregard Ethiopian sovereignty in efforts to assist areas of Tigray and Eritrea not under Ethiopian government control. Mark Duffield sees this as 'one of the first hesitant steps toward the present era of humanitarian interventionism' (1994, 60). The International Committee of the Red Cross had long had a recognized 'right of initiative' acknowledged in the Geneva Conventions and Additional Protocols. In 1986, in the *Nicaragua* case, the International Court of Justice had determined that 'there can be no doubt that the provision of strictly humanitarian aid to persons or forces in another country, whatever their political affiliations or objectives, cannot be regarded as unlawful intervention, or as in any other way contrary to international law' (ICJ Reports, 1986, 124).

But the most significant advances came in a series of UN General Assembly resolutions. GAR 43/131 of 8 December 1988 (Humanitarian Assistance to Victims of Natural Disasters and Similar Emergency Situations) declared that access to victims of natural disasters 'and similar emergency situations' (widely interpreted to imply 'man-made') could be demanded as a right by humanitarian organizations, on the grounds that abandonment of such victims without humanitarian assistance 'constitutes a threat to human life and an offence to human dignity'. GAR 45/100 of 14 December 1990 laid down that governments should allow unfettered access by accredited agencies, where necessary establishing 'relief corridors for the distribution of emergency medical and food aid'.

Finally, on 19 December 1991, at the time of the Iraqi relief efforts, came General Assembly Resolution 46/182 (Strengthening of the Co-ordination of Humanitarian Emergency Assistance of the United Nations), which led to the establishment of a new Department of Humanitarian Affairs (DHA) in March 1992. Under GAR 46/182 the DHA was charged with co-ordinating humanitarian assistance efforts, mobilizing the necessary international support, and making sure that emergency relief was not an isolated effort but was combined with proper address of the root causes of the humanitarian crisis in question. The United Nations was given four 'tools for co-ordination': (a) an Under-Secretary-General for Humanitarian Affairs to run the DHA (Jan Eliasson), with offices in New York (responsible for central co-ordination, policy, diplomacy, management of CERF and transition from relief to rehabilitation and development) and Geneva (responsible for emergency operational support, relief co-operation and local disaster mitigation); (b) a Central Emergency Revolving Fund (CERF) with an initial target figure of $50 million; (c) an Inter-Agency Standing Committee, including ICRC and NGO representation; and (d) a consolidated appeals process to facilitate co-ordinated fund-raising (Eliasson, 1993b). GAR 46/182 was controversial, and was intensely debated. A number of governments were unhappy at what looked like a *carte blanche* for intervention. 'Guiding Principles', appended in an annex, went some way towards remedying this. They read: 'The sovereignty, territorial integrity and national unity of states must be fully respected in accordance with the Charter of the United Nations. In this context, humanitarian assistance should be provided with the consent of the affected country and in principle on the basis of an appeal by the affected country.' Some interpreted this as a pegging back of the creeping legitimation of 'interventionary humanitarianism'. Others drew attention to the use of 'should' rather than 'must', to the qualification 'in principle', and, above all, that it is the consent of the affected 'country', not the government or state, that is referred to: 'As a final compromise, reference is made to the consent of the affected *country* and not the sovereign state. This terminology provides flexibility in exceptional circumstances, and allows the UN to provide humanitarian assistance in the absence of a government request' (Slim and Penrose, 1994, 201).

It can be seen from all this that the word 'intervention' is being widely used for actions by non-government agents as well as by governments and to include semi-consensual and non-consensual cross-border actions. This will be incorporated in the reconceptualization to be outlined in chapter 4. As a result, Hugo Slim and Angela Penrose conclude that GAR 46/182 'tilts the balance towards humanitarian intervention'. They go on to describe the UN Security Council, with its post-SCR 688 humanitarian agenda, as the brain of the UN's new 'humanitarian interventionism', and the General Assembly's GAR 46/182 and DHA as its as yet undeveloped body (1994, 207).

3 Conclusion

Thus, by the end of 1991, a new context for forcible humanitarian intervention, albeit controversial and still indistinct, had been found. In his last annual report in the autumn of 1991, the outgoing UN Secretary-General, Javier Pérez de Cuéllar, wrote:

> It is now increasingly felt that the principle of noninterference within the essential domestic jurisdiction of states cannot be regarded as a protective barrier behind which human rights could be massively or systematically violated with impunity. The fact that in diverse situations the United Nations has not been able to prevent atrocities cannot be accepted as an argument, legal or moral, against the necessary corrective action, especially when peace is threatened. (UN Doc. A/46/1)

These sentiments reverberated throughout the international community. On 31 January 1992 an unprecedented meeting of the heads of government of current members of the UN Security Council was held in New York, and a declaration to set the tone for a post-cold war world was issued. Despite reservations from China's Prime Minister Li Peng that China 'is opposed to interference in the internal affairs of other countries using the human rights issue as an excuse', the declaration stated that

> [t]he absence of war and military conflicts among states does not in itself ensure international peace and security. The non-military sources of insta- bility in the economic, social, humanitarian and ecological fields have become threats to peace and security. The United Nations membership as a whole, working through the appropriate bodies, needs to give the highest priority to the solution of these matters. (UN Doc. S/PV. 3046, 143)

President Mugabe of Zimbabwe proposed that the Secretary-General be asked to provide 'a careful drawing up and drafting of general principles and guidelines that would guide decisions on when a domestic situation warrants international action, either by the Security Council or by re- gional organizations' (UN Doc. S/PV. 3046, 131). The new Secretary- General, Boutros Boutros-Ghali, responded in June 1992 with his *Agenda for Peace*, in which, famously, he referred to the fact that UN peacekeeping operations had been conducted 'hitherto with the consent of all parties concerned' and envisaged the possibility of peace enforce- ment units.

These sentiments seem, with hindsight, to have been remarkably opti- mistic – what Adam Roberts refers to as the euphoria preceding the hangover (1993b, 10). They were soon to be severely tested.

Suggested reading

As background to the Iraqi situation, Metz (ed.), 1990, is informative. Adelman, 1992a,b; Freedman and Boren, 1992; Gallant, 1992; and Stromseth, 1993, offer helpful accounts of the intervention.

3
Contexts

The four years that followed Security Council Resolution 688 and General Assembly Resolution 46/182 severely tested the embryonic collective mechanisms for forcible and non-forcible humanitarian intervention. They also transformed the context within which the question of humanitarian intervention arose. Whereas during the cold war, as we have seen, it usually entailed human rights abuse by over-strong governments, since the end of the cold war, it has been human suffering in violent, confused conflicts in which government has been contested or non-existent. Within the humanitarian aid community, these are usually called 'complex emergencies'. Of the five instances most commonly cited (in addition to the intervention in Iraq) as examples of forcible humanitarian intervention between 1991 and 1994, four were of this kind: the interventions in Bosnia, Somalia, Liberia and Rwanda. Only the US intervention in Haiti in September 1994 was of the classic type. Whether this represents a qualitative shift in conflict patterns, and if so, why, is a complex question beyond the range of this book, although we will touch on it below. More broadly, taking refugees as symptomatic, not only have the numbers of cross-border and internally displaced refugees continued to rise relentlessly, but, as the UN High Commissioner for Refugees notes, whereas when UNHCR was set up in 1950–1 the main cause of exodus was repressive government, now it is 'the product of vicious internal conflicts' (Ogata, 1993, iii). Every one of the 'ten most severe humanitarian crises' listed in its 1993 *Report on World Crisis Intervention* by Médecins Sans Frontières, the largest non-governmental organization for emergency medical aid, was associated with volatile conflict areas: Afghanistan, Angola, Bosnia, Cambodia, the Caucasus, El Salvador, Liberia, Somalia, Sudan, Tajikistan (Jean, 1993). The main purpose of this chapter is to identify the type of conflict which (a) causes the human suffering, (b) draws governments and others to intervene as a result, and (c) creates such severe problems for them when they do.

1 International-social conflict: definition, classification and incidence

Combining categories from international law and recent conflict resolution analysis, we will call these conflicts 'international-social conflicts' (ISCs). These are conflicts which are neither inter-state conflicts (such as the Iran–Iraq war) nor contained within the resources of domestic conflict management (such as the Los Angeles riots), but sprawl between the two. There are many other terms for this level of conflict, most commonly 'internal conflict' or 'civil war', but these do not capture the further twin characteristics of ISCs: (a) that they are rooted in relations between communal groups within state borders (the 'social' component) and (b) that they have broken out of the domestic arena and become a crisis for the state, thereby automatically involving the wider society of states (the 'international' component). A characteristic mark of (b) is militarization beyond the capacity of state police forces to control.

International-social conflicts are communal conflicts which become crises of the state. They characteristically cause massive human suffering, and invite international intervention.

A fuller name for this class of conflict would be 'international-state-social' conflict, because such conflict operates at three levels, and thus requires three levels of explanation: system level, state level and communal level. This, in turn, roughly corresponds to two broad approaches in conflict analysis: structural and relational. These ideas will be elaborated below. It is at the state level, which mediates between the other two, that the critical dynamics are played out. An ISC is a crisis of the state, whether it takes the form of a state-formation conflict (Bosnia), a struggle for state control (Rwanda), or eventual state collapse (Somalia).

1.1 Definition: mixed civil-international conflict, protracted social conflict and international-social conflict

We can best clarify the nature of ISCs in relation to two sets of alternative terminologies, one from international law, which relates particularly to the 'international' dimension, the other from conflict resolution theory, which relates more to the 'social' dimension. The term 'ISC' is not intended as a strict analytical tool, but as a broad category which both distinguishes the critical conflicts which form the context for this part of the book and at the same time identifies their salient features.

1.1.1 International law: civil and mixed civil-international conflicts.

Over time, and especially since 1919, increasing restrictions have been formulated in international law on the rights of states to wage war. In the process, new definitions of what constitute war and armed conflict have emerged. After 1949 the traditional concept of war was replaced in international humanitarian law by the concept of 'international armed conflict' for reasons already explained, so no attempt is made to distinguish between the terms 'war' and 'conflict' in what follows. There have been many typologies of conflict in international law, such as the distinction between international armed conflicts, wars of national liberation and non-international armed conflicts in the Geneva Conventions and Additional Protocols. Scholars have offered more elaborate systems. Thus John Norton Moore lists six categories of internal war: non-authority-oriented, anti-colonial, secession, indigenous control of authority structures, external imposition of authority structures, cold war-sponsored (1972, 175). Elsewhere he distinguishes international wars, civil wars and mixed civil-international conflicts, noting how 'since World War II civil wars and mixed civil-international conflicts have replaced the more conventional international wars as the principal forms of violence in the international system' (1974). There is nothing new, therefore, in the preponderance of internal conflicts. But international law presupposes a clear demarcation line between inter-state (international) war and intra-state (civil) conflict. A 'mixed' conflict occurs when assistance is given by another state or states (the international component) to one or more of the parties to domestic unrest (the civil component). International law, preoccupied with state borders, is mainly concerned (a) with distinguishing pure civil wars from wars of secession or unification which threaten to change those borders, and, as we saw in chapter 2, (b) with distinguishing between low-intensity unrest, insurgency and belligerency in order to work out the norms of legitimate intervention. In addition, through Common Article 3 of the Geneva Conventions (1949) and Additional Protocol II (1977), international humanitarian law attempts to define non-international armed conflict in order to afford protection to the victims of what has by now become the main form of war. Traditionally, international law has not been interested in the roots of 'social' conflict; nor, in Michael Brown's view, have international relations and strategic studies specialists: 'Until recently, international relations theorists and strategic studies analysts paid comparatively little attention to the causes, effects and international implications of ethnic and other forms of communal conflict' ((ed.), 1993, vii). It is the 'social' component that the concept of ISC adds to traditional international law and international relations categories.

1.1.2 Conflict resolution: protracted social conflict. Although international relations and strategic studies theorists may have somewhat neglected communal conflict, a number of scholars in the conflict resolution field have been preoccupied with it. John Burton (1987) refers to 'deep-rooted conflict', Louis Kriesberg (in Kriesberg et al., 1989) to 'intractable conflict', and Edward Azar (1990) to 'protracted social conflict'. For Azar, the critical factor in protracted social conflict (PSC), such as persisted in Lebanon, Sri Lanka or Northern Ireland, is that it represents 'the prolonged and often violent struggle by communal groups for such basic needs as security, recognition and acceptance, fair access to political institutions and economic participation' (1991, 93). The traditional preoccupation with relations between states is seen to have obscured a proper understanding of these dynamics. Indeed, in radical contrast to the concerns of international law, the distinction between domestic and international politics is rejected as 'artificial': 'there is really only one social environment and its domestic face is the more compelling' (Azar and Burton, 1986, 33). The role of the state (as also linkages with other states) is to satisfy or frustrate basic communal needs, thereby preventing or promoting conflict (Azar, 1990, 10–12).

We accept with Azar that the most useful unit of analysis in international-social conflict, as in protracted social conflict, is the communal group or identity group, whatever may be seen to be its base – race, religion, ethnicity or culture. But here we part company in also recognizing the continuing potency of the state as the main organizing principle in the international arena, not only as an extraneous causal or complicating factor, but as intrinsic to the aspirations of the conflicting parties themselves. The communal group is the 'social' base in which the conflict is rooted; the state is the 'international' prize which is being fought for. Given the current international system, where sovereignty and all that goes with it are reserved for existing states, embattled, disaffected communities are often driven to aspire to statehood themselves – either independently or through amalgamation with neighbouring cognates. Even in a 'failed' or collapsed state like Somalia, the mainly Issaq Somaliland in the north claims independent statehood, while fluid, fragmented kinship and clan groups provide the basis for the implacable drive by 'war-lords' to inherit and reconstruct the former post-colonial state. It is sovereignty that is seen to guarantee the needs identified in the extract from Azar quoted above – for security, recognition and access to sources of power. So it is that the struggle for power in the service of interest, characteristic of the 'old' thinking criticized by needs theorists, takes its place beside the drive for communal identity and recognition as integral to what defines international-social conflict.

1.2 Classification and incidence

Before moving on to look more closely at the nature of ISCs, we should provide some empirical underpinning for the concept. An example of the kind of data base now available is the careful analysis of post-1989 conflict conducted by Peter Wallensteen and K. Axell at Uppsala University in Sweden (Wallensteen and Axell, 1994). They divide conflicts into three categories: minor armed conflicts in which overall deaths are less than 1,000; intermediate conflicts in which casualties are higher and 25 to 1,000 people are killed in any one year; and wars, in which there are more than 1,000 battle-related deaths in one year. According to their analysis, some 90 armed conflicts took place between 1989 and 1993, of which in 1993 there were 47 conflicts above the minor armed conflict threshold. These 90 conflicts took place in 61 locations, and involved 60 governments – about one-third of UN member states. Using quantitative data bases such as this, we group the conflicts into three qualitative categories. Type 1 conflicts are inter-state wars over control of strategic territory, borders and resources. On our count there were four type 1 conflicts between 1989 and 1993, and none in 1993. Type 2 conflicts are intra-state conflicts related to control of government or authority structures, fuelled by political, ideological or religious differences. There were 20 of these over the 1989–93 period, including conflicts in Algeria, Cambodia, Haiti and Mozambique. The pattern here seems to be roughly that ideological (class) conflict of the classic cold war kind is in decline (Cambodia), but that religious conflict is on the increase (Algeria). All conflicts are at the same time political conflicts for power, some purely so (Haiti). Our focus is on type 3 conflicts, or ISCs, which covers the remainder of the data set. Of course, these categories are not watertight. Type 3 conflicts may have some of the characteristics of type 1 conflicts (territorial acquisition) and of type 2 conflicts (religious or political programmes imposed upon government), but they are fundamentally about enduring identity groups organized to insist on the satisfaction of their needs, interests and beliefs, groups which *do* challenge the integrity of a state. At any one time ISCs are in turn broadly divided into (a) those which seem to be threshold conflicts, such as in Zaire or Sierra Leone in 1993; (b) those which are already severe, of which on our count there

were 17 in 1993 and 1994; and (c) those whose overt phase is over
or in abeyance, such as Croatia, Israel/Palestine, Lebanon, Northern
Ireland and South Africa in 1994. The 17 severe ISCs in 1993–4 were
in Afghanistan, Angola, Azerbaijan, Bosnia-Hercegovina, Burundi,
Georgia/Abkhazia, Indonesia/East Timor, Iraq (Kurds, Shi'a), Liberia,
Myanmar, Russia/Chechnya, Rwanda, Somalia, Sri Lanka, Sudan,
Tajikistan, and Turkey (Kurds). We will use this as our main data base
in chapter 4 for applying the reconceptualization of humanitarian
intervention.

The central thesis of this chapter is that the nature of these international-social conflicts needs to be understood in order to see why they
cause so much human suffering and why it is so difficult for outsiders of
all kinds, non-state actors as well as states, to intervene, whether forcibly
or non-forcibly. Five of the six putative examples of forcible humanitarian intervention (Bosnia, Iraq, Liberia, Rwanda and Somalia) are in
this group of 17. The exception is Haiti. We make no claim that this
conflict pattern will persist. There is no reason why major inter-state
conflict may not come to predominate again. But it is just as likely that
the scale of ISCs will mount, possibly to unimaginable size if huge states
like China or India became convulsed by the fatal mix of inter-communal
violence and state crisis or collapse. We do not have a separate class of
'failed' or collapsed states, because in our view state disintegration
precipitates and is accompanied by conflict of the kind we analyse
here. It is of no help to attempt to say which 'causes' which, since it is
the combination of communally rooted conflict and state crisis which
defines ISCs in the first place. We trace some of these interconnections
below.

2 The nature of international-social conflict

It is difficult to characterize a phenomenon as widespread and diverse as
international-social conflict, varying as it does from region to region and
from culture to culture. Nevertheless, two complementary approaches
can usefully be adopted, a structural approach and a relational approach,
operating at the three levels of system, state and community (see diagram
6). A structural approach analyses the background conditions likely to
generate ISCs, no matter who the particular actors may be. Although
structural factors operate at all three levels, for the sake of simplicity we
will concentrate here on the system and state levels. A relational approach focuses on interconnections between conflict parties. In this case,
because ISCs are not inter-state wars, the relational approach operates
mainly at the social-communal level. Within this framework it is helpful
to look for 'accelerators' and 'decelerators' – the role of politics in

System level		International
	STRUCTURAL FACTORS	
State level		
	RELATIONAL FACTORS	
Communal level		Social

Diagram 6: *Structural and Relational Factors in International-Social Conflict*

stoking up or damping down conflict – and to consider sequential phases in conflict escalation and de-escalation.

2.1 Structural background conditions at system and state levels

It is helpful to distinguish four linked structural features conducive to the outbreak of international-social conflict.

2.1.1 Social heterogeneity and a discrepancy between existing state borders and the distribution of peoples and cultures.   At the present count, in mid-1995, there are 185 member states of the United Nations. According to some estimates, there are some 5,000 or more relatively distinct communal groups with sufficient actual or potential cohesion to claim autonomy (Horowitz, 1985). The net result is that the conventional concept of the nation-state barely fits one-quarter of the members of the international system. The word 'nation' is sometimes taken to be synonymous with 'state' (as in 'the United Nations'), and sometimes assumed to be the same as 'people' (as in 'the Kurdish nation'). Clearly it partakes of both, which, as Anthony Smith explains, causes structural problems:

> There is an inherent instability in the very concept of the nation, which appears to be driven, as it were, back and forth between the two poles of *ethnie* [ethnic community/people] and state which it seeks to subsume and transcend. Very few of today's nations have succeeded in subsuming the two poles and making *ethnie* coextensive and fully congruent with the state. (1986, 150)

This can be seen clearly in the list of new states accepted into the United Nations in 1992: Armenia, Azerbaijan, Bosnia-Hercegovina, Croatia, Georgia, Kazakhstan, Kyrgyzstan, Moldova, San Marino, Slovenia, Tajikistan, Turkmenistan, Uzbekistan. The UN Secretary-General commented: 'Their entrance reaffirms the concept of the state as the basic entity of international relations and the means by which peoples find a unity and a voice in the world community' (Boutros-Ghali, 1992–3, 92). This may in a sense be so, but once again 'states' and 'peoples' have been misleadingly conflated. Apart from San Marino and Slovenia, all the new states (making up some 8 per cent of UN membership) were bedevilled by the unresolved aspirations of unassimilated peoples living within their borders. Of the 23 borders between republics of the former Soviet Union, only three are not disputed in some way. Contested borders link with the issue of re-emergent nationalisms and ethnic tensions, with up to 800 distinct ethnic groups existing across former Soviet territories (S. Griffiths, 1993). More generally, the vast majority of aspirants world-wide are still locked firmly outside the state system.

> Baluchis, Biafrans, Eritreans, Tigreans, Ewes, Gandans, Karens, Katchins, Kurds, Moros, Pathans, Sikhs, Tamils and many other ethnonationalities are the abandoned peoples of the contemporary community of states. The moral language of the game refers to them disparagingly as 'separatists', 'secessionists', or 'irredentists' which strongly suggests that they are illegitimate and not likely to be admitted to the clubhouse in the foreseeable future. Self-determination has become a conservative right of quasi-states. (Jackson, 1990, 41–2)

As in a game of musical chairs, when the music stops (existing UN membership and territorial integrity rule), only a few can find chairs to sit on. Needless to say, there is no possibility of all being admitted, because, where peoples are settled in scattered pockets, any new entry automatically dispossesses those who thereby become minorities, as happened with the breakup of Yugoslavia. It is like chaos theory in mathematics: any portion, however small, is as complex as the whole. Two foundational principles of international declaratory and UN Charter law are in tension here: the 'territorial integrity of states' (Charter Article 1(1)) and the 'self-determination of peoples' (Charter Article 1(2)). These represent the two poles of international-social conflict, and in their discontinuity encapsulate the inner tension, if not contradiction, at its core. In international law, attempts have been made to expand the term 'self-determination' to include ex-colonial peoples, but then draw the line at that point. This is a founding concept of the Organization of African Unity, for example. But ex-colonial borders were in many, if not most, cases drawn by ex-colonials – they have no greater historical validity – and in many regions are becoming increasingly difficult to maintain. The structural feature of social heterogeneity is not confined to border issues. It relates to inter-communal tension in general, covering inter-clan as well as inter-ethnic tension and including religious and cultural fault-lines such as the conjunction of boundaries between Catholicism,

Orthodoxy and Islam in Bosnia and between the Muslim north and Christian/animist south in Sudan.

The broad rule at individual state level seems to be that ISC is more likely to arise in culturally heterogeneous than culturally homogeneous states.

The key problem posed for humanitarian interveners here is that their actions may materially affect the inter-communal struggle. If they are state actors, they will have to decide which political outcomes they favour or are prepared to tolerate – such as firm central rule, minority rights, local autonomy, federation, secession – and try to make sure that their humanitarian efforts are compatible with them (McGarry and O'Leary (eds), 1993). If they do not, they will find themselves sucked into the political mêlée willy-nilly (both to recognize and not to recognize a self-proclaimed breakaway is to be seen as party to the conflict), and will discover how dangerous it is to drift rudderless in such a sea.

2.1.2 The political crisis of the contemporary state.   International-social conflict, rooted in inter-communal relations, may erupt into a crisis of the state. A second relevant structural feature, therefore, closely linked to the first, is what many analysts see as a systemic challenge to the central organizing unit in modern international society: 'loyalty and legitimacy are shifting away from the state ... toward the center of the globe and toward the local realities of community and sentiment' (Falk, 1985, 690). Global changes and transnational pressures connected with the environment and resource depletion, economics, communications, population flow, cross-border crime, terrorism and weapons proliferation may well be calling into question the usefulness of the nation-state. Still, in Paul Kennedy's words, 'the nation state remains the primary locus of identity of most people ... even if the autonomy and functions of the state have been eroded by transnational trends, no adequate substitute has emerged to replace it as the key unit in responding to global change' (1993, 134).

As nation-states, notionally constructed to provide security and welfare for their subjects, palpably fail to do so, the potency of communal collective identity provides a readily mobilizable political alternative. It is in these terms that John Dunn speaks of a contemporary 'crisis of the nation-state', 'unable to handle problems which it once handled with aplomb, incapable of ensuring an order of its own (ecological, economic, civil, even spiritual) on its subjects' behalf, baffled by the novel challenges of a turbulent global economy and a decaying global habitat' (1994, 4). As formal structures erode, government becomes increasingly predatory, partisan and reliant on violence to maintain control. As Edward Azar puts it, 'most states which experience protracted social conflict tend to be characterised by incompetent, fragile and authoritarian governments that fail to satisfy basic human needs' (1990, 10). An important subsidiary point here is that 'democracy' in these circumstances often increases polarization and hastens conflict escalation, *contra* the normal liberal assumption that 'elections' are a panacea for political ills (de Nevers, 1993). The critical negative factors seem to be (a) whether party politics aligns itself with communal divisions rather than cutting across them as in most mature civil societies and (b) whether state power is seen to be irrevocably monopolized by one party or group of parties and used to reinforce its control of resources. This combination precipitates a crisis of state legitimacy. The trigger for the outbreak of several ISCs has been elections, as in Slovenia and Croatia in 1991 and Bosnia early in 1992.

At the individual state level, therefore, it appears that ISC is more likely to arise in politically weak, unintegrated states, particularly 'quasi-states', than in strong states with developed representative institutions.

This, too, poses severe problems for humanitarian interveners. Do they work with (and hence support) repressive regimes? In situations of state collapse, how far do outside responsibilities go? Is the international community responsible for helping to reconstitute the state? If so, in what form, and who will rule? Is it possible for outsiders to do this?

2.1.3 Underdevelopment and asymmetries of wealth and power. Fragile states are susceptible to internal and external shocks, particularly as systemic pressures mount. In the view of a number of analysts, including a majority from southern countries, among the systemic pressures building up on Third World states and precipitating conflict are those associated with the North–South fault-line. The industrialized states of the North and the West, overwhelmingly powerful in relation to the states of the South, are seen to be taking the offensive, politically, economically and, if need be, militarily in preserving their global interests (Rogers and Dando, 1992; Hawthorn, 1994). If anything, resources continue to move from the poor, weak, fragmented but increasingly populous countries of the South to the rich, powerful, better organized North. In conditions of underdevelopment, where there is severe material scarcity, 'the object [of government] has been to appropriate what surpluses there are and to distribute them to those, one's kin or one's ethnos considered more widely, who can be relied upon to sustain one's power in the state' (Hawthorn, 1994, 133). The link between state failure and the social roots of communal conflict is clearly evident here. In these circumstances, the usual conditions attached to aid from the North, whether bilateral or through the International Monetary Fund and World Bank, are as likely to exacerbate as to alleviate the situation.

Edward Azar eloquently describes the link between underdevelopment and conflict:

> Reducing overt conflict requires reduction in levels of underdevelopment. Groups which seek to satisfy their identity and security needs through conflict are in effect seeking change in the structure of their society. Conflict resolution can truly occur and last if satisfactory amelioration of underdevelopment occurs as well. Studying protracted conflict leads one to conclude that peace is development in the broadest sense of the term. (1990, 155)

This judgement is widely echoed among development and aid experts and field-workers. Underdevelopment and economic crisis bring political instability as the desperate fight for scarce resources intensifies, ruling elites are discredited, the middle ground occupied by those reasonably satisfied with the *status quo* is eroded, and politics fragments and polarizes.

Two variants should also be mentioned. The disruption of traditional social patterns by over-fast development strategies that lead to distortion and sectoral or regional imbalances, including tensions between 'modernizers' and 'fundamentalist traditionalists', and the effect of perceived uneven economic development, in which poorer regions resent the wealthier, and the wealthier resent a forcible redistribution of wealth. As in the case of democracy, what should be a cohesive move (solidarity depends upon equitable distribution), may in divided societies accelerate disintegration, even in better developed economies – as in the case of Serbian resentment of the wealthier Slovenes and Croats and Slovenian and Croatian resentment of the forcible redistribution of their wealth to the more numerous Serbs within former Yugoslavia.

At individual state level this translates into a third proposition: that ISC is more likely to arise in societies which suffer from economic underdevelopment or where resources are perceived to be unevenly distributed than in developed states capable of delivering some measure of distributional justice.

Humanitarian interveners are faced with grave challenges here, given the complex relationship between immediate relief and long-term development, as also between the need for energetic outside support and the requirement for local self-reliance. Behind all this lies the fundamental perception in the South that Northern 'humanitarian assistance' is a substitute for addressing the structural causes of conflict, if not itself a means of reinforcing the system of power and dependency from which the North profits so much.

2.1.4 The influence of cross-border politics. Finally, global and regional politics play an important and, for some, a decisive role in generating or inhibiting international-social conflict. No attempt is made to outline an overall systemic pattern here, because it is too complicated. Conflicts are inflamed where rival regimes support disruptive local forces or back exiled militarized groups and enable them to relaunch offensives, where powerful regional or global powers stoke up internal conflict in the course of fighting their own battles, or, most characteristic of international-social conflict, where indigenous groups engaged in conflict appeal to fellow identity groups beyond their borders. Since few of the countries convulsed by severe international-social conflict have their own arms industries, the role of outside patrons in flooding them with weapons evidently plays a critical part here. So too does the presence or absence of valued resources such as oil in attracting external political partisanship.

At individual state level the somewhat obvious generalization is that ISC is more likely to arise where external relations across borders or with other states exacerbate the situation than where they do not.

Humanitarian interveners have to operate within a web of intense regional and geopolitical interest. Lasting solutions require stable international frameworks to sustain them. These are difficult to build.

2.2 Relational factors at social and communal level

Structural features are rightly seen as 'background factors', underlying the play of foreground factors perhaps, but not on their own sufficient to explain the often unexpected turn of events. Another fruitful way of analysing conflict is to look at it in terms of relations between the conflict parties themselves. In the case of ISCs these will essentially be communal groups, however defined, even in countries whese breakdown has proceeded furthest, such as Afghanistan and Somalia, where the critical elements are found at clan and sub-clan levels, and political groupings are, as a result, complex, unstable and volatile. Unless humanitarian interveners understand this level of the conflict, they are likely to be ineffective and perhaps counter-productive.

In concentrating on conflict relations, we are overlooking studies of the conflict parties considered separately, such as elaborate investigations into the nature of coincident or cross-cutting ties within conflict groups and how this affects their relations outside. It has been claimed, for example, that the more successful a communal group is in achieving internal cohesion, the more likely it is to engage in external aggression

(Ross, 1993). We are also passing over claims such as that certain societies are by their nature more bellicose than others – for example, that in Serb and Somali society a male warrior culture predominates. Four conflict relations will be considered here.

2.2.1 Relations of identity and interest.   There is a potentially infinite variety of identity groupings in international-social conflict, depending upon local situation and tradition. 'Ethnicity', itself a deeply problematic concept, is only one of them, despite its current all-eclipsing popularity. Nor are conflict groups monolithic. They are usually made up of a complex of overlapping subgroups. In normal social conflict below the level of ISC, this complex of cross-cutting groups serves to contain and dilute conflict within an overall social cohesion. In the crucible of inter-national-social conflict, however, these tend to be melted down into what Nathan Glazer calls 'terminal loyalty' to whatever turn out to be the predominant conflict groups (1983, 244). Identities are imposed on individuals, often against their will, by their own side, by their opponents and also (often unwittingly) by outsiders. In Bosnia, for example, where, on most definitions of the term, there are few discernible ethnic differences, the competing parties became Bosnian Muslim, Bosnian Croat and Bosnian Serb, even though most so-called Bosnian Muslims rejected this terminology.

Fundamental here is the unresolved debate as to whether these collective identities are 'primordial' or whether they have been constructed for purposes of manipulation and the mobilization of interest, as 'instrumentalists' argue (A. Smith, 1986, 9–13). Some instrumentalists – those who see ethnicity and other forms of communal identity as constructions, reconstructions and deconstructions of discourses of power – would contest the integrity of the idea of international-social conflict, by questioning its 'social' roots. We must disagree with this sweeping conclusion, but beyond that do not need to come down on either side. Clearly, conflict groups, as 'imagined communities' in Benedict Anderson's (1983) celebrated phrase, are sites for manipulation. But they are not created *ex nihilo*, and, as often as not, political leaders whose power depends upon them are themselves caught up in the same nexus of values, beliefs and interests.

As to relations of interest, conflict analysts have made much of distinctions between 'interests', 'values' and 'needs', which are seen to be progressively more difficult to negotiate. In the heat of ISC, however, these too are found to be melted down into what we will call 'core interests', which are regarded as non-negotiable and as directly threatened by the opposing side. What may look like peripheral 'interests' from the outside may be seen from the inside to be imbued with value and integral to group identity.

All this poses a severe challenge to the supposedly non-political credentials of humanitarian interveners. Not only individual governments, but collectivities like ECOWAS in Liberia and the UN itself are seen to be partisan. Peacekeepers come to be variously identified with contending parties within the conflict region and with powerful interests outside. UN agencies and relief organizations find it equally difficult to shake off the imputation that 'if you are not for us you are against us'. In the intensity of ISC there is no room to be non-political.

2.2.2 Relations of power. Intense conflict relations of identity and interest are manifested mainly at the social-communal level. It is into this cauldron that the state-international dimension enters via the fact that conflict groups, struggling for what are perceived as mutually incompatible core interests, either try to use existing levers of state power to secure them or reach out to forge new ones. This is what sparks the greatest violence as, in the desperate attempt to preserve identity and secure non-negotiable values, the struggle crosses the domestic-social/state-international boundary, and conflict becomes war. Two features are characteristic. First, the 'security dilemma', familiar to analysts of international relations, now impacts with devastating effect on the inchoate social-state-international scene (Posen, 1993). Second, given the hybrid nature of conflicts of this kind, the resulting power struggle is often asymmetric, both quantitatively and qualitatively. Most analysts agree that asymmetric conflicts are harder to resolve than symmetric ones. Quantitative asymmetry encourages the more powerful to resist calls for settlement, either in the hope of outright victory or in order to strengthen a bargaining position and 'negotiate from strength'. The apparently weaker party may harbour hopes of future assistance if they can hold out, or, given the non-negotiable nature of the values being fought for, determine to 'fight to the last ditch'. Qualitative asymmetry is often even more confused and desperate. Here widely disparate systems, such as a government which sees itself as defending order and legitimacy and insurgents who see themselves as instruments of justice or social change, are locked together. Here the structure cannot be changed without conflict, so to end the conflict or to freeze the *status quo* is to serve the interests of the dominant party (Rapoport, 1971).

This confronts interveners with huge problems. Not to intervene forcibly risks being seen as an 'accomplice to massacre'. In cases of quantitative asymmetry, should interveners 'level the playing field' – for example, by lifting the arms embargo on the Bosnian government? As regards qualitative asymmetry, to confine intervention to the 'impartial' delivery of humanitarian aid as in Bosnia is to be regarded as adopting a stance 'that has become all but indistinguishable, in practical terms, from that of the Bosnian Serbs' (Rieff, 1994b, 40). If the intervener is all-powerful, the situation can be disposed of at will. If not, the intervener must somehow work within the limits of existing power relations.

2.2.3 Relations of belief.   This is a complex, relatively unexplored area. In most accounts of conflict, relations of belief are assimilated within reductionist explanations as historical and social conditioning or political rationalization of interest, and are attributed to the conflict parties accordingly. But the battle of ideas is as intense as the battle of weapons, as the baleful influence of stories of partisan atrocity spread through the media (television in former Yugoslavia, radio in Rwanda and Somalia) by ambitious manipulators shows. Underlying this are genuine, deeply rooted convictions which should not be reduced to epiphenomena of other processes. Nothing is more characteristic of international-social conflict than mutual perceptions of injustice and victimization. Conflict parties are not referring to rationalizations and projections; they are pointing to how things are and how they should be. To ignore this is to miss a vital element in the make-up of international-social conflict, without which its obduracy is incomprehensible and the passion with which it is conducted impossible to understand.

Humanitarian interveners operate in an environment constituted by incompatible perceptions of the conflict situation itself. The United Nation Protection Force is seen by the Croats to be protecting Serb gains, by the Serbs to be serving hostile German interests, and by the Muslims to be condoning ethnic cleansing and conspiring to prevent the legitimate Bosnian government from defending itself.

2.2.4 Relations of attitude and behaviour.   Those who study attitude and behaviour in conflicts often ask themselves how it is that mutual hostility can be sustained at such a pitch of intensity for so long and how the 'barbarous acts' which arouse demand for humanitarian intervention can be perpetrated by otherwise apparently normal people, often against others who until recently were neighbours and even friends. Among the most depressing examples of this are the tearing apart of village and town communities in former Yugoslavia and Rwanda. The following account comes from Butare, Rwanda, in April 1994.

An awful fury had been unleashed in Butare (Rwanda's second largest town) and nothing could stop it. Hundreds of roadblocks sprang up on April 20, patrolled by guardsmen and militiamen who demanded tribal identity cards and executed Tutsis on the spot. At the university hospital, militiamen entered wards where Tutsi refugees were recovering from machete and bullet wounds; all were murdered in their beds or cut down while trying to escape. The university rector and several professors escorted death squads to the rooms of Tutsi students: 300 were taken to a nearby arboretum and massacred. At the Maison de Souers convent, nuns pleaded for mercy as 26 young Tutsi refugees were arrested and led to a truck by soldiers. 'They are just children,' one nun cried. 'Isn't it better to take the adults?' 'Don't worry', she says the commander replied. 'Your turn will come.'

Butare was a town which had expected to escape the massacres which had started in the capital Kigali following the assassination of President Habyarimana. It had enjoyed a spirit of tolerance and both the local prefect and the commander of the gendarmerie were moderates who worked for toleration between Tutsi and Hutu communities. These two men were swept aside when busloads of militiamen arrived from Kigali and ignited a frenzy of killing which resulted in the murder of up to 90% of the 350,000 Tutsi population in the Butare region in the space of 70 days. (Joshua Hammer, 'Horror in Butare', *Newsweek*, 26 September 1994)

There have been many attempts to explain atrocities such as this. Terrell Northrup isolates four stages by which relations of identity and interest promote conflict escalation and intractability: (a) mutual perception of threat, (b) mutual distortion of information 'in order to maintain the core sense of identity', (c) mutual rigidification and dehumanization in which atrocity against the 'other' is not seen as such, and (d) collusion in which the identity of conflict parties becomes mutually defined (1989, 68–76). It seems easier to move from (a) to (d) than back again. Shattered communities are not easily put back together. Past outrage, resentment, unrequited desire for revenge and a deep sense of injustice swell the stream of public memory, ready to break out again and fuel future conflict if the circumstances arise.

2.3 Accelerators and decelerators: the play of politics

Here we do no more than note how some commentators, impatient with the 'neutral' tone of the preceding analysis, attribute the outbreak of vicious international-social conflict to the unscrupulous ambitions of malevolent political manipulators. We need only compare the leadership roles of Slobodan Milosevic and Franjo Tudjman in Yugoslavia with those of F. W. de Klerk and Nelson Mandela in South Africa to see the force of this point. It is tempting to follow the lead of the media in attributing much of what happens in international-social conflict, including the inflaming of conflict and its damping down, to the actions of particular protagonists or third parties. But actions and events do not take place in a vacuum. Deeper factors shape the overall context, including the emergence of the key actors themselves, and severely constrain their options thereafter. Communal groups such as those that make up the clan system in Somalia may be politically manipulated, but they also pre-date the current phases of the conflict, and all those who aspire to influence the course of events must in one way or another adjust their goals to this underlying social reality.

2.4 Conflict phases: lock-in and breakdown

Conflicts go through phases, much studied by analysts concerned to trace stages of escalation and de-escalation in order to learn how best to prevent, mitigate and terminate destructive conflict in the most appropriate way. William Zartman (1985) sees four general phases in most conflicts: articulation, mobilization, insurgency and warfare. Particularly important for some of the worst cases of protracted international-social conflict is what happens when conflict persists for long stretches of time. This is the self-reinforcing dynamic of the conflict itself, once (a) it has got a dominant grip on the embattled communities, and (b) it has destroyed the pre-existing political structures capable of sustaining stable relations throughout the region while preventing the creation of new ones. The first is 'lock-in', the second 'breakdown'. The two are connected.

In lock-in, domestic politics becomes the politics of conflict. Any middle ground is undermined by the conflict, thus reinforcing the political extremes which subsequently sustain it. Vested interests emerge which are dependent upon its perpetuation. These will be the losers in any peace settlement – as in the case of the Khmer Rouge in Kampuchea, the National Union for the Total Independence of Angola (UNITA) in Angola, and the extremist Hutu in Rwanda. The most violent and unruly elements in society appear in leadership roles, and criminality becomes a political norm. Psychologically, this extends to relations between the conflicting groups, Terrell Northrup's 'collusion'. Outsiders who 'don't understand' are effectively excluded. Local issues, all but incomprehensible to the outside world, assume dominant importance, while wider regional and global politics, including the various forms of intervention, are seen through the lens of local preoccupations or otherwise ignored, often with contempt.

In extreme cases breakdown follows. With sustained attrition, political structures buckle and collapse, a social implosion which subsequently sucks everything else in: government malfunctions, politics become reactive and defensive, the centre loses control of its own agents, and power withers at the centre and devolves to the periphery. In Somalia, state collapse preceded the worst phases of the conflict. In the absence of the state as provider of basic needs for its citizens, a political culture develops in which violence is used even within support communities to provide assets and gain power. A war economy takes over. Even the relatively ordered conflict of the cold war period disintegrates (Rufin, 1993, 112–13). Local banditry replaces organized war. Eventually the conflict may consume itself, disintegrating into a chaos of precarious local stand-offs with sporadic outbursts of renewed violence.

In the most chaotic of such circumstances, where young boys with AK-47 rifles command the political scene and racketeers the economic scene, what are aid workers, peacekeepers and other interveners to do? Should they stay or leave when conditions become dangerous? Work through war-lords who seize aid provision and use it to fuel the continuing struggle? Move in swiftly with sufficient military force, but as soon as possible pull out? Be prepared to take over completely?

3 International-social conflict and human suffering

The upshot of all this is intense and widespread misery, compounded of every element in the repertory of human atrocity: unspeakable war crimes, gross crimes against humanity from ethnic cleansing and rape to genocide, terrible deprivation of basic essentials through siege or starvation (Cranna (ed.), 1994). As always, it is the innocent who suffer most. Some 25 million people may have been killed in the 150 wars that have been waged since 1945 (Sivard, 1993, 20). Increasingly, these have been non-combatants. As James Grant, Executive Director of UNICEF, puts it, '[t]his "war on children" is a twentieth century invention. Only 5 per cent of the casualties in the First World War were civilians. By the Second World War the proportion had risen to 50%. And, as the century ends, the civilian share is normally about 80% – most of them women and children' (1992, 26). Others put the figure as high as 90 per cent (Lake (ed.), 1990, 4). To this must be added UNHCR's estimate of the primary role of vicious internal conflicts in generating 18.2 million refugees and 24 million internally displaced people in 1993 (Ogata, 1993). In African countries like Angola, Eritrea, Liberia, Mozambique, Rwanda, Somalia and Sudan, up to half or more of the total population have been forced to flee at some point. Overall costs in economic, social and political terms are incalculable. Perhaps 40–75 per cent of government financial resources are consumed by war in some cases (R. Green, 1994, 48). In their influential *Hunger and Public Action*, J. Dreze and Amartya Sen (1984) show how conflict exacerbates vulnerability to famine by destruction of resources, deflection of resources from welfare to war, stunting of economic development, disruption of organized relief and the displacement of populations. Famine and drought can usually be overcome in the absence of conflict. But when there is conflict, in addition to massive 'collateral' damage, food itself becomes a weapon, 'as much a part of the warfare as automatic rifles and land mines' (Bonner, *New Yorker*, 13 March 1989), while in disintegrated war zones armed militia prey on the settled populations, destroying and commandeering crops and livestock. Finally, in the vicious environment of international-social conflict, civilian populations themselves become caught up in the carnage, usually as victims of massacre and ethnic cleansing, but sometimes, as in Rwanda, also as perpetrators.

Here is one of the most agonizing problems for humanitarian interveners, as the professed non-political nature of emergency protection and relief comes up against the fundamental fact that the reduction, displacement or elimination of the civilian population may be precisely a major war aim of the conflicting parties. There is no way round this dilemma. No matter what interveners may profess, in the context of international-social conflict, humanitarianism is irrevocably politicized.

4 Conclusion

The concept of international-social conflict is not intended to cover all armed conflict. Rather, it offers an analysis of a type of conflict which is increasing in frequency, and it provides some explanation of why this kind of conflict becomes protracted and embittered, causes large-scale human suffering, and poses the sternest test for the international community when the question of intervention arises. Causes of such conflict are likely to remain complex and multi-faceted, and the specific locations in which they may break out in future are difficult to predict. Holsti's profile of issues that have generated civil and international conflict between 1648 and 1989 confirms the emerging significance of the ISC type:

> Despite all the rhetoric about global interdependence, the shrinking world, and the presumably unifying impact of technological innovations on social and economic life, a more primordial sentiment seeks to assert autonomy, separateness, uniqueness, cultural survival, and, ultimately, sovereignty. Since most of the states of the world are composed of multiple ethnic/ language/religious groups, we could expect the future international agenda to be crowded with cases of civil wars, wars of secession and the breakdown of multicommunal states – all with the possibility of foreign intervention. (1991, 323)

The complex, conflict-related humanitarian emergencies which will inevitably result from such a pattern of conflict, involving large numbers of refugees and internally displaced people, as well as victims of war and famine, require a new range of responses from the international community. The existing international humanitarian system has been strained to the limit, with multilateral military peacekeeping forces increasingly becoming involved in providing assistance and protection to a wide range of international aid agencies working in war zones. Some humanitarian organizations oppose military involvement in humanitarian work because they fear that it jeopardizes its non-political nature. Others concede that the need for relief and the chaos and insecurity prevailing in conflict zones justify and require the protection that military peacekeeping forces can provide. Forcible humanitarian intervention in its classic guise plays a relatively modest and increasingly ambivalent part in all this. These questions are the subjects of the next chapters.

Suggested reading

The literature on ethnicity and conflict is large. Two influential studies mentioned in this chapter are Anderson, 1983, and A. Smith, 1986. Horowitz, 1985, offers a comprehensive review, while Moynihan, 1993, is stimulating. In addition, see Heraclides, 1991; Maynes, 1993; Montville (ed.), 1990; S. Ryan, 1990; and Toland (ed.), 1993. On the concept of international-social conflict, it is helpful to compare the international relations approach of M. Brown (ed.), 1993, and the conflict resolution approach of Azar, 1990.

4
Options

1 Introduction

Why should outsiders do anything at all about the massive human suffering associated with contemporary conflict in other countries? Why not respond like Neville Chamberlain in September 1938 to the crisis in Czechoslovakia: that it was a dispute 'in a faraway country between people of whom we know nothing'? In this chapter we will look at what outsiders *have done* during the period 1991–4. In chapter 5 we will look at the debate about what they *should have done*. But why has there been widespread public demand for cross-border humanitarian action and why, in a number of cases, have governments responded?

For the general public in many countries it is, quite simply, the identification of such conflicts with human rights abuse and human misery of vast proportions that fires passionate demands for intervention. Such concern often reflects particular cultural and historical sensitivities, mixed with partisan political sympathies. Public response is said to be fickle, soon overtaken by 'compassion fatigue', and swiftly succeeded by equally passionate calls for withdrawal if the costs, particularly in terms of interveners' lives, begin to mount. Nevertheless, confronted with human suffering on this scale, graphically if inconsistently communicated through the media (the 'CNN factor'), much of it deliberately and wantonly inflicted, public response from outside the affected region is commonly one of disbelief, anger and calls for immediate action. These are 'barbarous acts' which 'outrage the conscience of mankind' (UN

Declaration of Human Rights, 1948, preamble). It is human solidarity, Kant's idea of suffering in one part of the world being felt in all other parts, that fuels calls for action:

> Once again at the very heart of Europe, in what used to be Yugoslavia, we are witnessing the unbelievable: cities besieged, ethnic cleansing, concentration camps. This war must be stopped. The children of Sarajevo must be saved. Each day that goes by renders our unavoidable intervention more costly and less effective. In Africa, meanwhile, entire populations from Somalia to Liberia are extinguished, victims of a famine which is the direct result of clan warfare. . . . Humanitarian intervention, backed by UN resolutions, has become our duty. (Kouchner, 1992, 14–15, adapted)

Nor is protest confined to Western societies. Anger at the treatment of Muslims in Bosnia-Hercegovina is widespread throughout the Islamic world, compounded by resentment at what are perceived as Western double standards and indifference, if not covert hostility towards, Islam: 'The EC's and US-controlled UN's refusal to use military force to stop the holocaust is absolutely disgusting and hypocritical. Their enmity against Islam and the Muslims has now been fully exposed' (Khan, *Muslim News*, 26 March 1993). So it is that public clamour that 'something must be done' is translated into non-governmental initiatives of all kinds, and sometimes swells into a chorus that even reluctant governments can no longer ignore.

As to governments themselves, a number of factors draw them in, many, if not most, of which are hardly 'humanitarian'. There will always be innumerable special interests which enmesh particular states, sometimes to do with historic links, sometimes with perceived threats to valued assets. Beyond this there is the complex of concerns summed up in the phrase 'threat to regional stability', including the spread of weaponry, economic dislocation, links with terrorism or international crime, disruptive floods of refugees, as well as 'spill-over' into regional politics. There is concern about contagion by example if unacceptable behaviour is not dealt with effectively. There is often fear that a war will spread. 'Ring-fencing' the conflict often involves progressively deeper involvement, as attempts are made to build international coalitions, and embargoes are imposed and enforced. Beyond this again is the broader point that conflict which convulses one state – indeed, may end up by destroying it – automatically involves all the other members of international society, some of them in a similarly precarious position. This said, however, governments are no doubt also motivated by more purely 'humanitarian' concerns, prompted by the sincere efforts of individual ministers or under compulsion from outraged public opinion. For the former British Foreign Secretary,

[s]ituations are developing in Europe, in the Middle East, in Africa, in areas like South–East Asia, which don't immediately threaten Western European or British national security but which are in themselves as a situation unacceptable. They are unacceptable because of the amount of death and suffering which they cause and because they could spread outwards. . . . Some academics have in recent months made an intellectual distinction: they have divided the kind of actions we might have to think about into two broad categories: wars of interest and wars of conscience, but I am not sure that these distinctions are absolute. I think that it is too simple a division. . . . If we really want a world that is truly more secure, more prosperous and more stable, then humanitarian problems may from time to time be seen not only as a moral issue but as a potential security threat as well. We help people because they are hungry and because if they are not fed they will die, but it is also true that countries which are racked by famine or civil war will be unsafe neighbours in the world village. (Hurd, 1992, 34–5)

Whatever their reasons, how have governmental and non-governmental actors responded to the challenge of conflict-related suffering in the immediate post-cold war period? And how does forcible humanitarian intervention fit into all this?

2 Forcible humanitarian intervention revisited

Faced with atrocities on a scale to match anything during the cold war, it is no wonder that public attention has once again become mainly focused on the issue of forcible humanitarian intervention. The immediate response is: 'This must be stopped.' The vulnerable must be protected, the needy assisted. Since the suffering in contemporary conflicts is caused mainly by the warring parties, it seems that only the decisive application of superior military force can end it. The situation appears to be much as it was during the cold war, when forcible humanitarian intervention meant the temporary projection of military force across a border in order to prevent or stop a government from abusing its own citizens. But, as chapter 3 may already have suggested in terms of context, and as this chapter will show in terms of response, the situation has changed dramatically. The argument here is that this requires a reconceptualization in order to preserve the substance of the notion of forcible humanitarian intervention while placing it in its proper context. To anticipate, forcible humanitarian intervention should now be seen as a special case within a more general class of actions – cross-border response by the international community to human suffering in other countries.

2.1 The classic definition

To begin with the conclusion, before providing the evidence, another look at the classic definition of forcible humanitarian intervention will clarify why a reconceptualization is needed. Taking the six component parts of the definition presented in chapter 2, each one can be seen to have been materially affected by the turbulence of the post-cold war conflict environment (see box 7, pp. 43–4).

2.1.1 Purpose.
The purpose of forcible humanitarian intervention clearly remains 'humanitarian'. But, whereas during the cold war this was equated with response to target government violations of international human rights law within its own territory, it now also includes the other two main components of international humanitarianism as described in chapter 1 – international humanitarian laws of war (in response to war crimes) and international humanitarian assistance for the needy (in response to gross deprivation and starvation). The declared aim of forcible intervention has been to create 'humanitarian space' within which aid and relief agencies can operate. This makes a material difference, because armed forces are consequently given far more complex briefs, including the securing of points of entry for humanitarian supplies, the keeping open of supply routes, the escorting of aid convoys, the imposition of air exclusion zones, the protection of safe areas, the repatriation of refugees, and possibly the apprehension of war criminals. This implies a much deeper involvement in the conflict zone, perhaps longer-term.

2.1.2 Agency.
In the classic definition of humanitarian intervention, agency is confined to individual states or groups of states. Such action remains significant, and, as we will argue, when it comes to the use of force, predominant. But it is now ambiguously related to other forms of regional and global intervention, particularly as a result of the lead role currently assumed by the UN Security Council. Every suggested example of forcible humanitarian intervention between 1991 and 1994 was in one way or another collective. This makes a profound conceptual difference to the whole nature of forcible humanitarian intervention.

2.1.3 Target.
During the cold war period the target of humanitarian intervention was the authority structure of the offending state (to count

as intervention the action had to be 'debilitating', thus above the Article 2(4) threshold). Moreover, it was laid down as definitional of forcible humanitarian intervention that the action should not be consensual or by consent. It was intervention despite the opposition of the target government. Between 1991 and 1994, putative examples of forcible humanitarian intervention have been formally, if ambiguously, consensual, and in some cases there has been no government to give or withhold permission. These are reminiscent of cold war interventions in the Congo between 1960 and 1964 and in Lebanon from 1978, the former only partially and controversially classed as humanitarian intervention, the latter not at all. This is another material difference with wide implications. Some commentators have struggled to preserve the old definition by saying that an already existing 'consensual' action such as the presence of the United Nations Operation in Somalia (UNOSOM II) from May 1993 all at once 'became' humanitarian intervention when local resistance was met on 5 June 1993 and 25 Pakistani UN peacekeepers were killed (Falk, 1993, 757). This seems a somewhat desperate recourse.

2.1.4 Force level.   Here, as explained in chapter 2, the classic definition equates humanitarian intervention with forcible intervention, and assimilates this to the level of force prohibited in UN Charter Article 2(4), which outlaws aggression and war. This plunges us into a highly complex area, in which forcible humanitarian intervention merges with the unexpected expansion of UN peacekeeping operations, asked to take on more ambitious humanitarian roles under the aegis of ambiguous UN Security Council mandates. Five of the six candidates for classification as forcible humanitarian interventions between 1991 and 1994 – in Bosnia, Somalia, Rwanda, Liberia and Haiti – have been associated with UN peacekeeping missions. We will see how this has been not only a controversial, but also a conceptually indeterminate, relationship. Whether humanitarian peacekeeping and humanitarian enforcement can or should be conceptually separated is part of the debate to be addressed in the next chapter. In a number of cases it has been unclear whether troops have been operating under Chapter VI (peaceful settlement) or Chapter VII (enforcement) of the UN Charter, and if the latter, whether this does in fact imply an enforcement operation on the ground.

2.1.5 Context.   In chapter 3 we saw what a difference it makes that forcible humanitarian interventions from 1991 to 1994 have generally taken place in highly volatile conflict situations rather than, as was normal during the cold war, in situations where what was required was precise military action to halt human rights abuse by the target government. As noted above, the Congo in the early 1960s and Lebanon in the late 1970s and early 1980s would be comparable examples from the earlier period. This transforms the whole context within which the intervention takes place, and thus integrally alters its nature.

2.1.6 Legitimacy.   Finally, we noted how strict definitions in international law during the cold war period tended towards the idea that intervention was illegal *per se*, thus often begging the question at issue. Since 1991, this too has changed materially. The shift to preoccupation with the possibility of collective action under the aegis of the United Nations, rather than self-help by states, and to a focus on Article 2(7) of the United Nations Charter, rather than Article 2(4), has opened up the whole matter to reinterpretation. For example, the humanitarian brief taken on by the UN Security Council in Resolution 688 of 5 April 1991 and subsequently expanded in later resolutions to include explicit authorization for the use of force certainly made such action legitimate in international law, but what made it legitimate – that it was presented as a response to 'threats to international peace and security' and was authorized under UN Charter Chapter VII – thereby cast doubt on both its 'humanitarian' and 'intervention' credentials. Was this a separate, hybrid category – 'enforcement action for humanitarian reasons' (Verwey, 1992, 114)? In which case, what difference did this gloss make? As Anne-Marie Slaughter Burley and Carl Kaysen put it in the introduction to the aptly titled *Emerging Norms of Justified Intervention*, 'an intervention in the traditional language of international law is an illegal action. In our exploration of changing legal concepts and evolving norms, this connotation is no longer universally appropriate' (Reed and Kaysen (eds), 1993, 7). All this amounts to a crisis for the traditional concept of forcible humanitarian intervention, evidenced in the current confusion in terminology, in which experts use widely divergent definitions (see box 11). For Adam Roberts, 'increasingly the term "humanitarian intervention" seems a misnomer'. He suggests that 'the whole idea of humanitarian intervention needs to be rethought and indeed renamed' (1993b, 10, 63). What is to be done?

2.2 A reconceptualization

Let us take the intervention and humanitarian components of humanitarian intervention in turn.

Box 11: Humanitarian Intervention – A Problem of Definition

Thorough analysis of the terminological turmoil would take many pages. The following is a sample. Lori Fisler Damrosch refers to 'profound normative confusion': 'international lawyers have usually employed the term "humanitarian intervention" with reference to the application of force in order to terminate genocide and comparable atrocities, while the same term is now in general use to mean the delivery of food and medicines to deprived populations' (1993, 91). James Jonah, UN Under-Secretary-General for Political Affairs, says that UN Security Council action 'should not be considered as a form of humanitarian intervention' (1993, 79), whereas Juergen Dedring (1994), Senior Humanitarian Affairs Officer, refers to it as 'humanitarian intervention by the United Nations', and Ved Nanda wants only the UN Security Council and regional organizations to undertake 'humanitarian intervention' (1992, 33). Two Dutch legal commissions on humanitarian intervention define the term in incompatible ways (Malanczuk, 1993, 40–1). David Scheffer offers criteria for 'non-forcible humanitarian intervention by international aid agencies' (1992, 288); Paul Fifoot refers to 'physical intervention with consent' (1992, 143–8); and Elizabeth Ferris (1992) writes about 'NGO humanitarian intervention'. Jennings and Watts suggest 'peaceful action', including, if necessary, military personnel, among the criteria for possible 'humanitarian intervention' (Jennings and Watts (eds), 1992, 443). The Development Studies Association refers to 'peaceable humanitarian intervention' (1992, 18). The French term 'droit d'ingérence' is translated in a variety of ways, ranging from 'right of interference' to 'right of intervention' (Tomasevski, 1994, 80; Garigue, 1993, 672). Hugo Slim and Angela Penrose think that UN General Assembly Resolution 46/182 'tilts the balance towards humanitarian intervention' (1994, 201). Jack Donnelly distinguishes between intervention, quasi-intervention and positive non-intervention (1993b, 211–72). Raymond Plant considers positive non-intervention a form of intervention (1993, 105). Larry Minear and Thomas Weiss suggest that 'virtually all humanitarian action involves "intervention" of one sort or another' (1993, 32).

2.2.1 Intervention.   Faced with the difficulties noted above, one possibility is to follow the draconian advice of Ernst Haas: 'we would strike a blow for clarity if we junked the entire concept of intervention' (1993, 68). We prefer a less drastic remedy, one which looks more unorthodox than it actually is. The simplest solution is to reserve the term 'forcible humanitarian intervention' for what is left of the original concept, but include actions authorized by the United Nations Security Council as well as individual states, as most scholars now seem to do. The more radical suggestion is then to follow David Scheffer in introducing the term 'non-forcible humanitarian intervention' to cover a whole range of actions by state and non-state actors which in some cases merge with forcible humanitarian intervention (UN peacekeeping) and in some cases are now inextricably connected with it (the provision of humanitarian aid) (1992, 267). One good reason for making this move is that, in addition to the continuing literature on forcible humanitarian intervention in the 1990s, there is also a burgeoning, if disparate, literature on non-forcible humanitarian intervention, with the literature on UN peacekeeping playing something of a bridging role. In the latter, the terms 'intervention' and 'humanitarian intervention' are frequently used in Scheffer's sense – witness Elizabeth Ferris's article 'NGO humanitarian intervention: ethics and pragmatics' (1992). This also reflects a well-established usage in sociology (Bermant and Warwick, 1978), and in the English language generally, one which exactly captures what is at issue in humanitarian intervention – an interposition by an outside party with a view to effecting some alteration in the original situation. In short, retention of the term 'forcible humanitarian intervention' preserves the virtues of the traditional concept, which now takes its proper place as a special case within a wider class that also includes 'non-forcible humanitarian intervention'. Together they make up an inclusive whole called 'humanitarian intervention'. The crucial terminological move is this:

Whereas in classic terminology 'humanitarian intervention' means 'forcible self-help by states across international borders to protect indigenous human rights', in the rest of this book 'humanitarian intervention' means cross-border action by the international community in response to human suffering, made up of (i) 'forcible humanitarian intervention', an expanded version of the classic concept to include collective action as well as self-help and no longer confined to human rights abuse by governments, and (ii) 'non-forcible humanitarian intervention'.

There are many further advantages to making this terminological and conceptual move, which should become evident in what follows: (a) it avoids the tendency of restrictionist definitions to beg the main question and become enmeshed in terminological intricacies; (b) it clearly pinpoints the key debates which are missed by exclusive preoccupation with the classic definition; (c) it reflects the proper relationship between the military and non-military dimensions of post-cold war humanitarian intervention – namely, that the chief function of the military is to secure 'humanitarian space' within which non-military aid and relief agencies can operate; (d) it escapes the misleading 'all or nothing' options posed by restrictionist definitions, and opens the way for more nuanced choices; and (e) it rescues the concept of forcible humanitarian intervention itself, restoring it to its natural place as one option among others.

2.2.2 Humanitarian.   In addition, as we have seen, the meaning of 'humanitarian' in the traditional definition of humanitarian intervention also needs to be revised. In the post-cold war context, traditional concern for human rights violations by governments must be expanded to include humanitarian assistance and humanitarian protection in conflict situations, where 'humanitarian' is as defined in chapter 1. The principles of humanity, impartiality, neutrality and universality constitute the core values. Moreover, in place of the one-dimensional classic preoccupation with humanitarian motives, which, not surprisingly, nearly all state actors fail, we apply the five criteria used at the beginning of Part II in the case of the Kurds and Shi'a in Iraq. We ask (i) if there was a humanitarian cause; (ii) if there was a declared humanitarian end; (iii) if interveners worked towards this end with reasonable impartiality and without interests which were clearly incompatible with it – in other words, a humanitarian approach; (iv) if humanitarian means were employed; and (v) if there was a humanitarian outcome.

3 A revised typology for humanitarian intervention

Before reviewing the humanitarian intervention options undertaken by the international community between 1991 and 1994, we should clarify the new typology, because there are important distinctions to be made within the broad category of non-forcible humanitarian intervention. Here we begin by introducing some further subcategories. Having established a simple distinction between forcible and non-forcible humanitarian intervention, we now develop the categorization further.

3.1 Governmental humanitarian intervention

First, it is useful to class forcible humanitarian intervention together with three types of non-forcible humanitarian intervention, so as to obtain

Box 12: A Typology of Governmental Humanitarian Intervention

1 *Coercive humanitarian intervention*
  (a) Forcible military humanitarian intervention
  (b) Coercive non-military humanitarian intervention
2 *Non-coercive humanitarian intervention*
  (c) Non-forcible military humanitarian intervention (e.g. peacekeeping)
  (d) Non-coercive, non-military humanitarian intervention

a schematic typology of governmental humanitarian intervention (see box 12).

These types of government action become decreasingly consensual and increasingly problematic in terms of distinctions between humanitarian and political involvement as they move from (d) to (a). It is significant that the two types of military action, peacekeeping (c) and enforcement (a), are clearly separated here. Although this is somewhat controversial, as we will see in chapter 5, in our view the two should be kept conceptually distinct, however hard it may be sometimes to discern which actions on the ground come under which heading. The alternative, as demonstrated in Bosnia, is hopeless conceptual confusion.

Coercive humanitarian intervention by governments, which includes categories (a) and (b), coincides with the broad classic definition of humanitarian intervention, whereby, as we saw in chapter 2, coercion rather than military enforcement is taken to be the critical determinant of intervention. Category (a), forcible military humanitarian intervention, coincides with the narrow classic definition (but not the very narrow definition, because it includes collective action as well as self-help; for the very narrow definition to apply, a further qualification would have to be added). An example of category (b), coercive non-military humanitarian intervention, would be the imposition of sanctions in order to promote humanitarian causes.

Non-coercive humanitarian intervention by governments, which includes categories (c) and (d), represents a terminological departure from orthodoxy. Within category (c), non-forcible military humanitarian intervention, comes the humanitarian brief for UN peacekeeping as traditionally defined. This links with other non-forcible military activity, such as 'Operation Sea Angel' launched in response to the cyclone in Bangladesh in April 1991 (Rahman, 1993). There is great scope for military contributions in disaster areas in general, including air-lift capabilities, communications, logistics and command structures.

Examples of category (d), non-coercive, non-military humanitarian intervention, might be the granting or withholding of official recognition of a secessionist state (Damrosch, 1989), a graded range of diplomatic and other representations which fall below the level of coercion (Luard, 1981, 26–8), collective action through UN human rights procedures as noted in chapter 1, section 2.2, and governmental contributions to a host of international humanitarian relief, aid and assistance programmes (see box 13). Also included here, despite the apparent verbal contradiction, would be Jack Donnelly's (1984) main recommendation for outside government response to human rights abuse, which he somewhat equivocally calls 'positive non-intervention' – that is, the severing of links with an offending regime.

It is important to note that in the new terminology each of the four types of governmental humanitarian intervention (a) to (d) includes state action under the aegis of regional organizations or the United Nations, as well as action by states functioning singly or in *ad hoc* groupings.

3.2 Transnational, inter-governmental and non-governmental humanitarian intervention

This leaves (e) a whole complex of transnational, inter-governmental and non-governmental modes of non-forcible humanitarian intervention, as outlined in chapter 1.

3.2.1 The International Committee of the Red Cross. Having been excluded from internal wars by the great powers, ICRC humanitarian assistance in civil wars expanded in response to post-decolonization turbulence in the Third World during the 1960s (Caratsch, 1993). The ICRC has 6,300 employees, and in 1993 had a budget of $608 million provided mainly by donor governments (the US being much the largest donor) and national Red Cross/Red Crescent societies. Manned largely by Swiss nationals, it is professional, efficient and focused, all delegates (managers) being well trained in ICRC rules. On the other hand, it is expensive, its neutrality policy is sometimes controversial, and it does not address the causes of emergencies (Natsios, 1995, 73–4).

3.2.2 UN humanitarian agencies. These include the four main semi-autonomous line agencies – UNHCR, UNICEF, WFP and UNDP – supported by voluntary contributions from UN members, not assessed fees. Since they function independently of the UN Secretary-General and

Box 13: ODA, OFDA and ECHO

Donor government aid agencies, such as the British Overseas Development Administration (ODA), provide much of the money to finance ICRC, UN agency and NGO efforts, and also make their own independent contributions in the field.

The US Office of Foreign Disaster Assistance (OFDA), within the US Agency for International Development (USAID), has a budget of $189 million per year for immediate relief work and a staff of 25 regular and 25 contract employees. Under the Foreign Assistance Act it is deputed to co-ordinate US response to foreign natural and man-made disasters, and under the 'notwithstanding' provision can cut through bureaucratic red tape. Its own Disaster Assistance Response teams can act on the spot, and, as in Kurdish Iraq in 1991, report back directly to the US State Department via satellite (Natsios, 1995, 78–9).

The European Community Humanitarian Office (ECHO) was set up in 1992 with the aim of 'heightening the effectiveness of the Community's relief operations and contributing to a clearer perception of its overall humanitarian assistance' (ECHO, 1995). Included in its remit is the distribution of emergency aid financed by the European Development Fund (EDF) and the important task of improving working relationships between EC donor states, humanitarian operational agencies and recipient countries and other groups. In 1994 it provided some $977 million in emergency aid to 60 countries, including Rwanda, former Yugoslavia, the Caucasus, Afghanistan, Iraq, Sudan, Somalia, Angola, Liberia and Haiti. According to Emma Bonino, Commissioner for Humanitarian Aid, ECHO and other European nations provided 53 per cent of UNHCR's budget and 40 per cent of WFP's (Inter Press Service, 23 May 1995).

each other, co-ordination is problematic. Performance is also uneven. WFP has a budget of $1 billion for delivery of food aid, but no tradition of working on both sides in a civil war, whereas UNICEF has traditionally been seen to be capable of operating in internal wars without conferring legitimacy on insurgent forces (Minear and Weiss, 1993, 70). In recent years UN agencies have developed their own field capacity, rather than working solely through recipient governments, UNHCR giving an effective lead in Bosnia under Sadako Ogata and UNICEF in Sudan under James Grant. Performance in Somalia, however, is generally judged to have been inadequate. In some organizations, hard-working, able professionals work side by side with venial placemen assigned by corrupt governments. In chapter 1 we noted attempts to create a co-ordinated strategy through the setting up of the new Department of Humanitarian Affairs (DHA) in 1991, with mixed results as yet.

3.2.3 NGOs (PVOs). Included here are a host of non-governmental organizations such as the Save the Children Fund (SCF), whose origins go back to the rebuilding of Europe after the First World War; Oxfam, formed in 1942 to help Belgian and Greek children in the Second World War; CARE in the United States, created to send food parcels to Europe after the war; and Médecins Sans Frontières (MSF) (see box 14), launched after the Biafra war in 1971 (Finucane, 1993, 176–7; Beigbeder, 1991). American NGOs employ hundreds of thousands of people, raise private revenue of some $4 billion, and receive $1.5 billion per year from USAID. According to Mark Duffield, 'in net terms, NGOs now collectively transfer more resources to the South than the World Bank' (1994, 58).

A number of commentators would add the media to the list of significant non-governmental humanitarian interveners. Certainly the media are influential, and often intrusive, and should be included in any comprehensive attempt, as in the epilogue of this book, to establish general framework principles for humanitarian intervention as a whole (Benthall, 1993; Girardet, 1993).

Many experts will be unhappy about calling category (e) 'intervention', because this is not in accordance with international law (only states can be said to intervene in other states' domestic affairs; non-state actors overstepping the mark would simply be arraigned for breach of local municipal law). Intervention also carries its traditional pejorative overtones of illegal use of overbearing, dictatorial power. Nevertheless, for the purposes of this book, the simplification gained by calling all the types of action (a) to (e) 'humanitarian intervention' far outweighs the disadvantages. A simple distinction between 'forcible' and 'non-forcible' humanitarian intervention can then be employed. If the various international law usages are required, the terms 'coercive humanitarian intervention' and 'forcible humanitarian intervention' cover the main two, and clearly distinguish between them. As for the other categories and the all-inclusive unqualified term 'humanitarian intervention' itself, these are simply not usages in international law. This again is quite plain and straightforward, once the terminology is adopted. No pejorative over-

---

Box 14: Médecins Sans Frontières

In 1993–4, MSF had a budget of $187 million and 2,000 expatriate staff working in Eastern and Southern Asia (13 countries), Central Asia (5 countries), Eastern Europe (6 countries), the Middle East (4 countries), Africa (25 countries), and the Western Hemisphere (10 countries), including 360 workers in Burundi/Rwanda. MSF was founded in 1971 by two groups of doctors, one of which had worked in Biafra during the 1967–70 war with the French Red Cross. Unlike the Red Cross, however, MSF was dedicated from the start to 'bringing swift and direct aid to all populations affected by war and natural disaster regardless of government consent'. The prime responsibility was to the suffering; frontiers were to be disregarded. MSF refused, therefore, (a) to recognize national sovereignty, entering Afghanistan, Kurdistan, El Salvador and Eritrea clandestinely, and (b) to remain silent about obstruction or abuse, speaking out in Cambodia and Afghanistan and Ethiopia. MSF's operations expanded rapidly from the late 1970s with the multiplication of refugee camps in the Third World. In Ethiopia, realizing that the regime was using aid workers to assist a brutal transfer of population from the north of the country, in which perhaps 100,000 died, MSF denounced the action, and was expelled in November 1985. The EC and US subsequently joined the protest, and the resettlement programme was halted in early 1986. In Afghanistan, MSF workers were for some years the only foreign aid workers assisting the resistance fighters. First Bernard Kouchner, then Claude Malhuret, established their international reputations through leadership of MSF, subsequently becoming French government ministers (Brauman, 1993).

---

tones are implied. The ordinary English word 'intervention' is being used in an ordinary, accurate way.

3.3 Forcible intervention, non-forcible military intervention and non-military intervention

There are important issues to be discussed in each of the five categories (a) to (e), but, for reasons of space, we will say relatively little about categories (b) coercive non-military humanitarian intervention, and (d) non-coercive non-military humanitarian intervention, except for government development and aid programmes. Our main concern is with a reconceptualization of the traditional definition; so, for us, the most significant categories are forcible military intervention (option (a)); non-forcible military intervention (option (c)); and non-military intervention, particularly options (d) and (e).

Although a matter of judgement, and at the risk of some controversy, we use well-recognized criteria to distinguish option (a) from option (c). The US Army Field Manual of June 1994, for example, gives three criteria for distinguishing between peace enforcement and peacekeeping: levels of consent, levels of impartiality and levels of force, with peacekeeping requiring higher levels of the first two and enforcement a higher level of the third (p. 12). We accept this as a good general guide, although (i) consent is harder to determine in ISCs than in the situations envisaged in the classic definition, where it means the consent of host governments; (ii) impartiality is usually confused with neutrality, and in the case of ISCs is disputed and subject to the fluctuating, often contradictory perceptions of the conflict parties, even in the case of non-forcible intervention; and (iii) force level is relative to the politico-military situation and the scale of the stated objective of the mission – for example, France was able to enforce its aims in Rwanda with 2,500 troops, whereas UNPROFOR, with more than 33,000 military personnel, was unable to enforce its mandate in former Yugoslavia. British Army doctrine also makes a clear distinction between peacekeeping and peace enforcement, the main difference being whether or not there is consent (Dobbie, 1994). For collective UN action, in addition to these three criteria, (iv) a UN Charter Chapter VII mandate is a necessary, but (as shown in Bosnia) not a sufficient, condition for enforcement. Finally, a helpful extra indicator of the difference between forcible and non-forcible military intervention (in our view, sometimes the most helpful) is (v) whether the interveners can, and do, materially alter the outcome of the conflict. For example, the fact that in Liberia ECOWAS did, and in Bosnia UNPROFOR did not, materially affect the outcome of the conflict suggests that, at any rate until the end of 1994, the former was, and the latter was not, a forcible intervention.

As to the non-military option, we will for convenience refer to this as option (d/e).

It should be remembered that this is a conceptual model. The aim is to offer the simplest model with the greatest elucidatory power. It cannot be expected to apply neatly to the confusion of events, but must be shown to be based on convincing, widely supported conceptual distinctions and, when applied, to yield a better understanding than alternatives. In what follows, therefore, we apply the revised typology to complex man-made humanitarian emergencies during the 1991–4 period, taking as our data set the 17 severe international-social conflicts isolated in chapter 3. We then briefly apply the traditional concept, as described in chapter 2, to the same data set, in order to compare the two.

4 Humanitarian intervention in major complex emergencies 1991–4: application of the revised concept

In addition to the three classes of option that we are considering here – (a) forcible, (c) non-forcible military and (d/e) non-military – we should also include a fourth category: *pure non-intervention*. Under the traditional restrictionist concept of intervention as forcible self-help by states, 'non-intervention' included all action and inaction that was not forcible self-help. Under the revised typology, non-intervention is also reconceptualized. In addition to options (b) to (e), which would have been lumped together as non-intervention under the classic concept, there is what is termed here 'pure non-intervention', which means that UN agencies, NGOs and the ICRC have been unable to gain entry, and that governments are not pressing vigorously the range of non-military options short of coercion available to them, either bilaterally or collectively through UN human rights machinery. In other words, none of options (a) to (e) apply.

If interventions are matched with the most pressing humanitarian crises, it can be seen that the three options – (a) forcible, (c) non-forcible military and (d/e) non-military – are listed in reverse order of frequency. That is to say, the ICRC, UN agencies, NGOs and donor governments have been involved in almost all these conflicts; UN peacekeepers and other non-forcible military interveners have played an explicit humanitarian role in a number of them; and there has been forcible humanitarian intervention in only a few. In box 15 (which covers the 1993–4 period), for example, it should be understood that non-military intervention (option d/e) accompanies both non-forcible military intervention and forcible intervention. The crucial distinctions are cases in which there is forcible humanitarian intervention; cases in which there is no enforcement, but there is non-forcible military intervention; cases in which there is no military presence, but there is non-military humanitarian intervention; and cases in which there is virtually no humanitarian intervention at all.

4.1 Non-intervention

Among numerous instances of pure non-intervention, despite well-documented humanitarian cause, mention may be made of the situations in

---

**Box 15: Severe International-Social Conflicts 1993–4:
A Classification by Intervention Typology**

Non-intervention: Indonesia, Myanmar (Burma), Russia (Chechnya), Turkey.

Non-military intervention: Afghanistan, Azerbaijan,* Burundi, Sri Lanka, Sudan.

Non-forcible military intervention: Angola (UNAVEM), Bosnia (UNPROFOR), Georgia (UNOMIG),* Liberia (UNOMIL), Rwanda (UNAMIR), Somalia (UNOSOM I), Tajikistan (UNMOT).*

Forcible intervention: Iraq ('Operation Provide Comfort' and 'Operation Southern Watch'), Liberia (ECOMOG), Rwanda ('Operation Turquoise'), Somalia (UNITAF/UNOSOM II).

Note: Haiti is not included because it is not a case of ISC, nor are Algeria, Cambodia, El Salvador or Mozambique.
* Russian forces in former Soviet republics are a special case whose status remains controversial and are therefore excluded from this classification.

Indonesia and Myanmar (Burma). The lack of international response to human suffering in the East Timorese conflict in Indonesia is well documented (Pilger, 1994). In the cases of the Chechen conflict in Russia and the Kurdish conflict in Turkey there have been attempts to apply pressure from outside, but the governments involved are influential and strong enough to resist it. The situation in Iraq before 1991 also falls in this category. The survey in chapter 2 suggests that, historically, this has been the norm. In most of the cold war cases of massive human rights abuse, outside governments did not even use the available non-forcible collective mechanisms for redress, and non-governmental agencies were debarred despite their desire to intervene.

4.2 Non-military intervention

Here we have easily the largest class of interventions. As Jan Eliasson, Under-Secretary-General for Humanitarian Affairs at the UN, puts it, 'in most of our operations around the world we have no military presence'. In these cases success depends upon maintaining 'the important guiding principles of humanitarian relief – namely, impartiality, neutrality and humanity'. In 1992, in response to the threat of 'the most serious drought of the century', for example, the improved political situation in southern Africa enabled the timely distribution of $700 million in relief aid to 10 recipient countries co-ordinated through the Southern Africa Development Community. This helped save the lives of hundreds of thousands. The keys were prevention and a sufficiently stable political situation in which international humanitarian diplomacy could operate. Such successes are easily overlooked, because for that very reason they do not make headlines (Eliasson, 1993b).

Problems arise when turbulent conflict, as in Afghanistan or Sudan (see box 16), disrupts relief efforts and, above all, when humanitarian intervention efforts are seen by governments or powerful factions to run counter to major political objectives. As we saw in chapter 3, in international-social conflicts civilian populations may themselves be the direct target of the violence, so humanitarian relief is a political act. War zones disintegrate into a chaos of faction-fighting in which local populations are raided and aid provision is plundered to sustain the power of warlords and fuel the war economy. As we will see in chapter 5, aid providers confront severe problems in these circumstances to do with access and security, and impartiality and neutrality become controversial and difficult to maintain. They are thus faced with a series of cruel dilemmas.

4.3 Non-forcible military intervention: United Nations peacekeeping

According to the United Nations,

> a peacekeeping operation has come to be defined as an operation involving military personnel, but without enforcement powers, undertaken by the United Nations to help maintain or restore international peace and security in areas of conflict. These operations are voluntary and are based on consent and co-operation. While they involve the use of military personnel, they achieve their objectives not by force of arms, thus contrasting them with the 'enforcement' action of the United Nations Article 42. (White, 1993, 183)

Peacekeeping is not mentioned in the UN Charter, and peacekeeping operations are often described as falling between Chapters VI and VII. Chapter VI refers to the techniques which the Security Council can adopt in pursuit of the peaceful settlement of disputes, such as mediation, arbitration, negotiation and fact-finding. Chapter VII gives the Security Council power to enforce decisions, by using armed force if necessary, to maintain or restore international peace and security (White, 1993).

Box 16: Operation Lifeline in Sudan

The long-lasting conflict in Sudan has all the symptoms of international-social conflict: (i) social heterogeneity between the Arabized Muslim north and the black Christian/animist south; (ii) an inept, yet oppressive, government in Khartoum since President Nimeiri's withdrawal of regional autonomy and attempt to impose Sharia (Islamic law) on the south after 1983; (iii) a sharp dichotomy between the relatively more developed north and the south, which is perhaps 30 years behind; and (iv) outside influence, such as Ethiopian support before 1991 for the southern rebel Sudanese People's Liberation Army (SPLA). During the course of the fighting between 1988 and 1992, some 500,000 may have died from starvation or war, especially in the south, and millions were driven from their homes. Faction-fighting within the SPLA has added to the chaos.

In 1986 the head of UNDP in Khartoum was expelled for endorsing 'Operation Rainbow', an attempt to provide aid to civilians on both sides. For two years the government prevented food aid from reaching rebel areas. In 1989 a breakthrough in negotiations between Khartoum and the SPLA, a new policy of firmness towards Sudan on the part of the US, and the energetic leadership of James Grant of UNICEF led to the April launch of 'Operation Lifeline', often cited as a model of humanitarian intervention. 'Corridors of tranquillity' were opened for emergency relief on both sides of the battle lines. The operation is thoroughly described in Minear, 1991. But the success was short-lived. In June 1989 a military coup installed a new fundamentalist government which renewed military offensives in the south. According to MSF assessment, 'Operation Lifeline has continued, but gradually it has become an instrument of war, rather than a force for peace' (Jean (ed.), 1993, 20). The UN is accused of being too accommodating to the Khartoum government, even after two UN employees were executed in Juba. Meanwhile the SPLA plundered aid from the huge refugee camps in Ethiopia to feed its troops. In 1992 perhaps 11 aid workers died in Sudan, and in April the UN decided to suspend relief operations. In December 1992 the UN General Assembly unexpectedly condemned Sudan's human rights record, and appointed a special rapporteur. Under pressure, the Sudanese government agreed to UN food deliveries to the south. Sadly, internecine fighting within the SPLA subsequently made it almost impossible to make use of this opportunity. Meanwhile, during 1992, the non-Arab Nuba people in the north were subjected to a government-led jihad in which tens of thousands were deported and died. When Jan Eliasson, UN Under-Secretary-General for Humanitarian Affairs, visited Sudan in September 1992, he made no comment on human rights abuses, which he said lay outside his province. MSF commentators are highly critical of 'UN paralysis', but the issue is complex. The principles of neutrality and humanity are in collision here.

Article 99 gives the Secretary-General power to carry out 'good offices missions', including fact-finding and inquiry and encouraging hostile parties to seek a negotiated settlement. Peacekeeping operations, described as 'chapter six and a half' initiatives, often follow good offices missions.

The United Nations Emergency Force (UNEF I) deployed during the Suez crisis in the Middle East after 1956 was the first fully fledged peacekeeping operation, and served as a precedent for all subsequent missions. It established a set of principles which still define the essence of peacekeeping as a non-forcible form of humanitarian intervention in conflict. The principles were defined by Secretary-General Hammarskjöld and Lester Pearson (General Assembly President, 1952–3) as follows:

1 the principle of the consent of the parties to the dispute for the establishment of the mission;
2 the principle of non-use of force except in self-defence;
3 the principle of voluntary contributions of contingents from small, neutral countries to participate in the force;
4 the principle of impartiality;
5 the principle of control of peacekeeping operations by the Secretary-General. (Fetherston, 1994, 1–12)

Although a number of these principles have been contested and challenged (see chapter 5), particularly in the debate as to the nature and efficacy of peacekeeping in post-cold war conflicts, they proved durable enough over a period of 30 years for Brian Urquhart to describe the document in which they are defined as 'a conceptual masterpiece in a completely new field, the blueprint for a non-violent, international military operation' (Fetherston, 1994, 13). This comment perfectly defines peacekeeping as a form of non-forcible intervention under the control of the international community.

The history of the evolution of peacekeeping is now well charted (James, 1990; Fetherston, 1994; Durch (ed.), 1993), and its expansion since 1988 is striking. During the 42-year period from 1945 to 1987, 13 missions were established. Between 1988 and 1994, in the space of six years, 18 missions were initiated.

The launching of large-scale operations in 1992 in Cambodia, Somalia and Yugoslavia and the general expansion of the missions led to a qualitative development in the functions of peacekeeping, with the result that they are now best described as multi-dimensional in nature. This multi-dimensionality has pulled some missions towards enforcement responsibilities under Chapter VII. In addition, peacekeeping mandates frequently have political and humanitarian components, with civilian and civil police staffs to carry them out. In many operations, mandates which began as involving a limited responsibility to monitor cease-fires have grown *de facto* as cease-fires have broken down and missions find themselves getting drawn into the protection of civilian populations. In sum, there has been an acceleration of the *humanitarianization* of what was traditionally a form of military, albeit non-forcible, intervention (Fetherston, 1994, 31–4; Gordenker and Weiss, 1991; Weiss and Campbell, 1991; Durch (ed.), 1993, 474; Berdal, 1993). As Durch has put it, peacekeeping, which was 'devised to untangle warring states' (classic peacekeeping) has now 'evolved to assist suffering peoples ... protecting human rights while sustaining or rebuilding war torn countries' (1993, 474).

The post-1988 deployments are currently being redefined according to new forms of military doctrine seeking to elaborate the principles under which they should operate; they are variously called multi-dimensional operations, second-generation peacekeeping operations, wider peace-keeping, second-generation multinational forces, or peace support operations (Dobbie, 1994; Mackinlay and Chopra, 1992; US Army, 1994; H. Smith (ed.), 1993; House of Commons, 1992–3). Although their roles are classified in a variety of ways by different authorities (James, 1993a; Dobbie, 1994, 124–5; Berdal, 1993, 12), many current peace-keeping operations now have military, political and humanitarian components. The functions of these components can be classified as in box 17.

The multi-faceted nature and objectives of peacekeeping existed in a minority of pre-1988 deployments, but are coming to be characteristic of post-1988 missions. Peacekeeping forces, in addition to carrying out the interposition responsibilities linked to classical peacekeeping missions and involving cease-fire observation, buffer zone control and so on, now have to serve in support roles, including 'the establishment of a secure environment for non-military operations such as electoral monitoring, refugee repatriation, and the distribution of humanitarian relief supplies by civilian agencies' (Berdal, 1993, 11).

While functions have diversified, the contexts and environments in which the missions are deployed have become more complex. Although there have been exceptions (ONUC in the Congo and UNIFIL in Leba-non, for example), peacekeeping operations set up since 1956 in accord-ance with the Hammarskjöld–Pearson principles summarized above have generally operated in permissive environments in which they had the consent and support of host governments for their presence. Increasingly, however, they have come to be deployed in internal wars or complex situations of civil and international war. We have conceptualized these as international-social conflicts, which are at best semi-permissive environ-

Box 17: Classification of Wider Peacekeeping Roles

Military functions

cease-fires: observation, monitoring, maintenance of buffer zones
disarmament of warring factions / regulation of disposition of
    forces
prevention of infiltration / prevention of civil war
verification of security agreements / supervision of cantonment
mine clearance
training / reforming military units

Political functions

upholding law and order
assisting in the establishment of a viable government / ensuring
    political independence
coping / negotiating with non-governmental entities
elections / administration / temporary authority
providing security / re-establishing economic life for local
    populations
management of local disputes
provision of confidence-building measures
training police

Humanitarian functions

protecting aid convoys (protection of delivery and relief workers)
provision of humanitarian assistance
establishing, supporting and protecting regional safe havens and
    protected areas
assisting in refugee repatriation and monitoring flow of refugees
logistical support for humanitarian assistance, including transpor-
    tation, medical and engineer support
verifying human rights agreements

(Taken from Fetherston, 1994, 31–3; UK Ministry of Defence,
    1995; US Army, 1994)

ments in which there is a high level of suffering among the civilian
population and governments and other authorities are rarely in complete
control of territory. In such environments consent may be partial, and
conditions of lawlessness and violence in which militias and paramilitary

groups act autonomously mean that UN agencies are often confronted and opposed. It is precisely these environments into which the UN gets drawn as it seeks to respond to conflict-generated humanitarian emergencies.

We are concerned here with the United Nations peacekeeping operations which were initiated during and/or operated continuously between 1991 and 1994. Box 18 identifies the missions and the presence or absence of a humanitarian component in their mandate and operation. Of the 12 missions initiated since 1991 and still in operation at the end of 1994, 10 had a significant humanitarian dimension. The two which did not were in response to type 1 inter-state conflicts (UNIKOM (Kuwait) and MINURSO (Western Sahara)). Three of the 10 were involved in type 2 political, ideological and religious conflicts (ONUSAL (El Salvador), ONUMOZ (Mozambique), UNMIH (Haiti)). Seven of the 10 were in type 3 international-social conflicts (UNAVEM II (Angola), UNPROFOR (former Yugoslavia), UNOSOM II (Somalia), UNOMIG (Georgia), UNOMIL (Liberia), UNAMIR (Rwanda), UNMOT (Tajikistan)). In the pre-1991 deployments, which were of the classic peacekeeping type, humanitarian roles were non-existent or minor (with the possible exception of UNFICYP (Cyprus)).

In international-social conflicts, humanitarian functions emerged alongside traditional cease-fire supervision, either because in the absence of more adequate political solutions the cease-fire created a vacuum in which humanitarian needs for communities in a buffer zone were not being serviced by normal authorities (UNFICYP) or because cease-fires or political agreements broke down, sucking the peacekeepers into a humanitarian crisis in which they found themselves having to co-ordinate humanitarian assistance programmes (UNAVEM II, UNAMIR, UNOMIL, UNOMIG). The same process may well occur in the conflict in Tajikistan should the cease-fire there not hold. Undoubtedly among the seven humanitarian ISC interventions, the problems of UNOSOM II and UNPROFOR have loomed the largest. These two cases, therefore, are examined in detail in chapters 6 and 7.

4.4 Forcible intervention

We can now consider the six cases most often cited as putative examples of forcible humanitarian intervention during the 1991–4 period, and compare application of the traditional definition with application of the revised concept. These are the interventions in Liberia, Somalia, Iraq, Haiti, Bosnia and Rwanda, triggered by intensified humanitarian crises erupting in December 1989, January 1991, March 1991, September

Box 18: Humanitarian Components in UN Peacekeeping and Observer Missions Operating 1991–4 (in chronological order, by date of deployment in the field)*

Mission	Duration	Humanitarian component
Missions created before 1991 and still deployed		
UNTSO	June 1948–present[†]	No
UNMOGIP	January 1949–present	No
UNFICYP	March 1964–present	Yes
UNDOF	June 1974–present	Yes (minor)
UNIFIL	March 1978–present	Yes (minor)
Missions created since 1991		
1991		
UNIKOM[‡]	April 1991–present	No
UNAVEM II[‡]	June 1991–present	Yes
ONUSAL[‡]	July 1991–present	Yes
MINURSO[‡]	September 1991–present	Yes (minor)
1992		
UNAMIC	October 1991–March 1992	
+ UNTAC	March 1992–September 1993	Yes
UNPROFOR[‡]	March 1992–present	Yes
UNOSOM I	April 1992–April 1993	Yes
ONUMOZ[‡]	December 1992–present	Yes
1993		
UNOSOM II[‡]	May 1993–March 1995	Yes
UNOMUR	June 1993 until absorbed by UNAMIR	No
UNOMIG[‡]	August 1993–present	Yes
UNOMIL[‡]	September 1993–present	Yes
UNMIH[‡]	September 1993–present (suspended October 1993 and July 1994)	Yes
UNAMIR[‡]	October 1993–present	Yes
1994		
UNASOG	May–June 1994	No
UNMOT[‡]	December 1994–present	Yes

* See Appendix 1 for complete names of UN missions.
[†]'Present' here means beyond the end of 1994.
[‡]Missions initiated since 1991 and still in operation at the end of 1994.

Box 19: Time-Chart: Forcible Humanitarian Intervention, 1989–94 (including Bosnia)

	Liberia	Somalia	Iraq	Haiti	Bosnia	Rwanda	World
1989	24 Dec. Taylor invades						Nov. fall of Berlin Wall
1990	25 Aug. ECOMOG lands 27 Nov. cease-fire		2 Aug. invasion of Kuwait	16 Dec. Aristide wins elections		4 Oct. RPF invade	Unification of Germany Gulf crisis
1991	30 Oct. Yamoussoukro IV Agreement	Jan. Siad Barre overthrown Nov.–Feb. worst phase of fighting	27 Feb. end 'Desert Storm' Mar. attack on Kurds/Shia 5 Apr. SCR 688 'Operation Provide Comfort' 'Operation Southern Watch'	30 Sept. *coup*	25 June Slovene/Croat independence June/July Slovene war July/Jan. Croat war		Gulf War Collapse of Soviet Union 19 Dec. UNGAR 46/182
1992	15 Oct. Taylor attacks Monrovia	3 Mar. cease-fire 24 Apr. SCR 751 UNOSOM I May–Oct. Sahnoun UNSGSR 3 Dec. SCR 794 UNITAF			21 Feb. SCR 743 UNPROFOR I 6 Apr. Bosnian war 30 May SCR 757 sanctions (against Serbia) 13 July SCR 764 13 Aug. SCR 770 UNPROFOR II 9 Oct. SCR 781 no-fly zone		Jan. UNSG Boutros Ghali UN summit Mar. UNTAC in Cambodia June *Agenda for Peace*
1993	11 July Cotonou Agreement 22 Sept. SCR 866 UNOMIL	26 Mar. SCR 814 UNOSOM II 5 June–9 Oct. war against Aidid Oct. 1993–Mar. 1995 wind down to withdrawal		2 July Governors Island Agreement 23 Sept. SCR 867 UNMIH	22 Feb. SCR 808 War Crimes Tribunal 4 June SCR 836 Safe Areas	22 June SCR 846 UNOMUR 4 Aug. Arusha Agreement 5 Oct. SCR 872 UNAMIR I	Jan. Clinton becomes President of US Sept. UNTAC ends
1994	6 Sept. Akasumbo Agreement			19 Sept. 'Operation Uphold Democracy'		6 Apr. President killed 21 Apr. SCR 912 17 May SCR 918 UNAMIR II 23 June SCR 929 endorses French 'Operation Turquoise'	May PDD 25 US Congressional elections

1991, April 1992 and April 1994 respectively (see box 19). In the literature UNPROFOR is often included as an example of forcible intervention, although in terms of our classification it was non-forcible up to the end of 1994.

4.4.1 Application of the classic concept.   Under the classic concept, as in the cold war period and before, restrictionist definitions rule out all six examples, half on more or less substantive grounds, half by definition. In *Iraq*, as we have seen, either the forcible action was authorized under SCR 688, in which case it was not intervention, or it was not, in which case it fails under the normal criteria described in chapter 2, including those of consent and genuine humanitarian motive. Probably the allied action should not be classed as humanitarian intervention at all, but in terms of the rights and responsibilities of victors after a war (Mayall, 1991). In *Bosnia*, as argued more fully in chapter 6, there is no doubt that UNPROFOR was given a humanitarian brief, but, despite a UN Charter Chapter VII mandate, it was not an enforcement operation. UNPROFOR went into the country with the consent of the newly recognized government of Bosnia, and (unlike ECOMOG in Liberia) was not directly opposed in this period by the warring parties. In *Somalia*, as elaborated in chapter 7, UNITAF's action was authorized under SCR 794, thus not qualifying as intervention, and once again it was not an intervention against the will of the government, because there was no government to give or withhold consent. It should probably be classed not as humanitarian intervention but 'in terms of the long-standing proposition in international law that when a state completely collapses into chaos, there can be grounds for military intervention by other states if such a course has a serious chance of restoring order' (Roberts, 1993a, 440). In *Liberia*, the Cease-Fire Monitoring Group (ECOMOG) forces of the Economic Community of West African States (ECOWAS) entered the country in August 1990 with the tacit consent of President Doe. The UN Security Council subsequently endorsed ECOMOG as a 'peacekeeping force', and implicitly recognized the Interim Government of National Unity which ECOMOG sustained. This casts doubt on the status of the action as a classic instance of intervention without the consent of the government. In addition, the regional political ambitions of Nigeria, the preponderant power in ECOMOG, are seen to compromise the genuine humanitarian credentials of the undertaking (Ofuatey-Kodjoe, 1994). In *Rwanda*, the French-led 'Operation Turquoise' of 23 June 1994 was also (albeit narrowly) endorsed by SCR 929, while the motive for creating a safe area in south-west Rwanda is widely interpreted as a move to restore French influence after the set-backs of the Arusha Peace Agreement and to block the advance of the Uganda-backed, English-speaking Rwanda

Patriotic Front (RPF) leadership (Vassall-Adams, 1994). In *Haiti*, 'Operation Uphold Democracy' of 19 September 1994, which is not an intervention in an international-social conflict and looks much more like a classic cold war case, is also impugned, both because the *de jure* president, Aristide, did not withhold consent, and because, as with earlier US interventions in Grenada and Panama, the humanitarian motivation is suspect (von Hippel, 1995).

We are by now accustomed to the negative results which come from applying the traditional restrictionist definition. As in the cold war period, substantial debate is short-circuited as a result, and discussion is side-lined into terminological dispute. What happens if the revised typology is applied instead? The results are strikingly different.

4.4.2 Application of the revised concept. In Iraq, 'Operation Provide Comfort' and 'Operation Southern Watch' certainly count as forcible interventions as defined in section 3.3, and arguably as humanitarian as discussed in the introduction to Part II. The most important result here, however, is that the reconceptualization enables us both to separate the forcible intervention element from the non-forcible intervention going on at the same time under the terms of the 18 April 1991 Memorandum of Understanding (MOU) and to relate the two to each other. This, in our view, reveals the proper significance of Security Council Resolution 688, which is better seen as a precedent for the latter than for the former. It was a precedent not for forcible, but for non-forcible, humanitarian intervention.

In Bosnia through to the end of 1994, as will be argued in chapter 6, the intervention comes out as an option (c) non-forcible military intervention. This is a highly significant result, and, regardless of whether it was the right option to choose, a failure to recognize it as such and to act accordingly led to a great deal of misunderstanding in both government policy and public reaction. The resulting confusion threatened to discredit the whole enterprise of humanitarian intervention.

In Somalia, as will be argued in chapter 7, the intervention should be seen as consisting of at least three phases, only the second of which (December 1992–October 1993) was forcible. The reconceptualization enables us to make the critical comparisons which the traditional concept misses, and raises key questions which are otherwise left unasked.

In Liberia and Rwanda, which can only be mentioned briefly here, similar results are obtained. Haiti, because it is not a case of ISC, will not be commented upon.

In Liberia the ECOMOG intervention comes out as a forcible intervention, while application of the five humanitarian criteria gives mixed results, although the judgement that 'for the most part ECOMOG was (and continues to be) welcomed throughout Liberia' counts heavily in its favour (Wippman, 1993, 175). The reconceptualization allows a comparison with the non-forcible presence of UNOMIL from September 1993 in the wake of the Cotonou Agreement, suggesting that the continuing preponderance of ECOMOG, seen by Charles Taylor's NPFL as a hostile force, compromised the key elements of non-partisan consent essential to the nature of an option (c) intervention. This may be one reason for the collapse of the Cotonou process by September 1994 (Mackinlay and Alao, 1994).

In Rwanda there was already a 2,500-strong peacekeeping force (UNAMIR) in the country when the massacres initiated by Hutu extremists began, following the death of President Habyarimana in a plane crash on 6 April 1994. By the end of April some 200,000 people had been killed. By mid-summer the figure had risen to 500,000 or on some estimates 1 million. Whole populations fled in panic. On 29 April, 250,000 poured into neighbouring Tanzania in a single day – according to UNHCR the largest exodus in such a short time ever recorded. The UNAMIR force commander, the Canadian Major Dallaire, phoned New York asking for rapid reinforcement to stop the massacre. His forces were already roughly the same size as the French forces of 'Operation Turquoise', which established protected areas from 23 June. On 20 April the UN Secretary-General presented the Security Council with three options, which were exactly the options suggested here: enforcement under Chapter VII (option (a)), a small non-forcible military presence in Kigali (option (c)), and complete withdrawal (option (d/e)). The next day, in passing SCR 912, the Security Council chose the second option, reducing UNAMIR to 270 men (although in the event the number did not fall below 440). One of the main lessons from the Rwandan tragedy is the difficulty of 'learning lessons'. Faced by the unexpected, the temptation is always to 'fight the last war'. The 'success' of 'Operation Provide Comfort' in Iraq encouraged similar action in Bosnia, without adequate thought about the difference in context. The 'failure' of 'Operation Restore Hope' in Somalia led to paralysis when the Rwandan genocide began (O'Halloran, 1995).

5 Conclusion

Taken together, to the end of 1994, the Iraqi, Bosnian and Somali cases are shown by the reconceptualization to exemplify all four of the intervention options listed above: non-intervention in Iraq before 1991; non-military intervention in Somalia in 1991–2 (option (d/e)); non-forcible military intervention in Bosnia (option (c)); and forcible military intervention in Iraq from April 1991 and in Somalia between December 1992 and October 1993 (option (a)). This enables us to make comparisons between the four broad alternatives, and, as the next chapter shows, to engage with the key policy debates.

The interventions in Liberia, Rwanda and Haiti offer examples, among other things, of the continuing key role of regional hegemons for the enforcement option (true also of Russian intervention in a number of former Soviet republics), with Liberia also illustrating the scope for regional organizations (Wippman, 1993; Ofuatey-Kodjoe, 1994).

Beyond this, the chapter has drawn attention to the humanitarian dimension of United Nations peacekeeping operations (PKOs), not only in Bosnia, Somalia, Liberia, Rwanda and Haiti, but also in other places, either in severe international-social conflicts (Angola, Georgia and Tajikistan) or in what are classified in chapter 3 as political, ideological or religious type 2 conflicts (El Salvador, Cambodia and Mozambique). This should be remembered when making broad overall assessments of the viability and usefulness of option (c), non-forcible military intervention.

The chapter has also shown the remarkable range and scope of non-military humanitarian intervention by the ICRC, UN agencies and NGOs in all conflict zones except where oppressive regimes block them. In the case of Somalia, whereas exclusive employment of the classic restrictionist definition of humanitarian intervention leads to a focus on SCR 794 of December 1992, and thus, as it were, joins the TV crews waiting on the beaches at Mogadishu for the American marines to land, the reconceptualization puts this in its proper perspective as one option among others, giving equal prominence to the patient, heroic and often surprisingly successful efforts of aid workers during the previous two years to alleviate the suffering of millions of innocent Somalis in the most gruelling conditions that it is possible to imagine.

Suggested reading

For an example of the non-intervention option see Pilger, 1994. A thorough study of non-military humanitarian intervention can be found in Minear, 1991. A convenient summary of UN non-forcible military humanitarian interventions through to May 1994 is offered in United Nations, 1994. Two good collections of intervention case-studies are Damrosch (ed.), 1993, with studies of intervention in Yugoslavia, Iraq, Haiti, Liberia, Somalia and Cambodia; and Jean (ed.), 1993, with studies of interventions in Sudan, Afghanistan, Tajikistan, Georgia, Liberia, El Salvador, Angola, Cambodia, Bosnia and Somalia. See also Hoffman and Mayall (eds), *Humanitarian*

Intervention in International Society [provisional title] (Macmillan, forth-coming), which includes case studies of humanitarian interventions in Bosnia, Haiti, Iraq, Liberia, Rwanda, Somalia and Sri Lanka. On interven-tion in Liberia see Mackinlay and Alao, 1994; Ofuatey-Kodjoe, 1994. On intervention in Rwanda see I. Jones, 1995; O'Halloran, 1995; and Vassall-Adams, 1994. On intervention in Haiti see Von Hippel, 1995, to be pub-lished in Hoffman and Mayall (eds), forthcoming, cited above. For further literature on humanitarian interventions in Iraq, Bosnia and Somalia, see references in the relevant chapters.

5
Controversies

1 Introduction

The reconceptualization outlined in chapter 4 opens the way for a more comprehensive account of current controversies than is afforded by application of the traditional concept. This can be seen by comparing what follows with the analysis of the traditional debate in chapter 2. A chapter of this length cannot deal thoroughly with such a large agenda; all it can do is to map out the main areas of controversy and thereby help clarify what is at issue. A survey of the literature on forcible and non-forcible humanitarian intervention from the period 1991–4 shows that the debate has widened, deepened and become more complex.

1.1 The widening of the debate

The debate has widened in two main ways. First, it has been enriched by the much closer link between forcible intervention and the whole enterprise of humanitarian assistance, protection and relief carried out by UN agencies, the ICRC and NGOs. By contrast with the cold war period, the main declared humanitarian purpose for the use of military force has been to create humanitarian space for such activities. In Mats Berdal's words, 'The two major support roles for military forces are the provision of theatre-level logistics, and the establishment of a secure environment for non-military operations' (1993, 11).

Second, and if anything the main emphasis in this chapter, the debate has expanded to become an authentically global debate involving most of the 185 members of the United Nations. The phenomenon of international-social conflict, the main generator in this period of the human suffering which has made the question of humanitarian intervention such an urgent one, has been of deep concern to peoples in all parts of the world. The plight of Muslims in Bosnia, for example, has aroused passionate response throughout the Islamic world. Many African states are threatened by incipient international-social conflict. In addition, the shift of primary concern from forcible self-help by individual states to collective action through regional organizations or the United Nations has made demands on large numbers of countries hitherto only marginally, if at all, involved. This includes developed countries like Germany and Japan, reorientating themselves after the end of the cold war and contemplating military involvement in UN missions for the first time, as well as soldiers, civilian police and others from nearly half the UN member countries. For example, Pakistan was the largest contributor of troops to UN missions in April–June 1994 (7,256), while other developing countries also provided large contingents, such as India (5,914), Jordan (3,350), Bangladesh (3,287), Egypt (2,245), Nepal (1,995), Ghana (1,173), Zimbabwe (1,127) and Kenya (1,064). The five permanent members of the UN Security Council, who covered 55.2 per cent of the operational costs, provided 11,934, nearly all in UNPROFOR (*International Peacekeeping*, 1994, 354). In this period humanitarian intervention became a genuinely global enterprise.

1.2 The complexity of the debate

As the debate has widened, so it has grown in complexity. Hans Morgenthau's (1967) simple disjunction 'to intervene or not to intervene?' is no longer adequate. The question of *whether* to intervene now requires prior specification of the sort of intervention that is being contemplated, what the alternatives are (including the implications of 'doing nothing', itself often seen as a form of intervention), as well as a series of other questions. This is not the end, but the beginning, of a continuing sequence of difficult choices to be made by the large, disparate body of significant decision-makers within the overall corpus of would-be collective humanitarian interveners. There is the question of *why* to intervene, which involves a difficult weighing up of the relationship between the scale and nature of the humanitarian need and the other, international dimensions of the crisis. There is the question of *what* the most appropriate and practically possible form of intervention would be, along the lines set out in chapter 4. There is the so far unanswered question of *where* intervention should take place, raising the contentious issue of criteria for selection and when and why the international community would be right to refuse. There is the question of *when* to intervene, with widespread calls for early warning, proactive response and prevention on the one hand (but as yet no agreed mechanisms or criteria for such a programme) and recommendations to wait until conflicts have 'burned themselves out' on the other. There is the question of *whither* (to what end) the intervention is aimed, including controversial issues about the relationship between humanitarian and non-humanitarian goals. There is the question of *who* is willing, capable and best suited to undertake the intervention, which involves highly complex, controversial relations between governments (particularly the government of the United States), regional and subregional organizations, and the United Nations. There is a whole set of issues related to the question of *how* the intervention can best be carried through, including matters of finance, compatibility between political consensus in New York and fulfillable mandates on the ground, complementarity between civil and military components, efficient lines of command and communication, logistics, equipment and training. Finally, there is the question of *by what authority* the intervention is being undertaken, where a balance must be struck between capability and credibility, on the one hand, and international acceptability and legitimacy, on the other.

In response to these questions and in light of the complexity of the international-social conflict environment, it is not surprising that, in addition to the inner contradictions within most traditions noted in chapter 2, there have been surprising 'cross-overs' during the post-cold war period, with former cold war 'hawks' advocating caution and former cold war 'doves' urging vigorous military engagement (see with reference to Bosnia, Dewar, 1993; Sharp, 1993). The Third World has been similarly riven, with continuing suspicion of Western intervention in tension with resentment on the part of many non-Western societies at the failure of the West to intervene forcibly to protect threatened populations with whom they identify.

1.3 The deepening of the debate

All this has led to a deepening of the humanitarian intervention debate, in which the underlying issues, latent during the cold war period, if somewhat concealed beneath legalist-restrictionist arguments as described in chapter 2, have been more clearly revealed in the new environment. For example, the four structural features of international-social conflict described in chapter 3 have each given rise to deep questions for humanitarian interveners. First, there is the issue of social heterogeneity.

Here humanitarian intervention raises critical questions of minority rights and self-determination, which both underpin and at the same time challenge the whole doctrine of non-intervention (Hannum, 1990; Halperin and Scheffer, 1992). Second, there is the issue of state crisis, where, in cases of state collapse, humanitarian intervention raises difficult questions of responsibility for political reconstruction, including the question of trusteeship (Helman and Ratner, 1992–3). The traditional dichotomy 'sovereignty or suffering' loses purchase when inner sovereignty is in abeyance. Third, there is the issue of environmental pressure and economic underdevelopment. Here humanitarian intervention raises questions about the relationship between immediate relief and long-term economic and social development. There is a strongly felt, widespread perception throughout the undeveloped world that precedence should be given to addressing structural imbalances, rather than to temporary interventions by those who benefit from them, which only perpetuate dependency (Awoonor, 1993; Zuberi, 1989). Fourth, there is the international dimension, the relationship between the crisis itself and the wider repercussions for the international society of states. Here collective humanitarian intervention poses questions both about the regional arrangements within which sustainable solutions can be found (Rivlin, 1992; McCoubrey and White, 1995), and about the international environment in general. The status and role of the United Nations is central here. Widespread calls for structural reform of the United Nations raise questions about what the organization is or ought to be, which in turn involve debate about the whole nature of international society (Childers and Urquhart, 1994).

As a result of all this, although the core issues remain the same as they were during the cold war, the centre of gravity has shifted. During the cold war period the key question was this:

> If governments violate the basic human rights of their citizens, should other governments intervene forcibly to remedy the situation?

Since the end of the cold war the key question has been this:

> If internal wars cause unacceptable human suffering, should the international community develop collective mechanisms for preventing or alleviating it?

2 The humanitarian intervention debate revisited

Under the reconceptualization two new features in particular can be noted. We are no longer asked to come out simply 'for' or 'against' forcible action, but are required to compare the different options, including pure non-intervention, in response to any given humanitarian challenge. It is a question of weighing up probable benefits and costs and making comparative judgements. Secondly, in the confused context of contemporary conflict, it is the nature of humanitarianism itself, as defined in chapter 1, which now occupies the centre stage. This was surprisingly neglected in the cold war humanitarian intervention debate. The key issues concern the compatibility of humanitarianism with (i) the politicization inevitable in such conflict situations, and (ii) the militarization which is often unavoidable.

2.1 The enforcement option

A comparison between the cold war humanitarian intervention literature and the literature on forcible humanitarian intervention between 1991 and 1994 shows that, although much of the debate is similar, its deeper dimensions are now more evident (Forbes and Hoffman (eds), 1993). We take Caroline Thomas's (1993) 'pragmatic case against intervention' to illustrate this. Although she calls it a 'pragmatic case', it is steeped in ethical evaluation. The three elements described in chapter 2, pluralist, realist and statist, are again evident. In *pluralist* vein she argues that, compared with the nineteenth century, the present state system is culturally heterogeneous, and intervention 'to promote human causes' 'springs from the Western liberal tradition and smacks of ethnocentrism'. As for the *realist* component, states 'will always be concerned with promoting state interest', and, given the hierarchical nature of the international system with its gross inequalities of power, forcible intervention will be in the interest of the strong. 'This may not be how the world *ought* to be, but it is how the world *is*.' The *statist* element once again pulls the other two elements together. Given a culturally diverse world and the prevalence of state interest and inequality of power, breach of the non-intervention norm opens the door to disorder. The ethical dimension operates at three levels here: (i) the morality of international order, (ii) the morality of states (states are the only bearers of rights and duties in international society), and (iii) the morality of diverse community which underpins the morality of states: non-intervention 'values and maintains the heterogeneity of an ideologically, economically, ethnically and religiously diverse world. In this respect the state has moral force to it.' Many Third World states are in early authoritarian stages of evolution, which may be anathema to the West, but, along J. S. Mill's lines, they must be allowed to develop autonomy in the only way possible – through their own efforts. Forcible intervention can only interrupt and postpone this process, never be a substitute for it. One way in which the West could help would be to address the structural causes of poverty and instability: 'we should realise that genuine humanitarian assistance for those starving in the Third World would entail structural transformations in our own economies and political processes' (C. Thomas, 1993, 99).

This is a powerful argument, which sums up much of what we looked at in chapter 2. But counter-arguments are equally powerful. One response to cultural pluralism is the *universalist* sentiment expressed by Pope John Paul II at the International Conference on Nutrition on 5 December 1992: 'The conscience of humankind, sustained henceforth by its liability to international human rights, asks that humanitarian interference be rendered mandatory in situations which gravely compromise the survival of entire peoples and ethnic groups: this is an obligation for both individual nations and the international community as a whole' (Coste, 1993, 28). John Vincent, ambivalent on the question of forcible humanitarian intervention, also rejects radical pluralism, but on *internationalist* rather than cosmopolitan grounds.

> [C]hanges in the international system are not producing some kind of cosmopolitan advance on the society of states. Rather there has developed within sovereign states a realm that may now be legitimately scrutinised by other sovereign states. This is not something new, but a return to the medieval tradition of *jus gentium intra se*, that part of the law of nations which is common to all nations in the sense of being common to their domestic life. Henry Shue's basic rights constitute that part of the law common to all. (Vincent and Wilson, 1993, 126–7)

Realist emphasis on national interest is turned on its head, and comes out as an argument in favour of humanitarian intervention, when it is argued that there is a causal link between the overthrow of democracy, massive human rights abuse, violence and aggression. *Realpolitik* then suggests involvement. The Clinton administration's Presidential Decision Directive 25 of May 1994, for example, often interpreted as a brake on forcible humanitarian intervention, says that it is in the US national interest to support UN peace operations (including the enforcement option), among other things, when 'there is a threat to or breach of international peace and security . . . defined as one or a combination of the following: international aggression; or urgent humanitarian disaster coupled with violence; or sudden interruption of established democracy; or gross violation of human rights coupled with violence; or threat of violence' (PDD 25, Executive Summary, 1994, 4). Similar ripostes are found at the three levels of the statist argument. As concerns (i) the 'morality of order', Delbrück says that 'it is only realistic to assume that massive human rights violations of genocidal dimensions will sooner or

later escalate into international military conflicts in a world highly sensi-
tized by such events' (1992, 900). In Adam Roberts's view, 'one might
even say that if a coherent philosophy and practice of humanitarian
intervention could be developed, it could have the potential to save the
nonintervention rule from its own logical absurdities and occasional
inhumanities' (1993b, 11). With regard to Caroline Thomas's defence of
non-intervention on the grounds of (ii) the 'morality of states', John
Vincent writes: 'in effect this is a weak moral defence because it turns out
to be no more than a rationalisation of the existing order without any
interest in its transformation' (Vincent and Wilson, 1993, 124). And
often, given the ambivalent relationship between state, nation and people
and the deep problems which surround the concept of self-determination,
it is, as in Bosnia, precisely the nature and identity of the state itself which
is at issue. Finally, as to (iii) the 'morality of community', even a
communitarian like Michael Walzer has tempered his aversion to forcible
intervention in cases where 'the violation of human rights . . . is so terrible that it makes talk of community and self-determination . . . seem
cynical or irrelevant' (1992/1977, 90). A *solidarist* sentiment is suggested
beneath a communitarian veneer.

Finally, there is the impact of the post-cold war experience on the
debate in international law. This has been transformed by a switch of
emphasis from discussion about the relationship between UN Charter
Article 2(4) and forcible self-help to discussion of the relationship between Article 2(7) and collective intervention. So far, forcible collective
action under UN Charter Chapter VII has been justified, however notionally, as a response to threats to international peace and security, thus,
among other things, avoiding a Chinese veto in the Security Council. In
the view of Lori Fisler Damrosch, this could be expanded to include an
explicitly humanitarian mandate. Under what she calls a 'teleological'
interpretation of the Charter, there is no reason why the conferral of
coercive powers on the Security Council with respect to threats to peace
and security should not be extended to the wider purposes of the Charter.
There is also the possibility under Articles 10–14 for the General Assembly to make recommendations for what Richard Lillich has called
'uniting-against-genocide'. In short, she argues that it is not so much
constitutional law as practical wisdom that gives rise to reservations
about the trans-boundary use of force for humanitarian ends, in particular the dangerous consequences for international order that might follow
and the question of whether force can in any case be effective (Damrosch
and Scheffer (eds), 1991, 220–2). On the question of whether international law has already become more permissive with regard to forcible
humanitarian intervention, publicists range from the scepticism of Kelly
Kate Pease and David Forsythe (1993), through the cautious permissive-

ness of Christopher Greenwood – 'it is no longer tenable to assert that whenever a government massacres its own people or a state collapses into anarchy international law forbids military intervention altogether' (1993, 40) – to the forthright endorsement of a 'droit d'ingérence [right of intervention] in international humanitarian law' by Philippe Garigue (1993). A similar spectrum of opinion is found in the French debate from the scepticism of Chantal Carpentier (1992) to the enthusiasm of Mario Bettati (1991). There are those who advocate explicit codification and redrafting of the Charter in order to accommodate the humanitarian dimension (Chopra and Weiss, 1992; Kartashkin, 1991), whereas others demur (Roberts, 1993a; Meron, 1991a). The question of forcible self-help by individual states has not been forgotten (Benjamin, 1992–3), but in this period has been in abeyance as regional or global hegemons such as France in Rwanda, the US in Haiti, and Nigeria in Liberia have sought UN Security Council endorsement. Even Russia wants similar legitimation for its military presence in former Soviet republics. Dubious justification of 'Operation Provide Comfort' in Iraq as an action covered by Security Council Resolution 688 and the 'second-tier legality' granted *post hoc* to the ECOWAS intervention in Liberia press at the margins of the concept of UN authorization (White, 1994). Tom Farer offers a balanced overall view when he argues that the task of scholars is to help expedite the evolution of international law in the direction of humanitarian protection without stripping it of its usefulness as an instrument of conservative statecraft preserving the international order, which is a necessary, but not on its own sufficient, condition for human dignity (1991, 200). Box 20 takes the example of Bosnia to the end of 1994 to set the enforcement option in context.

2.2 The non-forcible military option: humanitarian peacekeeping

It is this option, option (c), which is both least familiar and most vulnerable to being discounted in favour of options (a) and (d/e). During the period 1989–94 peacekeeping became the most visible activity of the UN. In chapter 4 we saw how UN peacekeeping operations multiplied at an unprecedented rate at that time, while their roles also became complex and multi-dimensional. By the end of 1994, peacekeeping had become also the most controversial activity in which the UN was engaged. Michael Klare, writing in defence of peacekeeping, argued:

> The truth, then, is that we *need* the United Nations and its peacekeeping capabilities. Faced with the threat of rising global chaos, we must work with other states to contain the violence and address the underlying causes of conflict – tasks that can only be performed effectively under UN auspices.

Box 20: Forcible, Non-Forcible Military and Non-Military Humanitarian Intervention Options in Bosnia, 1992–4

We take the Bosnian example, described in more detail in chapter 6, to make the point that a simple discussion 'for' and 'against' enforcement is no longer adequate. When confronted with a humanitarian challenge, as in Bosnia, decision-makers have to compare the likely overall costs and benefits of all three options (a), (c) and (d/e) – forcible, non-forcible military and non-military intervention – before taking action. These calculations will change, depending upon when they are made. There is also, in theory, the option of not getting involved at all.

During the first six months of the Bosnian war, between April and September 1992, the international community drifted into adopting option (c), the non-forcible military intervention option. Prior decisions in the different circumstances of the collapse of Yugoslavia and the earlier Croat war dictated as much, although the logic of the move was not widely understood. Chapter 6 illustrates the danger of not keeping options (a) and (c) conceptually distinct. Through to the end of 1994 a number of governments, particularly European governments, vigorously defended the choice of option (c) throughout, arguing that it helped to contain the conflict and alleviate suffering so far as was possible at reasonable cost. They rejected alternatives as impractical and unacceptable. Critics repudiated this. Richard Betts (1994) rejected the whole idea of 'impartial' and 'limited' military involvement in such conflicts. Many in the Third World argued that 'humanitarianism' had been a deliberate ploy for doing nothing, providing the excuse that more decisive action would endanger the existing mission. But these criticisms are not mutually consistent. Some castigated Western policy as 'crusading liberal interventionism' which prolonged the suffering, postponed a decisive outcome, and obscured the possibility of a political settlement (Stedman, 1993, 3). Their recommendation would be abstention or withdrawal (option d/e) in the name of *realism*. Others condemned Western policy as a muddled, half-hearted compromise which effectively abetted the Serbs in a policy of ethnic cleansing and genocide (Rieff, 1995). They would prefer the enforcement option (a) implemented in the name of *justice*.

With regard to option (a), Rosalyn Higgins maintained that '[e]verything about the situation in the former Yugoslavia has made it unsuitable for peacekeeping, and appropriate for enforcement action', and such action should have been immediate and decisive (1993, 470). Arguments in favour of enforcement have

Box 20 (*continued*)

included (i) the moral case, (ii) the fact that the international community had recognized Bosnia and should therefore have defended it, (iii) the danger of an international Muslim backlash, (iv) the dangerous precedent of allowing ethnic cleansing to succeed, and (v) the danger that the war might spread. Arguments against included (i) that there was no agreed or sustainable political settlement to enforce, (ii) that the military force required would be prohibitive, (iii) that there was insufficient international solidarity and domestic support to sustain such an operation, (iv) that out-siders would simply be sucked into the Balkan morass, and (v) that it would be counter-productive in humanitarian terms, forcing the withdrawal of existing humanitarian protection and assistance.

The other alternative is option (d/e). One argument for abstention has been that the Balkans is an unruly area, and that it is best 'to leave the Serbs, Muslims and Croats to re-draw their internal borders in their own brutal way' (Jenkins, *The Times*, 14 April 1993). Outsiders have no business interfering. Moral crusades are dangerous and smack of colonialism: 'it is every politician's cop-out and every soldier's dread. Such crusaders measure their glory in body-bags'. 'Fewer lives may be lost if one side wins outright. Moreover, a decisive victory is sometimes the best result, followed by a forward-looking conciliatory peace' (Stedman, 1993, 10). By contrast, the abstention/withdrawal option was fiercely rejected by all who argued that the innocent must be protected in Bosnia, and that the multi-cultural Bosnian state, recognized internationally, must be defended against what was in effect outside aggression from Serbia and Croatia. This was the view of a number of Republican senators in the United States. The abstention option was passionately condemned throughout the Muslim world, where even option (c) was seen as an obscene dereliction of duty by the West, so ready to act decisively against Iraq when oil interests were at stake. The argument here was that decisive action right at the start (during the Croat war) would have obviated later difficulties at relatively low cost.

Clearly, all these options have been highly controversial. It is simply not the case that there are 'easy' solutions. All political persuasions have been divided on the issue. The fact is that international-social conflict of the kind that has erupted in Bosnia confronts the international community with a challenge that it has hardly begun to learn how to address.

No other organisation can mount a response to ethnic and religious warfare with the same degree of international support, or bring to bear the same range of military, diplomatic, and humanitarian capabilities. (1995, 62)

Klare argues that the UN is the only international body capable of combining the military, political and humanitarian functions necessary if the misery of complex conflicts is to be mitigated or removed. This defence is made in the face of a barrage of criticisms on both operational-logistical and conceptual grounds. We consider this debate below, looking first at operational-logistical critiques and the response to them and, secondly, at the conceptual attack, which suggests that operational difficulties stem from, or are secondary to, a misunderstanding of the nature of power, state interests and conflict in the international system. These critiques suggest that military, political and humanitarian objectives should not necessarily be combined.

2.2.1 The operational-logistical critique. Mats Berdal has identified priorities where organization reform is needed. He distinguishes between problems of readiness (mounting and deployment) and problems of operation (continuous support in the field). At both levels peacekeeping poses complex logistical problems: in the Gulf War, for example, ground forces came from 18 different nations, whereas at its height UNOSOM II took troops from 35 different nations. Command and control of military forces becomes highly complicated with this degree of reliance on multinational forces. Operations suffer from unclear, ambiguous chains of command both within missions and between missions and the Secretariat in New York, which has overall responsibility for the management of peacekeeping operations. It is well known that national contingents frequently look to their capitals for orders rather than to the UN force commander or to New York. This failure to establish effective communication with New York is at least in part the result of a lack of direction from the centre in New York and a failure to co-ordinate the activities of the four main UN bodies involved in managing peacekeeping operations (DPKO, DPA, DHA and DAM; see box 21). Communications between the military, the civil/political and the humanitarian components of an operation are also a problem, and there is a serious inadequacy in the training of many units sent on peacekeeping missions (Berdal, 1993, 32–50). Reforms aimed at improving the central management of UN peacekeeping in New York, improving co-ordination between New York and the field operations, and developing central training guidance and standards have been considered and to some degree implemented since 1993 (Berdal, 1993, 52–60; Mackinlay, 1994).

Box 21: Control of United Nations Peacekeeping Operations

Peacekeeping is controlled in the UN system in the following way:

UN Security Council

UN Secretary-General

DPA	DPKO	DAM	DHA
(Department of Political Affairs)	(Department of Peacekeeping Operations)	(Department of Administration and Management)	(Department of Humanitarian Affairs)

The DPKO is responsible for the day-to-day management of peace-keeping operations and for communications between the UN and the field operation. The DHA is responsible for the co-ordination of humanitarian operations, especially for organizing the delivery of assistance by UN relief organizations and for liaison with NGOs in the field. The DPA advises the Secretary-General on issues of international peace and security and on the control and resolution of conflicts within and between states. The DAM is responsible for the administration and financial support of peacekeeping operations.

Sheri Prasso and Dzenita Mehic give damning accounts of the inefficiency and corruption of aspects of UN peacekeeping in Cambodia and Somalia. In Prasso's view, UNTAC in Cambodia was not at all the success that it is often claimed to be. The 22,000 mission personnel, she claims, created a 'frontier-like' mentality in which brothels were packed and spread throughout the country. The spending power of UNTAC created a warped economy, whereby the gap between rich and poor widened and a 'free-for-all crime wave' ensued. Overall, she concluded, UNTAC was a mission in which incompetence was the rule, and whatever good reputation UNTAC had, existed only because other missions, such as those in Somalia and Yugoslavia, were even worse (Prasso, 1995). Mehic portrays a similar picture of UNPROFOR in Bosnia. His account is of an ineffective force which 'fell prey to the corruption and abusive power of any occupying army', one in which the motivation of many UN personnel seemed to be self-seeking and self-indulgent (Mehic, 1995). David Rieff similarly condemns the 'colonial' mentality of UN peacekeepers in Bosnia, scornful of the 'locals' and unwilling to listen to and learn from them, spending their time with each other talking about holidays and future assignments, and, if anything, more respectful of Serb commanders, who, as former Yugoslav National Army officers, they regarded as 'fellow professionals', often personally known through earlier contacts through NATO (1994b, 37). Another recurrent complaint is of lack of accountability when UN personnel are themselves guilty of breaches of local or international law. However, these criticisms should be set alongside the more positive accounts offered by contributing governments and by the UN Secretariat.

2.2.2 The conceptual critique of peacekeeping: withdraw or enforce? We consider two aspects here, beginning with the definition of 'wider peacekeeping'. One of the most comprehensive statements about the new kind of peacekeeping is based on British Army experience, and appears in the *British Army Field Manual on Wider Peacekeeping* (UK Ministry of Defence, 1995). The manual defines peacekeeping as 'operations carried out with the consent of the belligerent parties in support of efforts to achieve or maintain peace in order to promote security and sustain life in areas of potential or actual conflict'. The term 'wider peacekeeping' is used to describe 'the wider aspects of peacekeeping operations carried out with the consent of the belligerent parties but in an environment that may be volatile' (Dobbie, 1994, 122). Despite the post-cold war conflict experience of Somalia and Bosnia especially, the manual insists on retention of the principle of consent and on a clear separation between peacekeeping and peace enforcement. Peacekeeping requires consent, whereas peace enforcement does not. A distinction is made between the tactical field operations level, where consent may be partial, subject to change, and poorly defined, and the operational (theatre) level, where consent comes from formal agreements by recognized parties and is relatively stable. Particularly at the tactical level, consent does not mean seeking universal approval for every action, but it does involve 'a general public attitude that tolerates a peacekeeping presence and represents a quorum of co-operation'. This definition has implications for the degree to which force can be used in an operation which is essentially non-forcible – where local opinion supports its use against banditry or looting, for example. It may also be used in a way which Dobbie describes as 'breaching the tactical edge of the consent divide' – for example, the shooting down of three Serb aircraft which violated the Bosnian no-fly zone in April 1994. It is only when force is used in a way which 'breaches the tactical and operational levels of consent' that wider peacekeeping lurches into peace enforcement (Dobbie, 1994, 136). We saw in chapter 4 how the US Army also officially subscribes to the clear separation of peacekeeping and peace enforcement, distinguished in terms of relative levels of impartiality, consent and force (US Army, 1994) – although many have commented that the US Army in practice does not seem to comprehend, never mind accept, the concept of limited peacekeeping operations. (US Army staff are 'intuitively uncomfortable with being subordinated to a mission that cannot rely on the use of overwhelming force to achieve its ultimate success' (Mackinlay, 1994, 155).) PDD 25 uses the term 'peace operations' to cover 'the entire spectrum of activities from traditional peacekeeping to peace enforcement' (PDD 25, Executive Summary, 1994, 1). NATO doctrine emphasizes impartiality and the international nature of the operation, rather than consent, as characteristic of peacekeeping (BASIC, 1994). For the French experience, see Guillot, 1994. The UN itself, in the form of the Secretary-General's *Agenda for Peace* of June 1992, appeared to elide peacekeeping and peace enforcement by inclusion of the celebrated phrase 'hitherto with the consent of all parties concerned' (Boutros-Ghali, 1992, para. 20); but in his report to the 48th Session of the General Assembly in March 1994 he omits it, suggesting thereby that he had had second thoughts (cited in Dobbie, 1994, 122). John Mackinlay, who pioneered much of the rethinking, refers to 'second-generation multinational operations', to distinguish the expanded tasks of peacekeepers in creating 'the conditions for others [the civil and humanitarian components] to succeed' (1994, 158). He argues that in semi-consensual and turbulent conflict environments new concepts and training methods are needed. Similar ideas have been developed in Australia, where the term 'second-generation peace operations' has been used for expanded peacekeeping interventions in 'messy, value-based intra-state conflicts' (Downes, 1993).

The second aspect to consider is the more substantial one of the viability of wider peacekeeping as a credible and acceptable option. The argument that impartial intervention in post-cold war civil wars is a 'destructive misconception' and a 'delusion' is cogently put by Richard K. Betts (1994). In Bosnia the attempt at limited, impartial intervention resulted, he argues, in abetting 'slow-motion savagery'. In effect, the result of the UN presence on the ground was that the interveners refused to let either side, the Bosnian government or the Bosnian Serbs, win. Economic sanctions against the Serbs were balanced by a general arms embargo which worked against the Muslims. The hope was that a compromise settlement would emerge, but the effect was stalemate and slow haemorrhaging. Such failure, argues Betts, is bound to attend attempts at limited, impartial military intervention in ongoing internal wars. This amounts to a frontal attack on option (c) – 'compromises that kill' – and advocacy in most cases of abstention or withdrawal (option (d/e)) or, in rare cases such as Rwanda, enforcement (option (a), which is 'a tall order, seldom with many supporters, and it is hard to think of cases where it actually works').

> If outsiders such as the United States or the United Nations are faced with demands for peace in wars where passions have not burned out, they can avoid the costs and risks that go with entanglement by refusing the mandate – staying aloof and letting the locals fight it out. Or they can jump in and help one of the contenders fight to defeat the other. (Betts, 1994, 28)

Disillusionment with the experience of UN peacekeeping has led others to advocate abandoning peacekeeping, except in its limited, classical, pre-1988 form, in favour of regional and great power conflict management. This attitude towards peacekeeping is seen in recent American policy (Quinn (ed.), 1994). The experience of the United States in Somalia, from which it withdrew when 18 American Rangers were killed there in October 1993, led to changes in the attitude of the Clinton administration to UN peacekeeping, embodied in the scrapping of the originally planned Presidential Decision Directive 13 (PDD 13) and substitution of the markedly more sceptical PDD 25 in May 1994 (although PDD 25 is less sceptical than it has often been made out to be). President Clinton took up office with a foreign policy characterized by what his officials called 'aggressive multilateralism', with talk of increasing US support for peacekeeping. According to David Rieff, this optimism about what UN peacekeeping could achieve was shared by the British and French governments and by some in the UN Secretariat, whose 'infatuation with peacekeeping as an almost infinitely plastic panacea for the world's conflicts is summed up in Boutros Boutros-Ghali's astonishingly sanguine policy statement on preventive diplomacy, peacemaking, and peacekeeping, *Agenda for Peace*' (1994a, 4). According to Rieff, such optimism as regards peacekeeping was profoundly misplaced.

> If UN peacekeeping is helpless in Bosnia, an inappropriate vehicle for protecting Tutsis in Rwanda, and so on – and if the practitioners of peacekeeping do not believe it can be transformed – then the question that needs to be asked is why peacekeeping is needed at all, or, at least, why its activities should not be radically scaled back. (1994a, 13)

Unlike Betts, whose critique of option (c) is accompanied by a preference for option (d/e), Rieff's critique points to option (a). This key divergence between many of the most outspoken critics of UN peacekeeping is easily overlooked if the traditional 'to intervene or not to intervene' conceptualization is invoked. For Rieff, 'classical peacekeeping', of the kind practised during the cold war, retains its validity in the post-conflict phase after the military situation has been stabilized. Elsewhere it is likely, and to be welcomed, that effective humanitarian intervention 'will become the exclusive province of regional hegemons and the G-7 countries plus the Russian Federation'.

2.3 The non-military option: transnational, inter-governmental and non-governmental humanitarian intervention

The issue of non-military agencies and their role in humanitarian intervention is best approached through an examination of the various relationships with which interveners have to deal.

There are four main intervention relations as far as host or target countries are concerned: with host governments, insurgent forces, indigenous NGOs and the threatened or suffering population itself. Relations with the host government (if there is one) and insurgent forces pose some of the gravest problems. According to some UN officials, since General Assembly Resolution 46/182 of December 1991, 'in a civil war situation the rebel faction or group of victimised civilians can directly approach the UN system for emergency aid, by-passing a Government unable or unwilling to fulfil its intrinsic duties towards its own subjects' (Dedring, 1994, 7). But in the intensity of international-social conflict, the leeway for non-partisan humanitarian space narrows to vanishing-point. Both governments and insurgents accuse international aid organizations of helping the other side: the question 'What is your agency doing to relieve immediate suffering?' gives way to the question 'Whose side are you on?' (Minear and Weiss, 1993, 70). In such circumstances aid agencies are torn between making the political compromises necessary to reach victims where they can and keeping to principle by refusing to be used as political pawns, at the risk of expulsion. Most UN specialized agencies find this difficult, since their basic function is to support the governments of member states. Few of the more than 60 organizations in Ethiopia in 1984–5 spoke out against forced population removals, repression and aid manipulation, for fear of jeopardizing relief activities, presenting the crisis as one simply of famine and drought (Girardet, 1993, 45). We saw earlier how the ICRC struggles to preserve the humanitarian space needed for dialogue and non-political action, but without thereby compromising the foundations of international humanitarian law by condoning atrocities (Sandoz, 1993). Problems intensify when civilian populations are themselves the targets of one or more of the warring parties, for here humanitarian relief conflicts with explicit war aims. The problems faced by UNPROFOR in Bosnia, ill understood by outsiders impatient for clear-cut results such as the effective protection of victims and the punishment of war criminals, are well known to non-forcible humanitarian interveners in conflict zones. These are lessons which the wider international community needs to learn. If the alternatives of withdrawal or enforcement are ruled out as unacceptable or impractical, then there is no alternative to the patient negotiation of such dilemmas, which demands a combination of realism and readiness for political compromise up to a certain point with preservation of the essential principles and purposes of humanitarianism, without which it would be indistinguishable from non-humanitarian intervention.

As to relations with local NGOs, practice varies widely, with some international agencies accused of arrogance, riding roughshod over local sensibilities, and ignoring local expertise, others making it a point of principle to work where possible on an equal footing with local organizations. The Somalia case-study in chapter 7 exemplifies this. Although local NGOs are relatively well developed in some countries, like India and Bangladesh, in others they 'hardly exist, or exist only in name. . . . Often they exist only to promote the interests of their members. Others . . . are largely tools of government' (Finucane, 1993, 188).

All this is summed up in terms of relations between aid workers and those they are there to help. This is the overriding priority, but difficult dilemmas arise when helping victims plays into the hands of often unscrupulous conflict parties. Humanitarian interveners can easily find themselves assisting ethnic cleansing by helping to move the vulnerable, stoking war economies by pouring in aid through politically controlled channels, and, as in Rwanda, helping to keep expatriate refugees in camps run by murderous former perpetrators of massacre and resourcing the latter's vengeful insurgency campaign.

Almost equally important are relations among the interveners themselves. Here we should mention inter-agency relations, relations between aid agencies and donor governments, and, from a somewhat different angle, relations between the humanitarian and the political goals of complex intervention missions. Inter-agency relations can be strained, as the Somalia case-study in chapter 7 illustrates. Summing up the 1993 experience, François Jean of MSF concluded:

> The UN agencies . . . have to improve their operational efficiency. Despite vague attempts at reform, the UN continues to be governed by inertia, lack of accountability, sometimes even incompetence, which hinder its ability to respond, especially to emergencies. . . . The myriad UN agencies too often function like private fiefdoms when the UN has to juggle peacekeeping, emergency relief and long-term recovery programmes all at once. (Jean, (ed.), 1993, 6)

UN agencies like UNHCR, for their part, find that NGOs often jeopardize their operations by poorly thought-out interventions. In an attempt to remedy this, UNHCR and the International Council of Voluntary Agencies (ICVA) organized six regional 'Partnership in Action' consultations, culminating in a global conference in Oslo in June 1994 attended by 182 NGO representatives from 83 countries, which produced a concerted 'Plan of Action' with 134 recommendations. Under UN General Assembly Resolution 46/182, it is the new Department of Humanitarian Affairs that is meant to take the lead in country-level co-ordination, but it is not yet clear that the DHA has the expertise and authority to achieve the necessary comparative advantage over other agencies which would justify such a role: 'the jury is still out' (Dedring, 1994, 7).

Relations between agencies and donor governments are also problematic. In the 1980s USAID and European donors such as the British ODA and the EC Commission channelled significant amounts of emergency aid through NGOs, because they were seen to be more reliable than some recipient government agencies and better able to deliver aid where needed without the official recognition of insurgent groups implied by direct government involvement. NGOs vary in the amount of government aid they are prepared to accept, the Catholic Relief Service in the United States gaining the benefit of substantial US government funding, but sacrificing a measure of independence from US foreign policy, by contrast with the Protestant agencies in the US, which, traditionally, have been more jealous in preserving independence, thereby forfeiting influence at government level (Nicholls, 1987). Oxfam limits the percentage of donations from government to 20 per cent.

As to the wider political ramifications of regional or UN interventions, these often conflict with immediate humanitarian priorities, as when sanctions aimed at recalcitrant governments cause most hardship among those the intervention is intended to help. In Liberia ECOMOG jets attacked an MSF aid convoy on 18 April 1993 while enforcing the UN embargo on NPFL territory. MSF protested that humanitarian aid was explicitly exempted, but the UN special representative said that bringing peace took precedence over bringing aid (Jean (ed.), 1993, 55). The UN suffers from a split personality here, on the one hand acting politically as an association of states through the Security Council, on the other hand acting non-politically through the General Assembly, ECOSOC and its various agencies. Even the DHA is caught up in this schizophrenia, with a 'visible clash between the traditional culture of diplomacy' represented by the 'pin-striped suit' image of New York and 'the new culture of relief provision, which requires rapid response, impatience with routine and imaginative innovation' represented by its Geneva branch (Taylor, 1993, cited in Slim and Penrose, 1994, 202).

What of the question of access and security? Jean-Christophe Rufin offers a clear characterization of the new conflict environment, maintaining that (i) whereas during the cold war guerrilla groups were few, well structured and controlled homogeneous areas, now, deprived of outside support, many have disintegrated into fragmented, uncontrollable bands;

(ii) whereas during the cold war belligerents wanted to appear to respect human rights in order to maintain international respectability with one or other ideological bloc, now localized factions have little regard for such norms or reject them as 'values of the North'; (iii) whereas during the cold war guerrilla forces were sustained by relatively safe 'rear bases' supplied by the international community, which it was in their interests to preserve, now wars have moved out of border areas, and whole territories are prey to their depredations (1993, 112–13). In such an environment, what are aid workers to do? There are two alternatives: look to outside military forces, whether non-forcible (option (c)) or forcible (option (a)), or rely on internal protection under the aegis of local forces (option (d/e)). The latter is viable in conflict areas such as Tajikistan and Azerbaijan, where the process described above has not gone too far, but is very difficult in areas like Afghanistan, Liberia and Somalia where it has. One inevitable paradox is that to intervene in this way is to supply aid to the combatants and keep the conflict going. But not to do so in an attempt to 'starve out' the conflict means abandoning suffering populations, which is not acceptable on humanitarian principles. Another difficulty is that, given the political fragmentation, '[i]f, in order to protect themselves, [aid workers] place themselves under the sphere of influence of a certain faction – assuming that they can find one sufficiently strong to guarantee their security – this makes them the enemy of all the others, and what was intended to be their salvation is in reality their undoing' (Rufin, 1993, 114). In these circumstances even the ICRC has had to formulate criteria for employing military escorts (Sandoz, 1993). UNHCR has found relations with UNPROFOR in Bosnia very testing. There is no simple way around these problems or general agreement about what the best option is: to hire local guards (option (d/e); to rely on outside non-forcible peacekeepers or equivalent special humanitarian forces, such as Erskine Childers's and Brian Urquhart's proposal of UN Humanitarian Security Police (1994, 204) (option (c)); or to look to external enforcement (option (a)). As the case-studies on Bosnia and Somalia in chapters 6 and 7 show, none of these is unequivocally successful. One result is that NGO critics of current humanitarian intervention seem never to be satisfied, the 1993 MSF report castigating UN response in all 10 of the examples studied, but for opposing reasons – neglect in some cases (Sudan), going in too soft in other cases (Bosnia), going in too hard in yet others (Somalia) (Jean (ed.), 1993).

In view of the wide disparity in nature, culture and competence between the ICRC, UN agencies and NGOs and the number of diverse complex emergencies in which they are engaged, it is not surprising that the relevant literature is large and varied. This outline does no more than indicate some of the main issues and show why it is important that they be integrally included in future in discussion of humanitarian intervention, in a way that they were not during the cold war period.

We conclude the chapter with a brief survey of issues common to all types of humanitarian intervention.

3 Why? whether? what?: requirement for and practicability of humanitarian intervention

Why intervene? The issue of humanitarian intervention is raised by the scale and intensity of human suffering and by the failure of host governments to fulfil their primary duties in international law: 'there *is* an overwhelming moral case to be made on behalf of the victims of unspeakable crimes committed by their governments, or resulting from a civil war, and on behalf of the victims of disasters to which their governments are indifferent, or which these governments are incapable of eliminating' (Hoffmann, 1993, 62). There is widespread, but by no means universal, agreement that in these circumstances outsiders do have an obligation (*devoir*) and a right (*droit*) to be concerned: 'it is often asserted, quite erroneously, that the United Nations elevates national sovereignty over the rights of individuals or minorities. This has never been true' (Gardner, 1992, 22). The question is, what types of action are legitimate and appropriate in response? The obligation extends not only to other governments, but also, according to John Vincent, to other individuals and groups within the broader community of humankind (Vincent and Wilson, 1993, 123). Here is the foundation for the solidarist case.

Having established a prima facie case, the question of whether to intervene is a complex one. It involves weighing up the costs and benefits, as well as the practicability, of all the options analysed in chapter 4, including doing nothing. The case-study on Bosnia in chapter 6 shows how misleading the concept of doing nothing can be, given (a) prior involvement and responsibility, (b) the perception that non-intervention is often a form of intervention, and (c) the idea made famous by Margaret Thatcher that if you can do something but do not do it, then you are 'a little like an accomplice to massacre' (Thatcher, *The Times* 14 April 1993). One of the eight factors to be considered when deciding whether to vote for a UN intervention, according to US Presidential Decision Directive 25, is that 'the political, economic and humanitarian consequences of inaction by the international community have been weighed up and are considered unacceptable' (PDD 25, Executive Summary, 1994, 4). The weighing up of humanitarian versus other dimensions in this comparative assessment of intervention options and likely outcomes makes up one half of the task. The other half (somewhat overlapping) concerns practicability, or what Kenneth Booth calls 'technical' prudence, as against the 'rhetorical' prudence often spuriously invoked by politicians to mask self-interest (1994, 58). Here the question is one of 'do-ability', including (a) relation to the wider political goals of the intervention (humanitarianism must neither be a substitute for them nor damagingly cut across them); (b) whether there are adequate resources, logistics and operational strategies in light of the estimated magnitude of the task; (c) whether the conflict environment is conducive to success (for example, is military force likely to work?); (d) whether there is sustainable international and domestic support, given likely difficulties and costs; and (e) whether there is a viable fall-back position if things go wrong.

These are not easy choices. As the examples given in chapter 4 and the case-studies show, in many instances none of the options, including the non-intervention option, seem satisfactory. Unable to make peremptory all-or-nothing judgements, we may well find ourselves in the dilemma cogently expressed by Richard Falk: 'nonintervention is intolerable, but intervention remains impossible' (1993, 757).

With the question as to what form the response should take, we reach the set of intervention options outlined in chapter 4 and discussed above.

4 Where? when? whither?: selectivity and long-term purpose of humanitarian intervention

The question as to where to intervene is one of the most testing and controversial. When the United Nations Security Council, through SCR 912, decided to reduce the UNAMIR force in Rwanda from 1,700 to 270 personnel on 21 April 1994, a fortnight after the beginning of the mass murder of moderate Hutu and Tutsi, OAU Secretary-General Salim Ahmed Salim deplored the decision 'to abandon the people of Rwanda . . . in spite of the appeals from Africa', and said that many Africans would interpret it as a 'lack of sufficient concern for African tragic situations' (quoted in Vassall-Adams, 1994, 36). The question of selectivity and consistency of response is one of the most difficult for the international community to resolve, apparently arbitrary decisions to engage or not to engage drawing accusations of partisan interest, hypocrisy and double standards. Some have advocated formal codification to overcome this (Kartashkin, 1991; Chopra and Weiss, 1992), but others maintain that this would create more problems than it would solve (Meron, 1991a; Roberts, 1993a).

The questions as to when and whither (to what end) to intervene can be taken together. No generally agreed criteria have yet been formulated, for deciding either at what point in the escalation of a conflict the international community should intervene, if at all, or to what overall end such intervention should be aimed, although a great deal has been written in the search for coherent programmes of this kind. Advocates of proactive early warning and preventative intervention by no means necessarily disagree with those whose main recommendation is to wait until conflicts have run their course and winners have emerged or general exhaustion has set in, although there is often a tension if not a contradiction between these positions (Rupesinghe (ed.), 1992). Similarly, there has been much debate traditionally about the supposed tension between an emphasis on immediate relief and a focus on long-term development, and a great deal of recent effort to reconcile the two (M. Anderson and Woodrow, 1989; M. Anderson, 1993). The extraordinary completeness of the omni-dimensional catastrophe of severe international-social conflict has forced humanitarian interveners to expand their long-term concerns to include democratization, the building of civil societies, and the safeguarding of individual and communal rights. This in turn embroils them in deep and, as yet, generally unresolved debates about (a) criteria and processes for recognizing new states and the whole issue of how to handle self-determination (Nafziger, 1991; K. Ryan, 1991; Deibel, 1993; Kampelmann, 1993); (b) whether to adopt recommendations for UN trusteeships for failed states, the extent to which outsiders can or should take on responsibility, and whether it is possible or acceptable to leave them as 'black holes' in international society (Helman and Ratner, 1992–3); and (c) how to reconstitute collapsed economies, and whether structural changes are needed in world economic arrangements if the roots of disorder are to be properly addressed (Krasner, 1985). Some of these relationships are indicated in diagram 7.

5   Who? how? by what authority?: agency and legitimacy of humanitarian intervention

We will take these three questions together. The question as to who can and should respond raises the issue of agency, which is one of the most testing for humanitarian intervention in the post-cold war world, is also one of the most confusing, bound up as it is in continuing controversy about the very nature of the international collectivity. At the apex of this set of problems is the relationship between states, on the one hand, particularly the more powerful ones, which are the prime actors, and regional and global institutions, on the other. At the heart of this, in turn, is the troubled, ambiguous relationship between the United States, the

Developed from M. Anderson, 1993, 24.

Diagram 7: *Conflict Prevention, Conflict Alleviation, and Post-Conflict Reconstruction*

one remaining superpower without whose support and leadership many, if not most, forcible and even non-forcible military operations would not be possible, and the United Nations, still the only institutional embodiment of the international community as a whole. In many cases it is only a slight exaggeration in reply to the question how intervention is to be undertaken to answer 'with the backing of the United States', and in reply to the question by what authority it is to be undertaken to answer 'legitimized via the United Nations'.

5.1 The United Nations

Much of the confusion in the current debate about the nature, role and possible restructuring of the United Nations stems from the fact that in one way or another it can be said to embody all four aspects indicated in diagram 8 (see next page) – as tool, framework, actor, legitimator – with some functions contradicting or being difficult to reconcile with others. As principal world legitimizer, the UN may be said to represent the international community as a whole (level 3, if not level 4). Yet it is widely seen as the creation of great power politics, and in particular of United States national interests (level 2, if not level 1). Even so, a considerable body of opinion in the United States sees the UN not so much as a tool of US interests, but as a troublesome, inefficient, unreli-

1 International anarchy	United Nations as a tool of state interests
2 International society (i)	United Nations as a framework for mutual accommodation of state interests
3 International society (ii) (International community)	United Nations as an agent for promotion of common interests and values
4 World community	United Nations as an expression of human solidarity or possible future world government

Diagram 8: *The United Nations: Four Aspects*

able and financially burdensome liability, apt to entangle the country in unwanted, open-ended commitments. At the root of the problem, as far as international response to conflict-related suffering goes, is that what is still in large measure a club of states is ill-suited to intervene in the intense complexity of international-social conflict: 'humanitarian needs are often greatest at the point at which the international community has the least clear mandate to respond' (Scott, 1993, quoted in Slim and Penrose, 1994, 196). The different branches of the UN can pull in different directions, sometimes queering each other's pitches, as when relief agencies attempting to operate at level 3 by intervening impartially and non-politically on purely humanitarian grounds are compromised by association with the fact that the UN is at the same time acting coercively and highly politically as an agent of great power activism at levels 1 and 2. The two contrasting poles of post-cold war UN humanitarianism – the Security Council with its post-SCR 688 humanitarian competence and the General Assembly with its post-GAR 46/182 establishment of the Department of Humanitarian Affairs – are institutional embodiments of this, the former an expression of the will of the most powerful states, effective as a result, but constrained by their particularist interests; the latter an expression of international and transnational aspirations but to date often under-resourced and encumbered by formalities and 'lowest common denominator' inefficiencies.

It is often said that the United Nations is bureaucratic and wasteful, but Erskine Childers and Brian Urquhart do well to point out that the entire staff of 51,484 (which includes all civil service staff from drivers to directors employed all over the world in 185 countries serving 5.5 billion people) is no larger than the civil service of the American state of Wyoming (population 545,000) (1994, 28). Similarly, estimated total world-wide expenditure through the UN system (including peacekeeping and humanitarian assistance totalling $4.1 billion) was $10.5 billion, or 0.0005 per cent of world GDP (Childers and Urquhart, 1994, 142–5). The total peacekeeping and humanitarian assistance budget is roughly equal to the budgets of the fire and police departments of New York City. With huge budget deficits ('late payments and failures to pay gravely debilitate an organisation that is not permitted to go into debt' (Ogata/ Volcker Report, quoted in Childers and Urquhart, 1994)) exacerbated by the threat of drastic reductions in US contributions, the inevitable delays and problems caused by attempts to balance the often discordant interests of member states, and uncertainty about political priorities and the means to execute them, it is little wonder that the UN finds it hard to cope with the daunting difficulties of handling international-social conflict. A recurrent complaint from UN staff is that the most intractable problems are thrust on to its plate, often at a late stage, by powerful states which do not want to take them on, and that the UN is then used as a scapegoat, if, not surprisingly, things go wrong.

Proposals for reform of the UN have been elaborate and various, including attempts to reform the Security Council itself (Childers, 1992). We do no more than note the two main proposals made by Childers and Urquhart in the area in which we are interested. First, in response to 'a set of problems arising from the weakening of the post-Westphalian nation-state, from unresolved legacies of the age of empires, and from the aspirations of cultural and ethnic groups . . . [which] have received so little sustained attention' (1994, 201), they recommend revival of the Trusteeship Council under Article 22 of the Charter, to help accommodate diverse communities within states, find consistent criteria for the recognition of new states, and, where necessary, temporarily administer collapsed states in accordance with the ascertained wishes of their communities. Second, further to improve the operational co-ordination of the myriad bodies that provide humanitarian assistance, they recommend that the DHA be strengthened. Its establishment has been a step in the right direction, but as yet has been insufficient 'to overcome the separatism, competitiveness, and lack of coordination which governments have built up in this area too'. They propose that the DHA be restructured (a) for prevention, data assembly, early warning, needs assessment and joint appeals and (b) as an operations organization. To this end WFP food aid capacities and UNICEF and UNHCR emergency relief capacities should be transferred to the DHA. ECOSOC should establish a single Governing Council for Humanitarian Assistance as the responsible intergovernmental body (Childers and Urquhart, 1994, 203–4).

5.2 Regional organizations

These constitute another complex, disputed issue (McCoubrey and White, 1995). Chapter VIII of the UN Charter deals with regional arrangements, Article 53 providing that '[t]he Security Council shall, where appropriate, utilize such regional arrangements or agencies for enforcement action under its authority'. It was widely supposed that they would take a lead in post-cold war humanitarian intervention. The UN Secretary-General's *Agenda for Peace* envisaged as much. The Conference on Security and Cooperation in Europe (CSCE) and the EC first took on the Yugoslav crisis, and ECOWAS intervened as early as August 1990 in Liberia. But most of those who have written on the subject share Benjamin Rivlin's view that '[t]he theoretical advantages of the regional approach, i.e. familiarity with the parties and the issues, are offset by the practical disadvantages of partisanship and local rivalries' (1992, 108). The Arab League and the Gulf Co-operation Council failed in the Kuwaiti crisis; ASEAN played no part in resolving the Cambodian crisis; the OAU was of little use in Liberia, Somalia or Angola (though more active in Rwanda); and, for all its sound and fury, the Organization of the Islamic Conference contributed nothing of note in Bosnia. Regional organizations which did play a significant role were the Contadora Group in Central America, ECOWAS in Liberia and, albeit with ambivalent results, the EC in Yugoslavia (Higgins, 1993, 475). Neil MacFarlane and Thomas Weiss (1992–3) reach much the same conclusion about regional organizations: that their advantages exist more in theory than in practice.

5.3 The United States

United States policy is critical for a whole swathe of humanitarian intervention options, not just forcible ones, but also peacekeeping (Berdal, 1994; Quinn, 1994). Presidential Decision Directive 25 (PDD 25) of May 1994 marked a sharp reversal of earlier suggestions from the Clinton administration that the US was ready to help create a UN peacekeeping intervention force. Under the consultation process associated with the earlier PDD 13, a 10,000-strong UN permanent rapid deployment force was envisaged. There was even a willingness for US troops to serve under UN command, as when 300 GIs were detailed to UNPROFOR III in Macedonia and 2,700 logistic troops were assigned to UNOSOM II. Severe criticism of the inadequacies of the UN arrangements, however, soon discouraged further steps in this direction, and the débâcle in Somalia precipitated a large-scale retreat. The UN Secretary-General, in effect the de facto Chief of Staff to the Security Council for enforcement operations, was seen to lack all capacity for rigorous military staff analysis, while UN military operations themselves were bedevilled by multiple chains of command, cultural diversity and marked disparities in equipment and training (Powell, 1994). PDD 25 itself marked less of a volte-face than is often supposed. It rejected ideas of a standing UN army and even the earmarking of special troops, and insisted on a clear, demanding set of criteria for judging which UN peacekeeping operations to support; but the declared aim was to improve UN peacekeeping, not bury it. At the heart of PDD 25 lay an unresolved contradiction: the entire exercise was motivated, on the one hand, by regard for US national interests ('properly constituted peace operations can be one useful tool to advance American national interests and pursue our national security objectives'), on the other hand, by the concerns of the international community (action should be taken when 'the political, economic and humanitarian consequences of inaction by the international community have been weighed and are considered unacceptable'). This reflects a deep historical ambivalence in US policy: isolationism, hard-headed concern for US interests, and the idea that the United States has a mission to provide moral leadership – each of these is strongly present as a pull on US foreign policy formulation. After electoral victory in the autumn of 1994, the Republican Congress aims to introduce legislation to block US funding for the UN if strict conditions are not met. This would remove one-third of the UN peacekeeping budget, with regard to which the US is already $500 million in arrears. In 1991, for every $100 of US military expenditure, 5 cents went to UN peacekeeping.

6 Conclusion: universality and the international community

We conclude with what is in our view the most important aspect of all: the question of universality and the nature of the international community in whose name humanitarian intervention is carried out. We have noted the challenge to ideas of the universality of humanitarian values exemplified in the turbulent World Conference on Human Rights in Vienna in June 1993. Yet even in this area, where it was widely reported that countries such as Syria and China rejected the whole basis of international human rights law, the Bangkok Declaration of the Regional Meeting for Asia stresses 'the universality, objectivity and non-selectivity of all human rights and the need to avoid the application of double standards in the implementation of human rights and its politicization, and that no violation of human rights can be justified' (Article 7). In the process, it was also urged that the UN system be democratized (Article 3); that human rights not be used as a condition for extending development assistance (Article 4); that promotion of human rights not lead to

interference in the internal affairs of states (Article 5); that 'the significance of national and regional particularities and various historical,
cultural and religious backgrounds' be acknowledged (Article 8); that
obstacles to the right to development 'lie at the macro-economic level, as
reflected in the widening gap between the North and the South, the rich
and the poor' (Article 18); and that 'poverty is one of the main obstacles
hindering the full enjoyment of human rights' (Article 19). This gives a
good idea of some of the main preoccupations of Third World countries
in general. Although the human rights agenda is more politicized than the
humanitarian assistance agenda, the same background concerns are evident in both. Kopi Awoonor, Ghana's permanent representative to the
UN, affirms that '[h]umanitarian aid in our time springs from the universal acceptance of the principle of international cooperation as a necessary
component and expression of our common humanity' (1993, 63). But
elsewhere he says that 'the real sufferings of developing countries are not
readily available for cameras because they are eternally cyclical, undra-
matic and relentless'. These are the crises which blight millions of lives,
but do not reach the Western media: 'humanitarian practitioners estimate that ten to twenty times more can be done with the same limited
resources to attack what UNICEF has called poverty's "silent" emergencies rather than loud ones resulting from wars' (Weiss, 1994c, 17).
Awoonor points to structural imbalances first established during the
period of colonial exploitation and persisting to this day: 'Development
is the only instrument that will remove the stigma of charity that accompanies all humanitarian relief efforts' (1993, 69). Western governments,
reluctant to address structural imbalances from which they benefit, are
seen to prefer the palliative of humanitarian relief. President Mugabe of
Zimbabwe, noting that 'African states are almost all poly-ethnic', says
that 'the alarming rate at which ethnic tensions and conflicts occurred in
Africa has necessitated the re-examination by the OAU of its founding
concepts, as well as its capacity and potential to deal with such situations
on the continent' (1994, 4). The Twentieth Ordinary Session of the
Assembly of the Heads of State of the OAU meeting in Cairo in June
1993 adopted a landmark *Declaration on the Establishment of a Mech-
anism for Conflict Prevention, Management and Resolution*, which exemplified the new proactive attitude. The ambivalence here lies in the
contradiction between (a) the admission that 'Africa, with its burdensome economic and debt problems, was not in a position to undertake a
regional initiative to restore and maintain peace and order in Somalia' or
mount peacekeeping operations in Rwanda, with the result that the
withdrawal of Western contingents from UNOSOM II 'before the operation had achieved its mandate' was deeply regrettable, and (b) the

assertion that 'Africa believes that regional actors, with a better understanding of regional and local issues, are better placed to handle local conflicts than more distant participants'.

Marc Trachtenberg expresses the central challenge well when he says that, in light of the turbulence and suffering of contemporary conflict, traditional Western readiness to intervene in defence of 'civilized' European values must now be extended to a determination by the international community to uphold truly universal standards. The key element here is legitimacy:

> For an interventionist system to be viable, it needs in particular to have a general aura of legitimacy. In the case of intervention in the Third World, the system needs to be supported especially by the major Third World countries that can be expected to be very suspicious of it. This means more than just solving the tactical problems of getting Third World governments to vote for interventionist actions in the UN and various regional bodies, or even to send their own military contingents. It means figuring out how whole populations, or at least their politically active components, react to intervention – what excites hostility, which aspects of an interventionary policy can generate support – and then framing one's own policy with this understanding in mind. It means listening to people we are not used to listening to, and understanding the limits on our own power and, especially, on our own wisdom. (Trachtenberg, 1993, 32)

Suggested reading

On option (a), forcible humanitarian intervention since 1991, five collections of papers can be recommended: Rodley (ed.), 1992; Damrosch (ed.), 1993; Forbes and Hoffman (eds), 1993; Reed and Kaysen (eds), 1993, and *International Journal*, special issue on humane intervention, 48(4) (1993).

On option (b), non-forcible coercion, Damrosch, 1989, and *Bulletin of the Atomic Scientists*, special issue, *Sanctions: Do They Work?*, 49(9) (1993) are helpful.

On option (c), non-forcible military intervention, Berdal, 1993; Durch (ed.), 1993; Fetherston, 1994; James, 1990; and *Survival*, 36(3) (1994), which contains articles by Dobbie, Mackinlay and Roberts, offer good introductions.

On option (d/e), non-military governmental and non-governmental intervention, see Cahill (ed.), 1993; Ferris (ed.), 1992; Jean (ed.), 1993; Macrae and Zwi (eds), 1994; Minear and Weiss, 1993; Palwankar (ed.), 1994; Weiss and Minear (eds), 1993.

Part III
Cases

6
Humanitarian Intervention in Bosnia

This account covers the period to the end of 1994. During this time the intervention by the international community is classed here as an example of option (c), non-forcible military humanitarian intervention. At the time of writing, it was not clear whether this would remain the case, or whether there would be a shift to option (a), enforcement, or option (d/e), military withdrawal. In the event, there was a decisive shift from option (c) peacekeeping to option (a) enforcement on 30 August 1995. Whatever the outcome, the lesson to be learnt to the end of 1994 concerns the implications of attempting non-forcible military humanitarian intervention in cases of severe, unresolved international-social conflict.

1 The challenge

The humanitarian tragedy in Bosnia, which has posed such a terrible challenge to the international community, is directly related to the fact that this was an international-social conflict. As the state structure of the old Yugoslavia weakened after the death of Tito in 1980, powerful, historically rooted communal fears, ambitions and antagonisms re-emerged, offering fertile ground for unscrupulous or fanatical leaders to launch a challenge for the only guarantee of security and power – sovereignty. The old state had been born at the end of the First World War, in an earlier era of upheaval, out of the multinational Habsburg and Ottoman empires. This was a time when Wilsonian ideas of self-determination were current – at any rate, as regards Europe – and the 'South Slavs' were given their own 'kingdom of the Serbs, Croats and Slovenes' in 1918. Memories of separate statehood in medieval times lived on, however, as Serbs, proud of their heroic struggle for independence at the turn of the century after 500 years of subjugation, identified Yugoslavia with greater Serbia, while Croats became restive for autonomy. During the Second World War Croatia was reconstituted under German control, and the Croatian Fascist Ustashe emulated their masters by killing, on some estimates, hundreds of thousands of Serbs and others, including perhaps tens of thousands in the notorious death camp at Jasenovac. The Serbian Chetniks retaliated. Underlying these antagonisms were the fault-lines between three great 'civilisations': Orthodox Christianity (41 per cent, mainly Serbs), Catholic Christianity (31 per cent, mainly Croats and Slovenes), and Islam (12 per cent). After the war, the victorious partisan leader, Tito (Josip Broz, a Croat), reconstructed the Yugoslav state along federal lines, held together by his own authority, the Yugoslav National Army (JNA) and the Communist Party. He achieved a tenuous independence within the socialist bloc. In 1974 Tito attempted to head off revived nationalisms by instituting a complex balance within the six republics (Slovenia, Croatia, Bosnia-Hercegovina, Montenegro, Serbia and Macedonia), recognizing the Muslims in Bosnia as a 'nation' and giving a measure of autonomy to two regions in Serbia – Kosovo, with a large Albanian majority, and Vojvodina, heavily populated by Hungarians and others. On his death in 1980, a rotating presidency, shared between the six republics, preserved an increasingly precarious unity. In 1986 Serb nationalist ambitions were openly expressed in the Academy of Arts and Sciences manifesto, a 'call to national awakening', produced by Dobrica Cosic, later president of the rump Federal Republic of Yugoslavia. It was then that Slobodan Milosevic emerged from the Communist ranks to make his bid for power by appealing to these atavistic instincts, his chosen instrument being an assault on the independence of the autonomous regions within Serbia – Vojvodina and, above all, Kosovo with its 90 per cent Muslim Albanian population. In Serb mythology Kosovo is the heartland of the ancestral Serbian nation, lost in the catastrophic defeat by the Turks at the battle of Kosovo-Polje in 1389. The event is still passionately commemorated – for example, in the epic verse written by Radovan Karadzic, leader of the Bosnian Serbs. Milosevic maintained an intense media campaign to fan support for his ambitions, not just in Serbia, but among the Serbs in Bosnia (who made up 31 per cent of the population) and Croatia (who made up 12 per cent of the population). Most Croatian Serbs lived in the Krajina, where they were planted by Habsburg rulers centuries ago to guard the borders of the empire. Like many marcher peoples, the Krajina

Serbs were truculent and independent. Milosevic played on sentiments among Serbs, a majority in Yugoslavia, that they had been relatively disadvantaged, economically and politically, under Tito. If the international community had wanted to preserve Yugoslavia, then would have been the time to intervene by trying to curb Milosevic's populism. But, with the end of the cold war, the Soviet Union was internally caught up in what turned out to be its own death throes, and the United States no longer saw its vital interests threatened by what was happening in Yugoslavia. The lifting of the threat of Soviet invasion after the collapse of the socialist bloc in 1989 removed a major restraint on internal nationalist particularisms.

It was in response to Serbian assertiveness within a gravely weakened federal state that the long-standing Slovene and Croat separatism revived. The wealthier Slovenes and Croats, closer culturally to Western Europe, resented the forced redistribution of wealth within Yugoslavia to the poorer Serbs. At first pressing for a looser confederation against the Serbian drive to tighten control of the state, Slovene and Croat aspirations for independent statehood grew as tension mounted, once again fanned by ambitious politicians like Franjo Tudjman in Croatia. Under these pressures, the Communist Party disintegrated in January 1990, precipitating what we have called the second of the structural causes of international-social conflict – a crisis of the state. This was both a result of rising communal tensions and a cause of these tensions escalating as the stakes became higher. In international-social conflict, the danger is that, as in some former Soviet bloc countries like Czechoslovakia, the sudden move towards multi-party democracy, far from strengthening national unity, encourages a 'communalization' of politics as parties align with conflict groups. In this heightened atmosphere, only control of sovereignty and its association with communal identity are seen as adequate protection against what is most feared and a sufficient guarantee of what is most desired. Tudjman's Croatian Democratic Union (HDZ) emerged as the largest party in Croatia in May 1990. Driven by nationalist fervour and miscalculating the response of the mainly rural Krajina Serbs (according to Misha Glenny, because he listened only to the more sophisticated, liberal Serbs in Zagreb), Tudjman made no attempt to reassure minorities in Croatia that their rights would be respected after independence (Glenny, 1992). On the contrary, he pandered to Croat extremists by removing Serbs from key posts. This was a second point at which the international community might have intervened, by refusing to countenance acknowledgement of Croatian aspirations to autonomy in the absence of scrupulous guarantees of minority rights within the Croatian republic.

During the year following Tudjman's electoral success, a year that coincided with the Gulf War, any opportunity to prevent conflict in Yugoslavia passed. On 15 May 1991 the Serbs and Montenegrins blocked the Croat, Stipe Mesic, from acceding to the rotating federal presidency. A referendum in Croatia came out in favour of independence. Convinced by Belgrade propaganda that the terrible days of the Ustashe were about to return, the Krajina Serbs centred at Knin rose up in revolt. A fatal Rubicon had been crossed. On 25 June 1991 Slovenia and Croatia declared independence. The Yugoslav National Army (JNA), dominated by Serbs, tried to maintain control within existing state borders. The Yugoslav civil war had begun.

Three years later, hundreds of thousands had died (perhaps a quarter of a million in Bosnia), and there were 1 million refugees abroad and some 3 million displaced within the former borders. By 1994 more than 4 million people in former Yugoslavia were estimated by the UN inter-agency consolidated appeal to be dependent upon international aid. War deaths, detention camps, systematic torture, mass rape, indiscriminate shelling of civilians, sniper fire, land-mines (50,000 laid a week at the height of the war), eviction, including slaughter and the burning of homes (ethnic cleansing), obstruction of humanitarian relief, siege, as well as the debilitating cumulative effects of sanctions against the Federal Republic of Yugoslavia (Serbia and Montenegro) – an incredulous Europe watched in horror as international-social conflict destroyed what had hitherto seemed a civilized country, accompanied by scenes of bestiality not witnessed in Europe since the Nazi and Stalinist eras. This was happening just after the December 1990 signing of the Paris Charter by all members of the Conference on Security and Co-operation in Europe (CSCE), including Yugoslavia, which seemed to have ushered in a new co-operative era on the Continent. Much as the Lisbon earthquake of 1755 shattered the sanguine prognostications of the Enlightenment *philosophes*, so the débâcle in Yugoslavia swiftly disillusioned the optimists of the 'end of history'. What could or should outsiders do in response to this humanitarian catastrophe?

2 The response

Here we are mainly concerned with evaluating what was done. How did the international community respond between 1991 and 1994? Our interest is in humanitarian rather than political intervention, so, although the two were inextricably intertwined, we will concentrate on the former. According to James Steinberg's analysis, the conflict went through five phases: (i) a period of rising tension before the outbreak of fighting; (ii) a brief Slovene war at the end of June and the beginning of July 1991, ending with the Brioni Accords of 8 July brokered by the European Community, which recognized Slovene independence, no doubt mainly because there were so few Serbs in Slovenia; (iii) the savage Croat war which immediately followed, through to the cease-fire of 2 January 1992, which brought the shock of the shelling of Dubrovnik, destruction of Vukovar and the onset of 'ethnic cleansing', and by the end of which a third of Croatia was effectively controlled by the self-styled Serb Republic of Krajina; (iv) the Bosnian war initiated by the Serb assault of 6 April 1992 and still going on at the end of 1994; (v) the threatened further spread of the war to Macedonia and beyond, so far headed off. The case-study chosen here for detailed examination is the issue of humanitarian intervention in the Bosnian war (Steinberg, 1993).

2.1 The period before the Bosnian war

The main purpose of this section is to explore the concept of non-intervention, in the sense of doing nothing, by looking at the status of potential interveners at the time the decision was made. As with the outside observer in modern physics, it is what is meant by 'outside' that is in question here. The apparently paradoxical point is that in complex, protracted conflicts like that in Bosnia, outside governments are already deeply involved before the fighting breaks out. Given the interdependence of international society, they are not unconnected onlookers, but are implicated in the overall situation from the start. By the time the question of intervention in Bosnia was raised, several key moves had already been made which constrained future choice, three of which can be mentioned here.

First, during 1990 and 1991, UN Security Council members looked at the whole conflict through statist spectacles, with the goal of maintaining the integrity of Yugoslavia. Both the Soviet Union and the United States feared the repercussions if Yugoslavia were to break up, not least for the integrity of the Soviet Union itself. The United States was reluctant to get involved (a remarkable transformation from its cold war neurosis about the geopolitical orientation of post-Tito Yugoslavia), while the United Nations did not consider that it should intervene in the internal affairs of a member state. The CSCE was hamstrung by unanimity rules and the fact that Yugoslavia was a member. That left the EC, keen to reassert itself after the disarray of the Gulf War and in the process of working towards closer co-operation in security, foreign policy and defence as part of the Maastricht process. The EC also wished to keep Yugoslavia from disintegrating, although, by using differential economic carrots and sticks to put pressure particularly on the Serbs, it perhaps unwittingly accentuated internal differences. Whether or not outsiders realized it, to press for the preservation of Yugoslavia was, in effect, to support the Serb position. The upshot, in many commentators' eyes, somewhat paradoxically, was to lend encouragement to Serb intransigence. In view of later criticisms during the Bosnian war of premature recognition of breakaway republics, it is salutary to remember that throughout the Croat war the opposite was the case, with critics blaming outside governments for *not* recognizing the secessionist republics. Under these circumstances it is hard to see that either recognition or non-recognition count as 'doing nothing'. When structural asymmetry is part of what is at issue, as in many forms of international-social conflict, there is no room for abstention.

A second example of prior intervention is what happened when the United Nations finally became involved in the Croat war, with the Chapter VII Security Council Resolution (SCR) 713 of 25 September 1991, which imposed an arms embargo on Yugoslavia. This was done at the request of the Yugoslav presidency, still formally representing all six republics. So it was that what was to become a key ingredient in the future Bosnian war (since it favoured those who already had most of the weapons and disadvantaged those, such as the future Bosnian government, who did not) was already in place before that war began. Once again, it is hard to see how either the maintenance of the embargo or its cancellation could be said to represent 'doing nothing'. Whatever outsiders did or did not do, they were seen to be intervening in the eyes of insiders.

A third example of the way in which outsiders were involved from the start is the way United Nations peacekeepers were first sent to the region. This was at the request of the presidents of Serbia and Croatia and the Yugoslav Secretary of State for Defence, and was intended to reinforce a negotiated cease-fire between Croats and Serbs according to five traditional peacekeeping principles laid down by the UN Secretary-General's personal envoy, Cyrus Vance. It was on these terms that the Security Council approved a peacekeeping force in principle by SCR 724 on 15 December 1991. This also marked the international community's formal humanitarian involvement, inasmuch as the Secretary-General was asked to 'pursue his humanitarian efforts in Yugoslavia, in liaison with the International Committee of the Red Cross (ICRC), the UN High Commissioner for Refugees (UNHCR), the UN International Children's Emergency Fund (UNICEF) and other appropriate humanitarian organisations, to take urgent practical steps to tackle the critical needs of the people of Yugoslavia'. It was SCR 743 of 21 February 1992, in the wake of the 2 January cease-fire to the Croat war (phase iii), which formally launched the United Nations Protection Force (UNPROFOR) in former Yugoslavia. When UNPROFOR first went into action, after 8 March 1992, the Bosnian war had not begun. But when even worse atrocities and human suffering on an even greater scale followed in Bosnia, could the international community 'do nothing', given the fact that peacekeepers with a humanitarian brief were already in neighbouring Croatia? Indeed, UNPROFOR was headquartered in Sarajevo at first, and there were already UN personnel in Bosnia. Peacekeepers in Croatia found that more and more of their time was being taken up by what was happening in Bosnia, regardless of any decisions made in New York. As we will see, when, during the summer of 1992, the question arose as to whether to intervene militarily and if so, how, given the political difficulties involved, the prior deployment of UNPROFOR in Croatia under entirely different conditions proved a major influence on the decision finally taken – non-forcible military intervention.

We should also note two further points. In the eyes of many, if something *can* be done to restrain aggressors and perpetrators of atrocities and *is not done*, then that on its own amounts to a kind of intervention – on the side of the culpable. This was to be a powerful, widespread perception throughout the Islamic world: 'Western policies do amount to intervention – on the side of the aggressor' (Eqbal Ahmad, *Boston Review*, June/August 1993, 5, quoted in Weiss, 1994a, 20). Capability carries responsibility. The second point is that, whatever perceptions outsiders may have of their role, insiders regularly see them not only as implicated, but often as a main cause of the conflict in the first place. Serbs, for example, were almost universally convinced that Germany was largely responsible for the trouble from the beginning, encouraging Slovene and Croat separatism and pressing the international community towards recognition of independence. The fact that newly reunified Germany was constitutionally precluded from sending troops beyond its borders at the time made no difference.

In short, when the Bosnian fighting broke out in earnest in April 1992, the idea that outsiders at that point for the first time faced a simple choice between intervening or not intervening does not correspond with the facts. The choices that did need to be made on the humanitarian front were as laid out in chapter 4. Given prior involvement, the question was what form the intervention should take. As far as the use of troops was concerned, the three broad alternatives were not to send troops, to send in non-forcible peacekeepers with the consent of the warring parties, or to intervene forcibly. In the event, option (c) was not so much chosen as drifted into – we have already seen one reason why this was so – but not before a crucial few months of hesitation. We first look at the period when the other two options still seemed to be open. We then reach the most important part of this case-study as we attempt to assess some of the implications of engaging in non-forcible military humanitarian intervention in international-social conflicts of this kind. Admittedly, coercive and forcible elements were present, as in (i) the peremptory language of Security Council resolutions and the invoking of Chapter VII of the UN Charter, (ii) the mandatory arms embargo and economic sanctions against Serbia and Montenegro, (iii) the local use of force at the discretion of individual UNPROFOR contingent commanders, and (iv) NATO air support and imposition of an air exclusion zone. Nevertheless, as events clearly showed, none of this altered the fact that this was essentially a non-forcible military intervention of type (c). The forcible elements made it at times a precarious balance to maintain, as consent was strained to the limit and UNPROFOR was pulled towards being a party to the conflict. But, despite the bluster, through to the end of 1994 it was the non-forcible nature of UNPROFOR which was the deciding factor, and which, for better or worse, in the end constrained the forcible dimension. As later shown by the events of June – August 1995, forcible intervention would have required pulling back UNPROFOR and interjecting an entirely differently configured force. We argue that failure to clarify the concept of humanitarian intervention and, in particular, to distinguish between non-forcible and forcible military intervention contributed to much of the confusion and misunderstanding that bedevilled the enterprise. Not only the general public in a number of countries, but also some governments did not appreciate this. Expectations were out of line with the realities of the choice of option (c). UNPROFOR was blamed for failure to achieve what had never been part of its mission. If there are to be future humanitarian interventions of this kind, it is important that these lessons be learnt.

2.2 The first six months of the Bosnian war – April to September 1992

The first six months of the Bosnian war were militarily decisive. By the end of it, the Bosnian Serbs had made most of their territorial gains, controlled nearly 70 per cent of the territory, and had gone far towards expelling non-Serb populations. Strategic pockets of resistance remained, particularly in eastern Bosnia, centred on towns like Gorazde, Tuzla and Srebrenica, which, along with Sarajevo itself (less strategically vital to the Serbs), were under siege, while a secure land corridor linking the Serb territories to Serbia itself in one direction and the self-styled Serb Republic of Krajina in the other had still to be consolidated. Thus, by the time of the Vance–Owen Plan, which was presented on 27 October 1992 and envisaged a Serb retreat to 43 per cent of the land, denying the Serbs their land corridor, the situation on the ground meant that this could have been enforced only by the threat, if necessary backed up by the actuality, of full-scale land war. By that time option (c), not option (a), had in any case been chosen, so it was too late. Our concern is with the human-itarian rather than the political dimension, so we will not pursue the attempts at peacemaking further. What is instructive is the process whereby the choice to adopt option (c) was made during the first crucial six months of the war, and what its humanitarian implications were. This was the period during which the new UN Secretary-General, Boutros Boutros-Ghali, was preparing his *Agenda for Peace*, with its suggestion of UN peace enforcement units.

It is important to realize that in terms of international law the entire situation had changed at the beginning of 1992 with the recognition of the independence not only of Slovenia and Croatia, but also of Bosnia. Despite the Croatian war, Franjo Tudjman (representing the Croats, who made up 17 per cent of Bosnia's 4.4 million population) and Slobodan Milosevic (representing the Serbs, who made up 31 per cent) shared plans for a partition of Bosnia. The President of Bosnia, Alija Izetbegovic, however, claiming to represent a cosmopolitan Bosnia, not just the 44 per cent Muslim population, having earlier favoured the maintenance of Yugoslavia, now preferred independence to (i) partition or (ii) absorption in a Serb-dominated rump state. A referendum on independence in February, confirming this, had been boycotted by the Bosnian Serbs, who proclaimed their own 'Serb Republic of Bosnia' with its capital in Pale on 27 March. The EC and the US recognized Bosnia on 7 April. The UN Security Council recommended admission of Bosnia to the UN on 20 May (SCR 755).

When war broke out on 6 April 1992, therefore, Serb and Croat troops in Bosnia were now technically acting illegally. SCR 752 of 15 April accordingly demanded an end to outside interference by these forces in the new state of Bosnia. Bosnian territorial integrity must be maintained, and Serb and Croat forces must withdraw, place themselves under the authority of the Bosnian government, or disband. Otherwise, the UN could respond to aggression against a member state, and individual states and groups of states could come to the aid of the Bosnian government under Article 51, self-defence. Technically, this would not be interven-tion. This was a critical defining moment. From now on, supporters of Bosnian independence interpreted the war as one of aggression waged by Serbia and Montenegro against the integrity of the Bosnian state (and later, when the Croat–Muslim alignment collapsed between May 1993 and February–March 1994, by Croatia). From this perspective the inter-national community, having recognized Bosnia, should have helped to defend it and reassert government authority within it. The arms embargo of 25 September 1991, imposed when there was still a unitary Yugoslav state, should then have been lifted. President Izetbegovic asked for 10,000–15,000 UN troops to help 'restore order'. For the Serbs, on the other hand, the situation was structurally different. As in Croatia, they now, as Bosnian Serbs, found themselves against their will transformed into a threatened minority. They had not voted in the referendum. The internal borders of Yugoslavia were not sacrosanct, having been deliberately drawn under Tito to include Serbs in the other republics (a ruse that similarly backfired on the Russians as a result of the way in which Stalin had redrawn internal Soviet borders). Izetbegovic was seen as a dangerous Islamic fundamentalist intent on establishing an Islamic state. The breakup of Yugoslavia was seen as a German plot. In contrast to these two conflicting perspectives was a third, which was the one subsequently adopted by most outsiders. This was highly offensive to holders of both the others, particularly the supporters of the Bosnian government: it was that this was a civil war within Bosnia in which various 'factions' defined as 'Serb', 'Croat' and 'Muslim' were scrapping with each other. Few appreciate that in international-social conflict apparently 'neutral' descriptions of this kind are already contentious and deeply political. The international community never came to terms with these asymmetries, which undermined future attempts, whether by Vance–Owen or the Contact Group, to find a political settlement. It was evident that the mechanisms for recognizing secessionist states were arbitrary and highly politicized. According to the criteria laid down by the EC's Badinter Commission, for example, Croatia did not initially qualify for recognition (because of its treatment of minorities), whereas Macedonia did. Bosnia failed on what was widely regarded elsewhere as an essential precondition for recognition – government control of its own territory. Yet Croatia and Bosnia were recognized, whereas Macedonia, blocked by Greece, to begin with was not.

In the event, the rump Federal Republic of Yugoslavia (FRY), formed on 27 April by Serbia and Montenegro, eventually officially 'withdrew' the Yugoslav National Army from Bosnia, leaving large numbers of well-armed, trained troops to join local militias as a reconstituted Bosnian Serb Army. When President Izetbegovic asked for UN troops to restore internal order on 12 May, Marrack Goulding, UN Under-Secretary-General for Political Affairs, replied that much larger forces than he was asking for would be needed to do this and that the Security Council was highly unlikely to agree (UN Doc. S/23900, 12). On some readings of international law, if internal strife has reached the level of belligerency, then outside governments should not intervene on one side. During the spring and early summer the Serb assault intensified. This was the period when concentration camps were set up and some of the worst instances of ethnic cleansing were perpetrated. Sarajevo was put under siege. A land-grab was clearly under way. On 30 May, by SCR 757, the Security Council imposed comprehensive economic sanctions against the FRY under Chapter VII of the UN Charter. The coercion option had been adopted (in our categorization, option (b)), but not yet the use of military force (option (a)). Humanitarian agencies struggled to cope in the worsening environment. In May a UNHCR convoy had to 'negotiate its way through ninety road-blocks between Zagreb and Sarajevo, many of them manned by undisciplined and drunken soldiers of indeterminate political affiliation' (UN Doc. S/23900, 6, 12 May). On 18 May an ICRC convoy was attacked, and a delegate killed. On 29 June an international conference of UN humanitarian agencies and NGOs met in Geneva to set up an inter-agency consolidated appeal for the whole of former Yugoslavia. In June efforts focused on opening Sarajevo airport to humanitarian supplies (SCR 758, 8 June). President Mitterrand of France flew into Sarajevo unexpectedly on 28 June. As international outrage mounted, this was perhaps the moment when force came closest to being employed. David Owen, future EC negotiator, urged a bombing of Serb artillery (*The Times*, 4 August 1992). Margaret Thatcher insisted: 'Stop the excuses; Serbia should get an ultimatum' (*International Herald Tribune*, 7 August 1992). Outrage within Islamic countries mounted as Western unwillingness to defend 'Muslim' Bosnia was contrasted with the enthusiasm shown for restoring the independence of oil-rich Kuwait. Such was the public outcry that in August the UN Commission on Human Rights for the first time appointed a special rapporteur to investigate violations inside the borders of former Yugoslavia. Three main factors inhibited the choice of the forcible option: military assessments of the scale of operation required, uncertainty about what the political goals should be, and political differences between members of the Security Council, with Russia sympathetic to the Serbs and the United States increasingly sympathetic to the Bosnian government. Political paralysis meant that the conflict was interpreted more and more as a humanitarian rather than a political crisis, but with scant attention paid to what 'humanitarian' implied. 'NATO may send in 100,000 troops to cover aid convoy' announced a headline in the *Independent* newspaper (7 August 1992).

The crucial decision came on 13 August 1992, with two Security Council resolutions. By SCR 770, under Chapter VII, member states were called upon to 'take nationally or through regional agencies or arrangements all measures necessary' to facilitate, in co-ordination with the United Nations, the delivery of humanitarian assistance to Sarajevo and wherever else it was needed in Bosnia and Hercegovina. By SCR 771 the Security Council demanded that the ICRC and other relevant humanitarian organizations be granted immediate, unimpeded and continuous access to all camps, prisons and detention centres within the former Yugoslavia. It strongly condemned violations of international humanitarian law, including those related to ethnic cleansing, and called upon states and international humanitarian organizations to collate substantial breaches of the Geneva Conventions. SCR 770 opened the door to forcible action by states or organizations such as NATO acting only loosely within the UN framework in Bosnia. Whereas SCR 770 brought in humanitarian concerns under the usual 'threat to international peace and security' by saying that the provision of humanitarian assistance 'is an important element in the Council's effort to restore international peace and security', SCR 771, also under Chapter VII, did not. Chapter VII was invoked on humanitarian grounds alone. Here was a remarkable moment in which the international community was responding to a major international-social conflict as a largely humanitarian crisis in its contemplation of the use of force.

But the moment passed. There is, in fact, a convincing argument that, given the prior deployment of UNPROFOR I in Croatia in what was seen originally as a more or less traditional peacekeeping mission, the forcible option was in any case precluded, because, as the UN Secretary-General argued as early as May 1992, to depart from a basis of consent would 'risk involving the force in hostile encounters with those whose co-operation will be necessary if UNPROFOR is to succeed in fulfilling its existing mandate in the United Nations Protected Areas in Croatia. Such hostilities would have far-reaching implications for the security of UNPROFOR personnel generally' (UN Doc. S/23900, 10, 12 May 1992). This was to be a familiar argument in the months ahead, leading to accusations that UNPROFOR was concerned only with its own security, not that of those it was there to protect. In fact, the stipulation that minimum force could be used and then only in 'self-defence' was one of the recognized criteria for traditional peacekeeping. Once again, decisions made before the Bosnian war started constrained subsequent choice. As it was, at the London conference convened on 26–8 August and attended by all parties to the conflict, rhetoric blurred difficult choices. With scant connection to what was actually happening on the ground, familiar principles about the territorial integrity of Bosnia and the inadmissibility of altering international borders by force were proclaimed. All parties at the conference seemed to concur, agreeing that heavy weapons should be impounded. Meanwhile the land-grab continued unabated. Earlier dissension between EC and UN negotiators would be obviated by a new joint conference chaired by David Owen (for the EC) and Cyrus Vance (for the UN). Both now came out against the use of force. Military advice from NATO countries was in any case almost unequivocally opposed, suggesting that it would take perhaps 500,000 troops to subdue the region effectively (Dewar, 1993, 33). Memories of the number of German divisions pinned down in the region during the Second World War were invoked. On 10 September the UN Secretary-General's 'concept of operations' recommended implementation of SCR 770 through an extension to the mandate of UNPROFOR. The enlarged mandate would allow it to support efforts by, and supply protection for, UNHCR to deliver humanitarian relief throughout Bosnia and Hercegovina, and also to protect ICRC convoys of released civilian detainees. UNPROFOR would be deployed in sector Sarajevo and four new zones, later with headquarters at Kiseljak, outside Sarajevo. Critically, UNPROFOR troops would follow normal peace-keeping rules of engagement, which would authorize them to use force in self-defence only – for example, if armed persons attempted by force to prevent them from carrying out their mandate (UN Doc. S/24540). The suggested mandate did not otherwise explicitly include the use of force to protect Bosnians. Like other peacekeeping forces, therefore, UNPROFOR would operate in Bosnia only with the consent of the warring parties. These recommendations were accepted in SCR 776 of 14 September 1992, which, perhaps significantly, made no reference to Chapter VII of the Charter. Eight European countries agreed to contribute to, and pay for, the new force. By early November, more than six months after the war had started, UNPROFOR II, as the Bosnian force was now unofficially called, comprised 7,000 European troops, together with an infantry battalion from Canada and a field hospital from the United States. By this time, as already noted, this phase of the war had effectively been won by the Serbs, with a significant enclave in the West controlled by the Croats.

From 14 September 1992, therefore, the die had been cast. Option (c) had been chosen, not option (a). However peremptory the language of Security Council resolutions in favour of the territorial integrity of the Bosnian state and against violations of international humanitarian law, no provisions were made for effective enforcement. The entire military operation was not a forcible response to aggression or atrocity, but a peacekeeping mission in the extraordinarily testing environment of inter-national-social conflict, whose brief was not to resolve the conflict one way or the other, but (i) to alleviate its worst consequences by delivering humanitarian relief and where possible protecting civilians and (ii) to try to help create conditions conducive to the drawing up of a peace settlement. We return in the conclusion of this case-study to consider the implications of this. But first we look at what happened in the humanitarian field between October 1992 and the end of 1994, as peacekeepers and humanitarian aid agencies struggled to fulfil their rapidly evolving mandates.

2.3 Non-forcible humanitarian intervention in international-social conflict

The simplest way to convey some sense of the difficulties encountered by the interveners is to look in turn at three groups of tasks undertaken by UNPROFOR and the humanitarian community through to December 1994: the provision of relief assistance, the protection of threatened civilians, and the prevention and punishment of humanitarian crimes. These coincide with the three areas of humanitarianism described in chapter 1. The three tasks of humanitarian interveners outlined there were to assist, to protect and to punish – the latter not a task for UNPROFOR, although some argue that it should have been. We should say at the outset that in our view these humanitarian efforts, however fraught with problems, represented the best efforts of the international community to respond in a civilized way to the bestiality of international-social conflict, given the decision to adopt option (c) rather than resort to force (option (a)) or not employ military forces at all. The further, heated controversy about whether this was the right decision is another issue. What UNPROFOR II offers us in this period is some insight into the implications of choosing option (c) in international-social conflict. Within this brief, further distinctions can be made – for example, between the relief of refugees and the delivery of aid, which does not necessarily require the threat or use of significant force, and the protection of safe areas and imposition of air exclusion zones, which does. As events demonstrated, within an overall option (c) mission, even the latter is still from the outset clearly distinct from option (a).

2.3.1 Providing relief assistance to refugees and displaced persons, and delivering humanitarian aid.
It would be hard to exaggerate the problems faced by UNHCR, WHO, WFP, UNICEF, IOM and other UN agencies, as well as the ICRC and hundreds of humanitarian NGOs, in meeting the humanitarian needs of increasing numbers of desperate people, many of whom were not just 'collateral' victims of war but themselves explicit targets of attack. One of the main war aims of the major belligerents was precisely to kill and displace civilian populations on a massive scale. As a result, aid workers found themselves not only thwarted at every turn by road-blocks, evasions and obstructions, but themselves the recurrent objects of assault. One of the cardinal principles of humanitarian relief is that it should be delivered to the normal place of residence. Forcible displacement of people is expressly forbidden in humanitarian law (Fourth Geneva Convention, 1949, Article 49; Additional Protocol II, 1977, Article 17). Yet humanitarian aid in support of recipients at their

normal place of residence was diametrically opposed to the war aim of ethnic cleansing. In these circumstances humanitarianism was by its nature already heavily politicized. The 18 May 1992 attack on an ICRC convoy was no accident. Nor was the 25 October 1993 killing of a Danish UNHCR driver, after which the UN Secretary-General decided to suspend all humanitarian convoys in central Bosnia. Earlier, in February 1993, he had overruled the UN High Commissioner for Refugees, Sadako Ogata, when she had wanted to pull out in protest at comparable violence. Such decisions are difficult and controversial. Humanitarianism was politicized in many other ways, too. To deliver aid to one group was in itself seen as partisan. Relief for a besieged town enabled the defenders to resist longer. There were squabbles about what counted as essential humanitarian supplies and what was war material. Weapons were suspected (on occasion, correctly) of being smuggled in on aid convoys. To evacuate wounded or desperate people crowded into besieged enclaves was to abet ethnic cleansing. More generally, provisions of all kinds were seen as bargaining chips in the intense, complex negotiations that went on, often under duress, at local level. War-lords had to be 'paid off'. In November 1993 it was estimated that, one way or another, only 50 per cent of humanitarian assistance was getting through to those who needed it (United Nations, 1994, 82). This politicization of humanitarianism is a structural feature of all humanitarian intervention in international-social conflict. But where, as in Bosnia, there is a conflict between humanitarian purposes and major war aims, this 'creates humanitarian problems of such magnitude that it is far beyond the capacity of the humanitarian organisations alone to solve them' (Sandoz, 1993, 15).

What of the role of UN peacekeeping in this situation? Does the presence of military escorts under option (c) help or hinder the relief effort? Not surprisingly, those who have put a lot into the UNPROFOR effort are convinced that it saves large numbers of lives. For Kofi Annan, UN Under-Secretary-General for Peacekeeping Operations, '[t]he reality is that there are situations when you cannot assist people unless you are prepared to take certain [military] measures' (quoted in Weiss, 1994c, 6). Aid workers seem to be divided on the question. Certainly the keeping open of Sarajevo airport was vital, not only for the sustenance of Sarajevo itself, but also at critical phases for victims cut off in other parts of eastern and central Bosnia. As for armed escorts, since they were relatively lightly armed and had been given what was essentially a self-defence mandate, they too became embroiled in the same complications. Contingents varied in how much force they tried to apply at local level. For example, Swedish peacekeepers, arriving in Bosnia in October 1993, were at first determined to take a hard line. Their commander noted that local soldiers were refusing to remove mines blocking the way, and threatened to 'blow their heads off' if they did not. Within days three Swedish soldiers were abducted by Bosnian gunmen. After negotiations, they were returned unharmed (*Reuters*, 6 November 1993). On several occasions convoys with armed escorts were successfully blocked by un-armed civilians. At every point pressures and counter-pressures were applied, often within a highly localized politico-military context, and bargains were struck. Lorries were searched. Aid was diverted as tribute to areas controlled by those manning the road-blocks. Aid delivery itself became a pawn in the wider conflict. Sometimes it took days or even weeks to get a single convoy through. On the one hand, UNPROFOR undoubtedly succeeded in keeping many routes open, and facilitated the delivery of aid and the evacuation of the sick and wounded; on the other hand, humanitarian aid agencies found it harder to preserve their non-political image as a result. UNPROFOR depended from the start on the consent of all major parties, but within those parameters it was able to offer some protection from local banditry and impose a measure of regularity in some areas. It also assisted with reconstruction work, such as restoration of communications and power supplies and the rebuilding of hospitals.

It is hard to draw up an overall balance sheet. But the composite figures are dramatic, and, on the face of it, impressive. In December 1991, at the end of the Croat war, it was estimated that some 500,000 refugees, displaced people and other victims needed assistance and pro-tection. Appeals were launched by UNHCR, which was designated lead humanitarian agency, in December 1991 and May 1992. A seven-point plan was proposed by Sadako Ogata at the 29 July Geneva international meeting on humanitarian aid to victims in former Yugoslavia, entailing respect for human rights and humanitarian law, preventive protection, humanitarian access to the needy, the meeting of special requirements, temporary protection measures, material assistance, and return and re-habilitation. On 11 March 1993 Ogata reported to the Security Council that 3.8 million people were receiving assistance in former Yugoslavia, including 2.28 million in Bosnia – half the original population. This was a remarkable effort, taking up a large proportion of UNHCR's resources world-wide (Sandoz, 1993, 18). In October 1993 a new Consolidated Appeal was launched to cover the humanitarian needs of some 4.25 million people, more than half a million of whom were in Serbia and Montenegro. Humanitarianism was trying to retain its impartiality. De-spite all the obstructions and difficulties, WFP reported that average monthly deliveries in Bosnia increased during the latter half of 1993. In addition, the amount of aid delivered to cut-off places by means of air-drops from American and other aircraft also increased. By the time of the eighth UN Consolidated Appeal for the period 1 July to 31 December

1994, more than 4.1 million people were being sustained at a cost of $500 million. The conclusion of a report on UN peacekeeping operations prepared in May 1994 is that in former Yugoslavia '[t]he United Nations humanitarian assistance operations have succeeded in alleviating suffering and in saving hundreds of thousands of lives' (United Nations, 1994, 83). No doubt this is the kind of claim that an official UN document would make. At this point, let us simply say that if it is the case that hundreds of thousands more would have died without the combined efforts of relief agencies and UN peacekeepers, then this alone counts as a major justification of the whole enterprise. On humanitarian grounds the issue is decided. Further questions concern (a) whether it is indeed the case – could as much or more have been achieved without peacekeepers, or if the enforcement option had been taken up? And (b) whether humanitarian gains were made at the expense of other values, such as justice – was humanitarianism a substitute for adequate political and military engagement?

2.3.2 Protecting safe areas and enforcing no-fly zones. One of the recurrent criticisms of the international community's intervention in Bosnia was that pronouncements made in New York, often for political reasons, did not correspond with reality on the ground. UNPROFOR was encumbered with a steady accretion of sometimes conflicting mandates, in many cases beyond its capacity to deliver. Between September 1991 and July 1994 there were nearly 60 Security Council resolutions on former Yugoslavia. In January 1994, the Belgian commander in Bosnia, Lieutenant-General Francis Briquemont, following criticism of the UN Secretariat for refusing to back a call for air strikes, announced his resignation, citing exhaustion. He pointed to a 'fantastic gap' between the UN in New York and peacekeepers on the ground. When asked what advice he might have for his replacement, he suggested that the new commander 'constantly remind those politically responsible about the difficulties in which they put us because there is no coherence in their strategies'. 'I don't read the Security Council resolutions any more', he added, 'because they don't help me' (*Reuters*, 4 January 1994).

Behind these frustrations lay a tension, if not a contradiction, between (a) tasks mandated by the Security Council which required the co-operation of the conflict parties, such as those just considered, and (b) the authority to use a measure of force, as in those we are about to consider. This was reflected in the actuality of UNPROFOR's military dispositions. On the one hand, as aid escorts UNPROFOR forces were lightly armed, scattered through potentially hostile terrain in small contingents, surrounded by larger numbers of more strongly armed forces, many of them ill-disciplined and unpredictable, vulnerably located, and highly visible in deliberately whitened vehicles – all this made thoughts of a non-consensual use of force militarily unthinkable. On the other hand, UNPROFOR was also authorized by the Security Council to call on the undoubted military potency of NATO air support in self-defence as it fulfilled its various mandates. Use of force in self-defence was part of traditional peacekeeping. But now, much more ambitious mandates were to be fulfilled, and, unlike the situation in traditional peacekeeping, the conflict was still going on. Where such mandates involved actions seen by belligerents as opposed to their war aims, the use of force, even in 'self-defence', would be interpreted as an act of war. If this bluff were called, as seemed likely to happen, given the high value of the stakes at issue and the volatility of the situation, UNPROFOR would be in a potentially untenable position. Not to use force would be to betray its mandate; to use force might make UNPROFOR party to a conflict it was not equipped to fight. The alternative would then be total withdrawal or reconfiguration as a war-fighting force. It was a delicate balancing act.

These problems were exemplified in the experience of protecting 'safe areas'. Unlike 'Operation Provide Comfort' in Northern Iraq and 'Operation Turquoise' in Rwanda, UNPROFOR's limited capabilities as a peacekeeping force did not permit peremptory imposition. The siege of Srebrenica in eastern Bosnia, isolated after Serb forces seized the bridge at Zvornik, became a critical test of the international community's willingness to use the 'necessary means' authorized under SCR 770 to assist delivery of humanitarian assistance. Some 30,000 refugees had joined the 9,000 inhabitants, and were cut off for weeks at the beginning of 1993. UNHCR reported that 30 to 40 people were dying daily from military attack, exposure to cold, or lack of medical treatment. International pressure mounted, and in March humanitarian organizations at last got through, only to be faced with the dilemma that evacuation of the vulnerable would further ethnic cleansing. Nevertheless, evacuation went ahead. On 16 April, SCR 819 declared Srebrenica and its surroundings a 'safe area'. The Secretary-General was asked to increase the UNPROFOR presence to protect the civilian population. With reference to the consistency of UN response to humanitarian crises, it is worth noting that the even more destructive siege of Huambo in Angola, which was taking place at the same time as the siege of Srebrenica, elicited no such international action. On 6 May, having considered the report of an international fact-finding mission, the Security Council passed SCR 824, adding Sarajevo, Tuzla, Zepa, Gorazde and Bihac as safe areas. On 4 June, SCR 836 invoked Chapter VII of the UN Charter, so that, 'acting in self-defence', UNPROFOR could take 'necessary measures' in response to bombardment of safe areas, armed incursion into them, or deliberate obstruction of humanitarian convoys. UNPROFOR was to deter attacks, monitor the cease-fire, promote the withdrawal of military and paramilitary units other than those of the Bosnian government, and occupy key points on the ground. In addition, member states acting nationally or through regional organizations could use all necessary means, including air power, to support UNPROFOR. On 14 June, the UN Secretary-General reported that, to implement SCR 836, the UNPROFOR force commander had estimated that he would need an additional 34,000 troops. The Secretary-General said that it would be possible to start implementing SCR 836 under a 'light option', with a reinforcement of some 7,600. NATO was asked to provide and coordinate the use of air power. The crucial distinction between option (c) and option (a) was becoming blurred. Two specific criticisms were made by Lieutenant-General Briquemont. The first was that permitting one side (the Bosnian government) to retain armed forces within the safe areas while insisting that the other side remove theirs would clearly be seen by the Bosnian Serbs as a hostile military act. The 1994 Bosnian government break-out from the Bihac safe area showed why this was a sensitive issue. On the other hand, it was hard to see how the government of an officially recognized UN member could be told not to retain troops on its own territory. The only solution was negotiated demilitarization. The second criticism was that the barely adequate 7,600 reinforcements authorized in June 1993 took more than a year to materialize. In view of these contradictions, it is not surprising that the use of air power envisaged in SCR 836 in June 1993 was not invoked until February 1994. According to some commentators, UN personnel continually blocked it, arguing that peace was just around the corner, and even deliberately placed their own forces near Serb positions (Rieff, 1994a, 12). Decisions on the use of air power were subject to 'dual key' control, in which UN civilian authorities shared control with NATO. At the beginning of 1994, following the 5 February mortar shell explosion in Sarajevo central market which killed 58 and wounded 142, the new UNPROFOR commander in Bosnia, General Sir Michael Rose, seemed to regain the initiative. Despite Serb disclaimers of responsibility, NATO's North Atlantic Council, at the request of the UN Secretary-General, authorized its Southern Command to prepare for air strikes against Serb artillery and mortar positions. On 9 February the Serbs were given a 10-day ultimatum to withdraw heavy weapons from within 20 kilometres of Sarajevo. Perhaps the key ingredient which made this possible was strong Russian support for the ultimatum, on condition, however, that the Sarajevo area be entirely demilitarized, including Bosnian government forces. The West accepted increased Russian participation, including troops on the ground, in exchange, and persuaded the Bosnian government to accept the offer. On 17 February the Bosnian Serbs agreed to comply. In the wake of this success, the so-called Contact Group, which now included Russia as well as the United States, France, Germany and Britain, pressed hard for a peace settlement in which the Serbs would have 49 per cent of the land. At last there seemed to be some consistency to Security Council policy. The further political story through to the end of 1994 is not our concern here. But the underlying logic of the choice of option (c) continued to dictate events. In March and April another cat-and-mouse game was played around Gorazde, ending with its effectively being rendered indefensible, given current policies. There were accusations that the Bosnian government was deliberately not defending Gorazde in an attempt to encourage NATO involvement. After some Bosnian government successes around Bihac later in the year, albeit complicated by rebel Muslim forces who joined the Serbs in blocking supplies and followed by vigorous Bosnian Serb counter-attack, the town was left to what seemed a similar fate.

It is hard to see the coherence of a policy which uses peremptory language in New York to declare key strategic areas 'safe', but neither demilitarizes them itself nor ensures their effective defence. Peacekeepers were supposed to 'deter' attack by acting in 'self-defence' but lacked the military means to do so. Attempts were made to distinguish 'close air support' in defence of UN personnel from pre-emptive and punitive air strikes. But this was of no help in clarifying the conceptual confusion which undermined operational planning. Given the general vulnerability of UNPROFOR in Bosnia, such that Serb forces could take peacekeepers hostage at will, the threat of air strikes was soon seen to be largely a bluff.

As for the imposition of a no-fly zone in Bosnia, first declared by SCR 781 on 9 October 1992 to ensure 'the safety of the delivery of humanitarian assistance', it was not until six months and more than 400 violations later that, on 31 March 1993, SCR 816 extended the ban to fixed-wing and rotary-wing aircraft and authorized NATO to enforce it. This followed an attack on two villages east of Srebrenica by three aircraft from the FRY. On 28 February 1994, a few days after the ultimatum on Sarajevo, four out of six aircraft which ignored the ban were shot down.

2.3.3 Preventing and punishing crimes in international humanitarian law.   As we saw in chapter 1, it is of the essence of humanitarianism that it is 'above' politics. War crimes and crimes against humanity, of which there were large numbers on a horrific scale during the Bosnian war, are defined as 'below' politics. Whatever the purported political motivations, the perpetrators are regarded as international criminals. Yet such actions are often carried out at official instigation or with official connivance. In the vicious, polarized milieu of international-social conflict, the perpetrators are likely to be regarded as heroes within their own communities. When the Serbian folk-rock star 'Ceca' became engaged to 'Arkan' (Zeljko Raznjatovic), commander of the paramilitary Tigers, responsible for hideous acts of inhumanity, and named as a war criminal by former American Secretary of State Lawrence Eagleburger, she said: 'My parents are very proud because I am going to marry the bravest man in the country. He is polite, direct – a real man' (*The Times*, 17 February 1995). Named 'war criminals' like Slobodan Milosevic and Radovan Karadjic, who are leaders of parties to the conflict, may subsequently be treated with official deference, and even be transformed into 'men of peace' if their support is needed by international peacemakers for the delivery of a preferred political outcome.

Thanks to graphic reporting of the unspeakable atrocities perpetrated during the Bosnian war by journalists like *Newsday*'s Roy Gutman, whose first-hand accounts of the death camps did much to stir international response, both the UN Commission on Human Rights and the UN Security Council quite soon took note (Gutman, 1993). In SCR 771 of 13 August 1992, such actions were indicted, and international humanitarian organizations were enjoined to collate substantial violations of humanitarian law, including breaches of the Geneva Conventions. A number of other resolutions followed. On 1 October 1992, in accordance with SCR 780, an impartial Commission of Experts from five countries was established to investigate such breaches. On 22 February 1993, on the basis of SCR 808, the Secretary-General was asked to submit proposals for the prosecution of those responsible. An international tribunal was to be set up in the Hague 'for the prosecution of persons responsible for serious violations of international humanitarian law in the territory of the former Yugoslavia since 1991'. A draft statute for the new tribunal, the first truly international criminal court (since Nuremberg and Tokyo in 1945–6 were 'victors' tribunals'), was approved by SCR 827 on 25 May 1993. It was to be an enforcement measure under Chapter VII of the UN Charter. The offences to be tried were given in Articles 2–5 of the statute, and included breaches of the 1949 Geneva Conventions and the 1948 Genocide Convention, crimes against humanity and violations of the laws of war. These did not entail 'new' laws (an accusation made against the Nuremberg tribunal), but laws already recognized in former Yugoslavia. Although, as we saw in chapter 1, the law of armed conflicts and non-derogable human rights law merge here, whereas human rights law is mainly concerned with the responsibility of a state for the damage suffered by a victim, the international law of armed conflicts seeks to prosecute individuals. This is a strict requirement, and poses a huge challenge to the tribunal. The Commission of Experts was starved of funds, and had almost no investigative staff, probably because Security Council members did not want the humanitarian dimension to cut across the search for a political settlement. Nevertheless, by July 1994 it reported, among other things, evidence of crimes against humanity and probably genocide against non-Serbs in Bosnia; evidence of the culpability of detention camp commandants, local political leaders and police in breach of the Geneva Conventions; and a prima facie case against Yugoslav army officers responsible for the December 1991 bombardment of civilians in Dubrovnik and the commander of the June 1993 attack on Sarajevo. The tribunal itself was to be led by 11 judges chosen by the UN General Assembly, none of them a party to the conflict. It could retry cases already heard in municipal courts, but could not impose the death sentence. Needless to say, there are grave difficulties in gathering sufficient evidence, particularly of 'systematic' crimes like genocide. Many of those potentially able to provide it, such as UNPROFOR, are not free to give it, because this would be seen as a 'political' act, particularly by the Serbs, and would impugn impartiality. This illustrates how hard it is to keep humanitarianism above politics in conflict situations. The ICRC also has to maintain a delicate balance between upholding international humanitarian law, which implies helping arraign those who breach it, and maintaining political impartiality and dialogue with all parties in order to preserve 'humanitarian space'. Beyond this is the formidable task of persuading authorities to hand over the accused for proper trial when the authorities in question may not recognize the 'non-political' nature of the proceedings and the accused may be war heroes. In a report in August 1994, the UN Commission on Human Rights' special rapporteur, Tadeus Mazowiecki, noted the widespread lack of knowledge about the tribunal and the inordinate delays which 'have gravely compromised its credibility'. Nevertheless, it is significant that the Bosnian war has led to (a) the first UN Commission on Human Rights appointment of a country rapporteur and (b) the first international criminal tribunal since Nuremberg.

Once again, UNPROFOR was unable to prevent the crimes from taking place. In January 1993 the Bosnian Deputy Prime Minister, Hakija Turajlic, was hauled from his armoured personnel carrier and killed, as UNPROFOR looked on. Ethnic cleansing continued in UN protected areas. Even professional troops were shocked by some of the atrocities. In the words of British Army spokesman Major Martin Waters: 'There have been terrible atrocities. Women and children have been murdered. The soldiers here have witnessed horrific sights that will stay with them for the rest of their lives' (*Guardian*, 22 April 1993).

3 Conclusion

Faced with international-social conflict on this scale, where deep-seated communal antagonisms fuel incompatible political ambitions in the context of an integral crisis of the state, the international community faces a series of dilemmas. It is not able to 'do nothing', since, given the structural asymmetry of the situation, it is already seen to be deeply implicated. But, for the same reason, it cannot avoid being confronted with difficult dilemmas when it tries to determine what it *should* do. In addition, the international community is not monolithic. On the contrary, it is made up the most disparate medley of barely compatible forces and interests. In view of all this, it is not surprising that the enterprise of collective humanitarian intervention in Bosnia proved problematic. What lessons can be learnt? We are essentially concerned with two relationships here: between humanitarianism and politics and between humanitarianism and the use of military force.

3.1 Humanitarianism and politics

Although easy to say and hard to do anything about, the political context within which humanitarian intervention has been attempted in Bosnia has been characterized by lack of conceptual clarity and inconsistency of purpose. Up to the end of 1991, the underlying political assumption was that Yugoslavia should remain in some sense one entity. The last attempt to achieve this was the EC's Carrington–van den Broek initiative of October 1991, which envisaged some kind of continuing loose association. But the corollary was not pursued vigorously: namely, a determined attempt to persuade Slobodan Milosevic to accommodate non-Serb interests in the late 1980s and Franjo Tudjman to accommodate non-Croat interests in 1990–1. Short of that, Yugoslavia could not survive. Given the asymmetry, support for an integral Yugoslavia, as insisted upon by the leaders of both superpowers until the fall of Mikhail Gorbachev as president of the Soviet Union, was bound to be read as favouring Serbia. When the Bosnian war broke out, however, the underlying political assumption all at once changed. One state entity hitherto considered inviolable – Yugoslavia – was abandoned, while another, hitherto non-existent – Bosnia – was now said to be inviolable. But the volte-face was not followed up consistently. Croat and Serb forces in Bosnia were abruptly treated as aggressors, and economic sanctions were imposed on the rump Federal Republic of Yugoslavia as a result. But the arms embargo on the whole of former Yugoslavia, inherited from the previous dispensation, was retained. Within the borders of the new state, differing interpretations of international law would have permitted either no military intervention or intervention on the side of the Bosnian government with its consent. In the event, troops were sent in under Chapter VII as 'impartial' humanitarians. This reading of the situation did not coincide with those of any of the main conflict parties. The ostensible humanitarian brief was viewed as covert assistance to the Bosnian government by one side and as a shameful abrogation of international responsibility to a formally recognized authority by the other. From the latter perspective, UNPROFOR II was no more than yet another example of international evasion in the face of aggression and inhumanity, an excuse for not confronting political and ethical priorities properly. In other words, humanitarianism was deeply politicized from the start. In particular, we have seen how, with or without a military presence, international humanitarian intervention by the ICRC, UN agencies and NGOs was (a) perceived as politically compromised by those whose political and military aims ran counter to the agencies' humanitarian principles and (b) used as a political pawn by all parties to the conflict in pursuit of their political purposes. In our view, such problems are unavoidable. They are in one way or another characteristic of all humanitarian intervention in conflicts of this kind.

3.2 Humanitarianism and the military

The international community in the form of the UN Security Council has been widely criticized for using the wrong instrument for the wrong purpose. This was not, it is said, a task for non-forcible military intervention, but for forcible military intervention. We have noted that this debate is complex: it seems that no political persuasion is internally consistent in advocating either non-use of military force or forcible humanitarian intervention. This includes cold war 'doves' and 'hawks', many of whom changed sides on this issue, as well as the humanitarian community itself, some of whose members advocated struggling through with aid provision without armed escort, others favoured forcible protection, and yet others (perhaps at first a majority, but now less numerous) non-forcible military intervention. We shall not carry this debate further here. Our main goal in this case-study has been to evaluate the option that in the event was chosen – namely, option (c), non-forcible military humanitarian intervention, or 'peacekeeping'.

Some use of military force, such as that which more or less succeeded in keeping Sarajevo airport open, was generally welcomed. In addition, both ICRC and UNHCR were at first prepared to countenance armed escort. It seems that the experience has led both to be more chary. At the 31 August 1993 International Conference for the Protection of War Victims in Geneva, the UN High Commissioner for Refugees said:

> My colleagues and I find it increasingly hard to accept that humanitarian concern today requires the protection of armour, bullet-proof vests and helmets. Even with these precautions, humanitarian staff continue to lose their lives in deliberate, I repeat, deliberate attacks. This is a sad illustration of the appalling state of affairs which this conference must urgently address. Let me solemnly state here that UNHCR and other humanitarian organizations cannot be expected indefinitely to operate in an environment that is not only hostile but blatantly vicious. What this viciousness amounts to . . . is the politicization of humanitarianism. On the one hand, humanitarian endeavours must not contribute to delaying, or indeed, replacing, political negotiations. On the other, they must not be used as an instrument for the pursuit of political or military goals. (Sadako Ogata, quoted in Sandoz, 1993, 31–2)

Undoubtedly, association with UNPROFOR – itself connected with the geopolitics of the Security Council and the military threat from NATO – makes it much harder for humanitarian agencies to keep humanitarian concerns separate from political interests. But we have seen that humanitarianism is unavoidably politicized anyway – witness the deaths of humanitarian aid providers before UNPROFOR II became operative. The UN High Commissioner is being unrealistic in saying that humanitarian endeavours 'must not' be used as politico-military instruments. In this kind of conflict they inevitably will be. The question as to whether, faced with politicization, UNHCR and other humanitarian organizations should pull out is highly controversial, as we will see in the next case-study. Whether, overall, working with UNPROFOR widened or narrowed the 'humanitarian space' or 'islands of humanity' within which victims terrorized by the war could be given assistance is difficult to say, as is evaluation of the idea that special purely humanitarian military units should be created for the purpose, dedicated only to humanitarian support and designated accordingly – what Thomas Weiss has christened 'HUMPROFOR' (1994c).

We conclude by citing as an example of what humanitarian agencies of all kinds managed to do in the most demanding of conditions the achievement of ICRC between January and mid-August 1993 in delivering 30,000 tonnes of assistance per month to 600,000 people, bringing medical supplies to 200 hospitals, visiting 15,000 detainees, supervising the release of 3,000 of them, collecting and distributing 1.5 million Red Cross messages, and reuniting 600 members of separated families. This was done by 214 expatriate and 762 local employees (Sandoz, 1993, 17–18). The cost in lives of the peacekeepers up to September 1994 was 112 for the whole of UNPROFOR (UNPROFOR Fact Sheet, September 1994). The total amount of relief delivered by all humanitarian interveners is impossible to calculate. Setting aside wider questions about the political and military decisions made, this in itself is an inspiring achievement, and, in our view, represents the best endeavours by the international community to maintain civilized, humane standards even in the midst of a hell in which they are routinely violated, despised and ignored. The fact that three times as many local as expatriate employees were involved in carrying out ICRC's work also puts humanitarian intervention in its proper place – it is not a substitute for indigenous efforts, but a necessary supplement in times of desperation.

This chapter was completed in March 1995. In May the vulnerability of UNPROFOR was underlined when large numbers of peacekeepers were taken hostage by the Bosnian Serbs in response to UN authorized air strikes on Serb positions near Sarajevo. This graphically demonstrated how up to that point, given existing troop dispositions and capabilities, UNPROFOR was operationally an option (c), non-forcible, peacekeeping mission. More tragic proof of this came with the subsequent fall of the 'safe areas' of Srebrenica and Zepa and the carrying off of defenders to an unknown fate under the noses of UNPROFOR troops.

Three major changes over the summer of 1995 prepared the way for a decisive shift to option (a), forcible intervention. These were (i) a change in the balance of power between the conflict parties on the ground following the Croat seizure of Serb-populated Krajina and the Bosnian government/Croat advance in Bosnia while Milosevic of Serbia-Montenegro continued to hold back; (ii) the increasing determination of the US government in the wake of the London conference to force through a peace settlement, with the support of European NATO allies and the continuing acquiescence of Russia; and (iii) an operational reconfiguration of UNPROFOR, including the pulling back of vulnerable contingents and the deployment of a more heavily armed Rapid Reaction Force configured for combat. With the initiation of 'Operation Deliberate Force' on 30 August 1995, a new phase of international intervention in Bosnia began.

Suggested reading

It is difficult to suggest reading for such a rapidly developing situation. But Ramet, 1992/1984, offers a reliable account of the political background, while Glenny, 1992; Woodward, 1994; and Zametica, 1992, chart the transition to open war. The horrors of the Bosnian conflict are graphically portrayed in Gutman, 1993, while Rieff, 1995, launches a savage indictment of the failure of the international community to respond. Steinberg, 1993, gives a useful analysis of collective intervention during the critical first two years.

7
Humanitarian Intervention in Somalia

1 The challenge

In our typology, however great the differences between the Bosnian and Somali conflicts, both are international-social conflicts. This is the key to understanding why there was so much suffering, how the international community was drawn to intervene, and the difficulties it faced when it did so. Whereas Bosnia through to the end of 1994 is an example of the problems that can be associated with option (c), non-forcible military intervention, Somalia has primarily been an example of the problems that can be associated with option (a), forcible military intervention, and the option of not intervening militarily at all (option d/e). We will use the four-part structural analysis of ISCs offered in chapter 3 as the framework for a description of the background to the conflict (Lewis, 1993; Makinda, 1993a,b).

1.1 Social heterogeneity

The Somali conflict is rooted in relations between social identity groups, in this case not ethnic, linguistic or religious, because nearly all Somalis are ethnically and (except for one major distinct dialect) linguistically homogeneous, and nearly all are Muslim. The basis of Somali society and the roots of the current conflict lie in the family, sub-clan and clan system. The easiest way to demonstrate this is to look at the connection between political movements during the years 1991–4 and clans (see diagram 9).

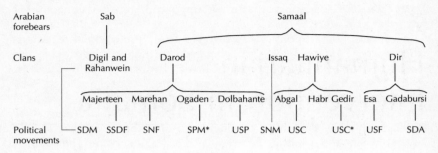

Key

SDM = Somali Democratic Movement
SSDF = Somali Salvation Democratic Front
SNF = Somali National Front
SPM = Somali Patriotic Movement (one branch led by Colonel Ahmed Omer Jess)
USP = United Somali Party
SNM = Somali National Movement
USC = United Somali Congress (Ali Mahdi)
USC = United Somali Congress (General Mohammed Farah Aidid)
USF = United Somali Front
SDA = Somali Democratic Alliance

*In August 1992 Aidid's branch of the USC and Jess's branch of the SPM joined to form the Somali National Alliance (SNA).

Diagram 9: *Political Movements and Clans in Somalia*

A few broad distinctions can be made. The Digil and Rahanwein (SDM), living in the fertile region of the Shebelle and Juba valleys, are agro-pastoralists, descended from a different mythical ancestor and somewhat looked down on by the other mainly nomadic cattle-rearing clans. Dependent on agriculture, they were the main victims of the conflict, plundered and terrorized by their more bellicose neighbours, silent gaunt figures who haunted television screens in the West in the summer of 1992. They speak a dialect which is not intelligible to the other clans. The Issaq (SNM) of the north-west (former British Somali Protectorate), who initiated the fall of Siad Barre in 1988 and were the main targets of his subsequent vengeance, declared themselves an independent Somaliland in May 1991, as yet not internationally recognized. They have a reasonably settled government and working infrastructure, which has so far withstood the worst ravages of the conflict, led by a former Prime Minister. But minority groups in the region oppose an independent Somaliland. In the north-east the Majerteen (SSDF) run another reasonably semi-independent enclave, but have not pressed for independence because other Darod live further south around Kismayu. The Majerteen were somewhat left out when, under Siad Barre, the other

Darod clans formed a platform for his support and received concomitant rewards.

In general, Somali politics has reverted to its pre-colonial traditions whereby loose, *ad hoc* family, sub-clan and clan alliances were made and broken as interest and opportunity arose. In an essentially nomadic society, there has been no tradition of kingship or central authority. The nineteenth-century explorer Richard Burton described the Somalis as 'a fierce and turbulent race of republicans'. Decentralized decisions were made at all-male assemblies of elders. The backbone of identity and interest in Somalia is lineage and family tree. To understand the conflict, and to know how best to intervene in it for humanitarian ends, it is necessary to understand these social roots. However political power is manipulated and abused, to be effective, it ultimately has to draw on the mobilizing strength of family and clan loyalty.

1.2 Political weakness of the state

From the time of independence from Italy in 1960, Somalia has been a prime example of one of Robert Jackson's (1990) 'quasi-states'. To begin with, a European-trained elite turned its back on clan politics, and attempted to construct the 'positive' elements of inner sovereignty to go with the juridical status of 'negative' sovereignty conferred by international society. Somalis referred to 'ex-clans'. When Siad Barre initiated his long, disastrous dictatorship in 1969, he courted the Soviet Union, and tried to construct a socialist state on this foundation. Somalis were induced to call each other 'challe' – comrade – and a concerted assault was mounted on nepotist clan politics. This weakened the traditional authority of clan elders, but failed to replace it with an effective substitute. As his grip weakened, particularly after the catastrophic 1977–8 war with Ethiopia, Siad Barre himself came to depend on an increasingly narrow base of clan support within the Darod from his own Marehan, as well as from the Ogadeni (who were powerful in the army) and the Dolbahante, generally referred to as MOD. His son-in-law ran the security services. Government became predatory, held together by the manipulation and partisan distribution of the spoils of office. This experience has conditioned the whole of post-Barre Somali politics. As Jonathan Stevenson puts it, 'Because Siad Barre had favored his own clan, the Marehan, so heavily and abused others so brutally, each rebel group vengefully sought to take Siad Barre's power for itself. . . . A Mogadishu businessman described the new clan dynamic well: "Siad Barre dominates the psychology of this country. All clans want what his clan had"' (1993, 142). This encapsulates the twin characteristics of international-social conflict:

that it is rooted in the social foundations of inter-communal rivalry, and that the all-embracing power vested in the modern state drives conflict parties to struggle desperately for control of sovereignty. The post-Barre Somali conflict illustrates perfectly how the effective disintegration of the state, far from damping down the struggle for control, if anything inflames it. What is often presented as a paradox turns out not to be.

Later, particularly after a car accident in 1986, Siad Barre began to lose the support even of his own clans. By the time the decisive attack led by the Hawiye-based USC was launched, Siad Barre had become little more than 'mayor of Mogadishu'. In desperation, he opened his large arsenal of modern weaponry to arm his supporters, destroyed his own capital, and, when he fled in January 1991, bequeathed to his successors a non-existent state.

1.3 Economic underdevelopment

As Samuel Makinda says with reference to the Somali conflict, 'economic misery and political problems are so intertwined that it is hard to explain one without the other' (1993a, 41). During the Barre era, unsuccessful attempts at socialist self-sufficiency were succeeded by a switch of allegiance to the West, followed in the 1980s by the normal IMF and World Bank conditions for reform: devaluation, reduction of the public sector, removal of price controls. Given the weakness of the political as well as the economic structures, this if anything accelerated the slide to ruin. Corruption and mismanagement were past redemption. In 1989 US aid was cut by Congress because of the regime's vicious attacks on the Issaq clans. By 1990 repayment of external debt took 50 per cent of exports (bananas and livestock). The collapse of the official Somali economy paralleled the collapse of the state. Black markets flourished. Oases of localized self-help coexisted with organized crime. Settled agricultural areas became a prey to brigandage. Decreasing amounts of revenue reached the government. Outside aid became one of the few sources of revenue, channelled by Siad Barre, together with money and weapons to his supporters.

1.4 External factors

Somalis had fought against Christian colonization in the Horn of Africa since the sixteenth century, resisting Ethiopians, French, British and Italians. From 1900 to 1920 it took four campaigns before British and Ethiopian troops were able to put down a fierce jihad. Eventually the state of Somalia was put together out of two of the five areas where Somalis lived – former British and Italian colonies and protectorates – leaving the others living in ex-French Djibouti, Kenya and Ethiopia. Once again, ex-colonial borders did not coincide with the distribution of peoples. On the death of Haile Selassie, Siad Barre was persuaded by Ogadeni relatives to undertake what proved to be a disastrous war in southern Ethiopia to reclaim some of those lands. The Soviet Union, earlier the regime's main supporter and supplier of arms, seeing the opportunity for a more advantageous alliance, did a volte-face and backed the new Ethiopian regime of Mengistu Haile Mariam. The United States hesitated before accepting the offer of a base at Berbera. The Somali defeat that ensued damaged Siad Barre severely, and led to a large influx of Ogadeni Somalis, which unbalanced the delicate clan relations in the area. Resentful Issaq formed the Somali National Movement (SNM). In 1988 the Ethiopian and Somali regimes, both vulnerable to internal disorder, reached an agreement to stop supporting each other's rebels, which precipitated a mass SNM entry into northern Somalia. Siad Barre's retribution was fierce, including the destruction of Hargeisa, the regional capital. The stage was set for the spread of the revolt to the Somali heartlands by the 1989 offensive launched by the Hawiye-based United Somali Congress (USC). Since Somalia has no indigenous arms industry, all the weapons flooding the country were supplied by out- siders, particularly the great powers. By 1976 Siad Barre had 250 tanks, 300 armoured personnel carriers, 52 fighters and an army that had grown from 12,000 to 30,000 (Makinda, 1993a, 43). It is somewhat ironic in view of this that one of the Security Council's first reactions when a conflict lands on its plate is to impose an arms embargo, as in former Yugoslavia in September 1991 (SCR 713), Somalia in January 1992 – one year after fighting had broken out (SCR 733) – and Liberia in November 1992 (SCR 788). For those who, until then, had been largely responsible for flooding the country with weapons, this was to shut the door after the horse had bolted. Collecting up weapons again, once they have been dispersed throughout a conflict-torn country, as was subsequently attempted (somewhat half-heartedly) in Somalia, is much harder than selling them to a fragile, discredited, conflict-prone govern- ment in the first place.

1.5 Lock-in and breakdown

In the case of Somalia, breakdown preceded the worst phases of the conflict. After the flight of Siad Barre in January 1991, the conflict continued to rage in complex patterns which we do not need to trace in detail here. The USC split into factions identified with two Hawiye sub-clans in particular, the Abgal followers of the Mogadishu businessman Ali Mahdi Mohammed, who proclaimed himself President, and the Habr Gedir followers of General Mohammed Farah Aidid, who challenged him. The political factions associated with the rival Darod clans inherited Siad Barre's aspirations for power. Fighting and religion had been the two main male occupations, in addition to cattle rearing, for the nomadic clans. During the Barre era, the country was awash with weaponry, liberally supplied by cold war patrons. Spears had been replaced by kalashnikovs, but the warrior culture remained. In the absence of any central authority, fighting became endemic in many areas, and localized war economies prevailed, with all resources regarded as means for increasing military power, and military power seen as a means for gaining control of resources. More than 100,000 weapons, left-overs from the cold war, fell into the hands of Somali teenagers, 'many of whom were addicted to *khat*, an herbal amphetamine', who roamed the streets of Mogadishu in 'technicals' – gun-mounted jeeps, so-called because their owners demanded money from relief agencies for 'technical assistance' (Stevenson, 1993, 138). This was the environment which created humanitarian disaster on such a catastrophic scale, particularly among the settled agriculturalists of the Shebelle and Juba valleys. The worst of the fighting was probably between November 1991 and March 1992, when what was left of Mogadishu was destroyed, leaving Ali Mahdi in control of the north of the city and Mohammed Farah Aidid in control of the south. Elsewhere faction and counter-faction killed, looted, slaughtered livestock, and plundered crops, as fighting raged across the lands of the inter-riverine agriculturalist clans. By mid-1992, with drought added to destitution, the calamity was at its height. An ICRC report in August 1992 estimated that 4.5 million out of a population of 6 to 7 million suffered from severe malnutrition and disease, while WFP figures suggested that 500,000 – half the population in the south-central region – had died by the end of 1992 (Stevenson, 1993, 138). Others put the number of deaths at 350,000 (Clark, 1993). In addition, there were 1 million refugees.

This was the situation which cried out for humanitarian intervention, but posed severe problems for those who responded.

2 The response

In contrast to the situation in Bosnia, the intervention in Somalia did not so much illustrate the option of non-forcible military humanitarian intervention as, first, non-military humanitarian intervention, then forcible humanitarian intervention, then a period of disarray leading swiftly to withdrawal and reversion to non-military humanitarian intervention. Does the Somali experience suggest that the non-military option and the forcible military option fare better than the experiment in non-forcible military humanitarian intervention tried in Bosnia?

In fact, the first period of non-military intervention can usefully be subdivided into two phases (see box 22). During 1991, not only was there no military humanitarian intervention, there was effectively no UN humanitarian intervention, military or non-military. In January 1992 the UN Security Council finally became involved politically. UN humanitarian agencies re-emerged. UNOSOM I was also established at this time, although it amounted to little more than 500 troops, who arrived in September and stayed barricaded in Mogadishu until the US-led Unified Task Force (UNITAF) landed on 9–10 December 1992. Thus our main interest in this period is with UN, ICRC and NGO non-military humanitarian intervention. Between December 1992 and early May 1993, mandated by SCR 794 of 3 December 1992, UNITAF provides an instance of forcible humanitarian intervention, even though, in the event, not much force had to be used. Meanwhile, UNOSOM I was expanded under its wing to contribute a continuing non-forcible 'second tier'. From 4 May 1993 UNOSOM II, authorized under SCR 814 of 26 March 1993, took over. Soon thereafter, between 5 June 1993 and 9 October 1993, it found itself plunged into the most spectacular example of collective forcible humanitarian intervention to date. The whole operation then wound down, with increasing speed, leading to final withdrawal in February–March 1995.

Box 22: Time-Chart: Humanitarian Intervention in Somalia, 1991–5

January 1991–November 1992: Non-military humanitarian intervention
(i)   1991: ICRC/SRCS, NGOs
(ii) 24 April 1992: SCR 751, UNOSOM I
      May–October 1992: Mohammed Sahnoun appointed as UNSG's special representative

December 1992–October 1993: Forcible humanitarian intervention
(i)   3 December 1992: SCR 794, UNITAF
(ii) 26 March 1993: SCR 814, UNOSOM II (took over 4 May)
      5 June–9 October 1993: war against General Aidid

October 1993–March 1995: Wind-down to withdrawal

2.1 1991: 'doing nothing' – international neglect

Here is one account of what happened in 1991:

> Despite the turmoil that ensued after the overthrow of President Siad Barre [January 1991], the United Nations continued its humanitarian efforts in Somalia, and by March 1991 was fully engaged in that country. Over the following months, the volatile security situation forced the United Nations on several occasions to temporarily withdraw its personnel from Somalia, but it continued its humanitarian activities to the fullest extent possible, in cooperation with the International Committee of the Red Cross and non-governmental organizations. The deteriorating and appalling situation in Somalia led the United Nations Secretary-General, in cooperation with the Organization of African Unity (OAU), the League of Arab States (LAS) and the Organization of the Islamic Conference (OIC), to become actively involved in the political aspects of the crisis and to press for a peaceful settlement. (United Nations, 1994, 98)

But there is another story (Clark, 1993; Stevenson, 1993; Makinda, 1993a; de Waal, 1994). Far from 'continuing with its humanitarian efforts' and being 'fully engaged' in Somalia, according to this account, the UN was conspicuous by its absence for the first year, if not effectively a year and a half, of the post-Barre conflict. There were no Security Council resolutions on Somalia in 1991, and what were to become the six relevant UN agencies, UNDP, UNICEF, UNHCR, FAO, WFP and WHO, did no more than make sporadic forays from New York, Geneva or neighbouring Nairobi. Somalia was to all intents and purposes abandoned. 'Somalia during 1991–3 was perhaps the most spectacular demonstration of the failure of the international relief system in recent years' (de Waal, 1994, 139). The great powers no longer perceived vital security interests in the area, and were preoccupied with the Gulf War and the worsening situation in Yugoslavia. The UN agencies, used to dealing with governments, judged that the situation was too dangerous for their staff, that in the chaos there were no authorities to negotiate with, and that the logistics were too complicated and the environment too volatile for their large aid programmes to be viable. UNICEF received funds from USAID early in 1991, but had no office in Mogadishu until December, keeping essential drugs in a warehouse for four months for lack of a programme while Somali-run hospitals ran out of supplies (de Waal, 1994, 148). WFP, working through CARE-International, kept 12,000 tonnes of free, monetized food in store in Mogadishu port from September, while trying to draw up a comprehensive distribution plan. When fighting broke out on 17 November 1991, 8,000 tonnes was still there (de Waal, 1994, 148). UNDP, the traditional co-ordinator of UN relief and development agencies, left $68 million unused for nine months for lack of a signature from a non-existent government (Clark, 1993, 220). 'The United Nations in terms of its life after the cold war is a shambles. If you look at Somalia, what you see is an ill-equipped, ill-informed and uncoordinated response' (Nicholas Hinton, Director of Save the Children Fund/UK, *Independent*, 8 August 1992, quoted in Clark, 1993, 238). In 1992, the new Department of Humanitarian Affairs (DHA) was no more successful than UNICEF or UNDP in co-ordinating efforts.

Nor were the regional organizations 'actively involved with the political aspects of the crisis'. Beyond taking in refugees (itself a major contribution), neighbouring countries were seen to do little, while, in Jeffrey Clark's view, the OAU (in marked contrast to its later activism in Rwanda) did nothing.

> More than two years into the turmoil, the OAU has yet to make a significant statement to the international community about human needs, national reconciliation processes, or peacekeeping in Somalia. The OAU Secretary-General has not visited Somalia; the organization has dispatched no delegation of respected African elders to attempt a dialogue between conflicting factions; it has launched no concerted campaign to place or keep Somalia on the Security Council agenda. (1993, 216)

This dereliction of duty is considered highly significant by those who believe that '[h]ad the OAU, the Arab League and the Organization of the Islamic Conference made serious efforts to negotiate peace in early 1991, the tragedy could probably have been averted' (Makinda, 1993a, 32).

All this is in marked contrast to the remarkable heroism and devotion seen in local Somali 'coping strategies', in the ICRC–Somali Red Crescent Society (SRCS) programme, and among the handful of NGOs which stayed on through 1991 – Médecins Sans Frontières (MSF), Save the Children Fund/UK (SCF), Comitate Internazionale per lo Sviluppo dei Popoli, SOS-Kinderdorf, International Medical Corps, World Concern and ACCORD (de Waal, 1994, 150–1). In 1992 SCF distributed more food aid than UNICEF. ICRC/SRCS succeeded in delivering 180,000 tonnes of food and supplies and sustaining 1.5 million people through more than 900 kitchens (de Waal, 1994, 146). In contrast to the bureaucratic, logistical UN approach, dependent on contacts with governments and elaborate comprehensive distribution plans, ICRC/SRCS improvised, worked through local Somali networks, took risks (an ICRC delegate and 14 local staff were killed in December 1991), employed local armed guards for convoys and storage houses (for the first time in ICRC history), unloaded supplies via small boats along the coast when Mogadishu port was closed, and, in general, followed the principle that whatever it took, the needs of those who were suffering must be met.

No doubt the judgements made will continue to be controversial. In the view of Adam Roberts, for example, by the summer and autumn of 1992 'humanitarian workers, having to pay ransom to gunmen if they were to carry out their tasks, had themselves become part of the problem, and were involuntarily assisting the war economy' (1993a, 439). The 'humanitarian workers' deny this. Either way, here is an example of what happens when there is no outside military involvement, either forcible (option (a)) or non-forcible (option (c)). Clearly, the *ad hoc* security arrangements with local guards were a regrettable necessity if supplies were to get through. We consider below what proportion of the aid was consequently siphoned off to sustain the armed militia and the insatiable ambitions of the war-lords. But, whatever view is taken of this, the splendid achievement of ICRC, SRCS and the NGOs remains.

2.2 1992: Sahnoun's way

The political involvement of the UN was stepped up in January 1992 when James Jonah, Under-Secretary-General for Political Affairs, was sent to Mogadishu to arrange a cease-fire. General Aidid refused to co-operate, and was from then on cast as the villain of the piece. His rival, Ali Mahdi, worked to get the UN involved, because, being somewhat weaker militarily than the USC/SNA, he thought that this would be to his advantage. For the same reason, General Aidid saw the UN as a threat. We will not follow the political story through to the 3 March cease-fire except to note that in the non-UN account of events James Jonah appears as an outsider who did not understand the situation:

> James Jonah, the first UN troubleshooter, was so flabbergasted by the moral and physical putrefaction of Somalia, and so befuddled by its labyrinthine clan politics, that he privately dismissed Somalia as a problem child too filthy, bizarre and suicidal to deal with. He did most of his peace brokering in New York and Addis Ababa, and he left Mogadishu after only a few sheltered days. (Stevenson, 1993, 144)

Strong criticism has been levelled that the 3 March 1992 cease-fire was not followed up immediately with sufficient vigour (Clark, 1993). There were six Security Council resolutions on Somalia in 1992, beginning with the imposition of an arms embargo on 23 January, by SCR 733, which also requested the Secretary-General to increase humanitarian assistance to those in need. A belated 90-day Plan of Action for Emergency Assistance to Somalia followed, widely judged to have been a failure. In response to the security situation, SCR 751 of 24 April 1992 agreed to monitor the cease-fire between Ali Mahdi and Mohammed Aidid in

Mogadishu with 50 unarmed observers, and in principle to establish a security force, the United Nations Operation in Somalia (UNOSOM). The United States blocked plans for a more ambitious force.

This was the situation when Mohammed Sahnoun, an Algerian diplomat and former protégé of Boutros Boutros-Ghali, was appointed special representative for Somalia on 28 April. He arrived in the country on 1 May. In the rapidly expanding critical literature on the conflict, Mohammed Sahnoun appears as the major exponent of non-forcible humanitarian intervention. In Jonathan Stevenson's account, the period May–October 1992 is referred to as 'Sahnoun's way' (1993, 144–54). In marked contrast to James Jonah, with whom, it seems, he came to be at loggerheads, Mohammed Sahnoun immediately immersed himself vigorously in local Somali politics. He established contacts with clan elders as well as war-lords, sustained energetic and indefatigable contact with all major players, particularly General Aidid (with whom he was accused of being too preoccupied), and accepted as axiomatic that everything had to be done by negotiation with consent, in accordance with Somali custom. The key to his strategy, according to Stevenson, was his understanding that 'clans in Somalia take precedence over both nationhood and religion as sources of allegiance'. He saw that the clan system, however complex and shifting, diluted power, and must form the basis for enduring peace. The aim was therefore 'to reverse Siad Barre's corruption of Somali tradition, so that some kind of equilibrium can prevail' (Stevenson, 1993, 150). He also understood traditional Somali fears of military occupation. Mohammed Sahnoun combined finesse with flamboyance, castigating the UN for 'arriving a year and a half too late', and outspokenly criticizing over-bureaucratized, inflexible and unco-ordinated UN practices, and the inadequately trained, inadequately skilled personnel who administered them. In the eyes of many, such frank criticism from a prominent UN representative contrasted refreshingly with the routinely bland self-congratulatory reports presented to the Security Council by the Secretary-General. It irritated a number within the New York establishment, however, who felt that they were doing all that could be done in the chaotic, vicious environment of the Somali conflict, and saw Mohammed Sahnoun as lacking balance and experience and having only a partial view of the overall situation. In Somalia, though, he seems to have won general respect as independent-minded and effective, someone who got things done and did not share the somewhat 'colonial' attitudes of many top UN bureaucrats, who jetted in and out of the country and showed scant understanding of, or respect for, Somali traditions. For Mark Stirling, UNICEF's representative in Somalia, for example, 'with Ambassador Sahnoun there was confidence in the UN's political leadership' (Stevenson, 1993, 151). Gradually, he came to represent a more locally attractive image of the UN, and co-operation spread. In July, prompted by Mohammed Sahnoun, the UN Secretary-General, in a famous outburst, castigated the relative neglect of Somalia by the major powers by calling the conflict in former Yugoslavia a 'rich man's war'. Certainly there was some response, in the form of a large US airlift of basic supplies in August. Meanwhile, by August 12, General Aidid had been cajoled into accepting 500 UNOSOM troops – although in the event, on their arrival in September, they did little more than hole up in their quarters in Mogadishu, inadequately equipped to defend even themselves. On 28 August, by SCR 775 (supplemented by a further decision on 8 September), the Secretary-General's request for 3,000 more troops was finally approved, which would have brought UNOSOM strength up to 4,219, including the original 500 and 719 for logistic units. On 10–12 September, Jan Eliasson, UN Under-Secretary-General for Humanitarian Affairs, led an inter-agency mission to Somalia, and launched a new 100-day Action Programme for Accelerated Humanitarian Assistance, which was still under way when the US-led Unified Task Force (UNITAF) arrived in December.

At this point, however, 'Sahnoun's way' was abruptly terminated. In August, American Senator Kassebaum made a much publicized visit to the Kenya–Somalia border. Belated media attention to Somalia in the wake of the US airlift suddenly confronted the Western publics with the extent of the humanitarian catastrophe, then at its peak. Television pictures told their own graphic story. This was a disaster which eclipsed even the 1984–5 Ethiopian famine. The media message was one of 'helpless starving victims', 'cruel gunmen and warlords', and 'brave and compassionate foreign aid workers' unable to cope without outside military support (de Waal, 1994, 153). Pressure mounted rapidly to 'do something' dramatic. Mohammed Sahnoun's patient, consensual, localized approach seemed inadequate, or was just not understood. Senior UN officials, including the Secretary-General, had concluded that the moment had come for forcible action, as presaged earlier in the year in the *Agenda for Peace*. Key personnel within the wing of the humanitarian community closest to the US government, such as Philip Johnstone, President of CARE–US, who had been seconded to the UN as co-ordinator of the 100-day plan, also pressed for forcible intervention. CARE–US was spending perhaps $100,000 a month on hiring Somali armed bodyguards. By this time, the US government had itself determined that decisive action must be taken, as prefigured in the August airlift. So it was that, in the middle of Mohammed Sahnoun's complex negotiations to persuade faction leaders to accept the expanded UNOSOM numbers decided in SCR 775 of 28 August, the atmosphere in New York changed abruptly, and a peremptory announcement was made that the 3,000 troops would be sent anyway, whatever local Somali war-lords said. At a stroke, this destroyed Mohammed Sahnoun's work: 'Aidid threatened to send the soldiers home in body bags, and lost interest in keeping the port open and safeguarding relief operations. The situation immediately deteriorated: The Pakistanis [in UNOSOM I] were attacked at the airport, a food ship was shelled and turned away, and UN officials were mugged in Kismayu' (Stevenson, 1993, 147–8). In late October, Mohammed Sahnoun sent a letter of resignation to the UN Secretary-General offering to become a special envoy answerable only to the Secretary-General so as to side-step the UN bureaucracy. But Boutros Boutros-Ghali by now favoured the forcible approach, and simply accepted the resignation.

This brought to an end an experiment in what was, given the marginality of UNOSOM I up to that point, effectively non-military humanitarian intervention. In the eyes of some informed commentators, the experiment of co-ordinating humanitarian relief through a powerful personal representative of the UN Secretary-General to whom military, political and humanitarian section heads reported, rather than, as was normal, through one of the main UN line agencies, proved unmanageable in Somalia: 'Neither the Secretary-General nor his staff was capable – temperamentally, intellectually, or organizationally – of centrally supporting extended field operations in Somalia' (Natsios, 1995, 76). In the view of others, however, compared with the forcible humanitarian intervention which followed, there was no doubt which was to be preferred:

> The UN's strongest suit is its ability to slog relentlessly through the political underbrush of troubled countries with gritty diplomacy, without taking sides or parcelling out favors, clearing the path to political self-sufficiency. 'Wherever there's oppression or a violation of human rights', Sahnoun has said, 'the Secretary-General must take the initiative of sending wise men very quickly.' And they must improvise, inventively using the tools they find in place. In this case, the UN found it easier to arm the Americans with a Security Council resolution and let them pave a way for the UN as it had done in the Persian Gulf. In the future, the UN will need to discard its white-collar attitude toward crises. Workmanlike programs like Sahnoun's must be the rule, not the exception. (Stevenson, 1993, 154)

2.3 3 December 1992–4 May 1993: the Unified Task Force (UNITAF) and 'Operation Restore Hope'

Why, after systematic neglect and on occasion obstruction in the Security Council (such as reducing the original proposed scale of UNOSOM I), did the US leadership suddenly swing to the opposite extreme in a frenzy of activity from late July 1992? The story is too complicated to be traced

fully here. Official US relief agencies, notably the Humanitarian Assistance Bureau of the Agency for International Development (AID), had
long been lobbying for more active involvement. In testimony before the
House Select Committee on Hunger on 30 January 1992, AID's humanitarian chief, Andrew Natsios, had called the Somali famine 'the greatest
humanitarian emergency in the world' (Clark, 1993, 212). But the State
Department was preoccupied with Iraq and Bosnia, and long-standing
US–UN antagonisms made American leaders chary of committing themselves to collective interventions which in their view were likely to be
incompetently managed, perhaps not in US interests, yet dependent upon
US resources. Senator Kassebaum's visit and the accompanying intensified media attention pushed the issue up the presidential list of priorities,
however, aided by an imminent Republican Party Convention. President
Bush was said to be keen to end his term in office in spectacular style. As
noted above, Philip Johnstone of CARE–US was pressing for forcible
intervention. Mohammed Sahnoun's replacement as UN envoy, Ismat
Kittani, a loyal UN bureaucrat, argued the same way – possibly also
because, as an Iraqi Kurd, he looked back favourably to the precedent of
'Operation Provide Comfort' in Iraq. In two key letters to the Security
Council, on 24 November and 29 November, the Secretary-General
presented the case for a humanitarian use of force. Some 3,000 were
dying every day, and 2 million were threatened with starvation. Yet
warehouses were stacked with supplies. International relief efforts were
subjected to extortion, blackmail and robbery. Up to 80 per cent of the
aid was being lost to the warring factions. Personnel and equipment were
attacked. Passage for relief was obstructed. Whole areas were inaccessible. There were no legitimate authorities to negotiate with. Mogadishu
port was closed. UN humanitarian agencies and NGOs would be unable
to provide the assistance needed without such support. On 25 November, acting US Secretary of State Lawrence Eagleburger indicated that,
should the Security Council decide to authorize such an operation, the
United States would be prepared to take the lead in organizing and
commanding it. Comparing the situation in Somalia with that in Bosnia,
he said:

> the fact of the matter is that a thousand people are starving to death every
> day, and that is not going to get better if we don't do something about it,
> and it is in an area where we can affect events. There are other parts of the
> world where things are equally tragic, but where the cost of trying to change
> things would be monumental. In my view, Bosnia is one of those.
> (Eagleburger, 6 December 1992, quoted in Roberts, 1993a, 442)

In other words, Somalia was considered to be a relatively easy prospect
militarily.

The Secretary-General offered five options to the Security Council: to intensify efforts to deploy UNOSOM I as originally intended (in our terminology, non-forcible military humanitarian intervention); to abandon the idea of using military personnel to protect relief activities and leave humanitarian agencies to make the best arrangements they could with faction and clan leaders (what had in fact been happening up to that point – in our terminology, non-military humanitarian intervention); and three versions of the forcible humanitarian intervention alternative: (i) UNOSOM to make a show of force only in Mogadishu, (ii) a country-wide undertaking run by an authorized group of member states, (iii) a country-wide undertaking carried out under UN command and control. The Secretary-General favoured the forcible option, and, within that, alternative (ii), because the UN did not currently have the capability to command and control an enforcement operation on the required scale.

On 3 December 1992, the Security Council unanimously adopted SCR 794, which, in operative paragraph 10, 'acting under Chapter VII of the Charter of the United Nations, authorises the Secretary-General and member states to implement the offer to use all necessary means to establish as soon as possible a secure environment for humanitarian relief operations in Somalia'. This is the enforcement language of SCR 678 of November 1990, which authorized 'Operation Desert Storm' in Kuwait. In contrast to 'Sahnoun's way', there is now no suggestion of consent – although a number of African states insisted that this was only because, 'unprecedentedly', there was no government in Somalia. It is a moot point in traditional terminology whether, in the absence of a government to give or withhold consent, such action counts as 'intervention'. Although there is one mention of a 'threat to international peace and security' in SCR 794, this contrasts with 18 mentions of the word 'humanitarian' (Roberts, 1993a, 440). The reference to international peace and security comes in the preamble: 'the magnitude of the human tragedy caused by the conflict in Somalia, further exacerbated by the obstacles being created to the distribution of humanitarian assistance, constitutes a threat to international peace and security'. The threat to international peace and security does not come from cross-border disturbance, but only from the fact of the humanitarian crisis within Somalia itself. UN Charter provisions were being stretched to the limit to accommodate legitimate collective forcible humanitarian intervention within a rubric which had not envisaged it.

UNITAF, made up predominantly of US troops and under US command, but with contingents from 23 other countries, prominent among which were France and Belgium, eventually reached a force strength of 37,000, and covered some 40 per cent of Somali territory, concentrated in nine locations. On 10 December the US marines made a dramatic night landing on flood-lit beaches near Mogadishu, filmed by American TV crews. The most spectacular experiment in collective forcible humanitarian intervention to date had begun. UNITAF's main task was to establish a secure environment for urgent humanitarian assistance. In the theoretical division of labour, a reinforced UNOSOM I, in liaison with UNITAF, was to continue to underpin the UN's political and humanitarian initiatives until, under a renegotiated mandate, a future UNOSOM II would replace them both.

At this point, two overlapping controversies must be addressed. The first concerns what UNITAF achieved for humanitarian security by forcible means during its five-month period of responsibility by comparison with what had been achieved by non-forcible means. This requires a comparison 'backwards' with the previous two years. The second is the question of whether UNITAF should in addition have disarmed the Somali militia, as many, if not most, Somalis seem to have wanted, and who was to blame for the subsequent débâcle between June and October 1993. This requires a comparison 'forwards' with the following months when UNOSOM II took over. The first controversy is essentially one between many, if not most, within the NGO humanitarian relief community and official UN and US versions of what happened. The second is between UN and US versions of events. For the sake of clarity, we will defer consideration of the second controversy until the next section.

Was UNITAF successful in its main mission task? In other words, did it rescue a desperate situation in which non-forcible international humanitarian intervention had manifestly failed and create a secure environment in which large numbers of Somali lives were saved? This is certainly the 'official' version, as relayed to the American people by the US President and by the UN Secretary-General in his congratulatory report to the Security Council on 26 January 1993. Many within the relief communities, originally sceptical, were convinced that forcible intervention was working by early 1993. Adam Roberts, writing before the disasters of June and July and also sceptical, was prepared to concede that up to February 1993 'countless lives have been saved' (1993a, 439). UNITAF undoubtedly succeeded in improving food distribution in the areas it controlled and, at any rate initially, in breaking the extortion rackets through which aid had hitherto been funnelled into keeping the armed militias and 'technical' battle-wagons going.

There is another version of events, however. It builds on the arguments we looked at earlier concerning UN failure and ICRC and NGO relative success in 1991 and 1992, and about the promise shown by Mohammed Sahnoun's approach between May and October 1992. The central claim is that UNITAF was both unnecessary and ineffective. It was unnecessary, because the most virulent phase of the conflict-induced famine and (to a lesser extent) threat of disease had passed by September 1993. Most of the main elements in the UN Secretary-General's letter of 24 November 1992 to the Security Council, which triggered the decision in favour of forcible intervention, are seen as 'falsehoods' (de Waal, 1994, 152–3). The idea that 80 per cent of aid was being looted, the upper limit given by Ismat Kittani and widely propagated through the media, is challenged. The ICRC estimate was 20 per cent. The latter is conceded to have been too low – among other things, imaginary villages were invented by Somalis who hoped to pocket the subsequent aid – but best local estimates suggest perhaps up to 50 per cent, a figure comparable to the amount of aid getting through to those in need, rather than the fighting factions, in Bosnia. The important fact is that 'access to food . . . improved dramatically in the first nine months of 1992' (de Waal, 1994, 147). The strategy of 'flooding the country with food' had already paid off. Food prices were stabilizing, and seed distribution had ensured a partial return to normal harvests in the Shebelle valley. The UN Secretary-General's figure of 2 million facing starvation is seen as grossly inaccurate, therefore. For example, in Baidoa, widely regarded as the epicentre of the famine, private relief groups were already winning the battle: weekly deaths shrank from 1,780 on 6 September to 335 by 1 November (Stevenson, 1993, 152). If anything, they rose again in December. The danger now, in fact, was not so much famine as disease. Nor was Mogadishu port inaccessible, as the Secretary-General claimed. Throughout 1991 and 1992 the ICRC had succeeded in bringing in supplies. Finally, the claim that there was no one to negotiate with in Somalia was seen to reflect ignorance of how Somali politics worked. Mohammed Sahnoun had succeeded in facilitating improvements in accessibility and aid delivery precisely as a result of his negotiations with both clan and militia leaders.

UNITAF was also, according to this account, ineffective. Although in the Weinberger–Powell tradition, overwhelming force initially carried all before it, UNITAF soon became embroiled in local Somali politics, coming to be seen as one more actor on the political stage well before the official hand-over to UNOSOM II in May 1993. The original unanimity in accepting UNITAF was the result of each faction hoping to use the invasion to its own advantage. Once these hopes were disappointed (as they were bound to be, since 'neutrality' was interpreted as a refusal to comply), support quickly changed to antagonism – an inevitable result, as anyone familiar with Somali attitudes to an intrusion by foreign troops would know. According to some estimates, perhaps 200 civilians were killed during the first three months (African Rights, 1993). When

Boutros Boutros-Ghali visited Mogadishu in January 1993, he was pelted with stones and rotten fruit. Many Somalis believed General Aidid's charge that, as Egyptian foreign minister, he had had designs on Somali lands. Above all, UNITAF was no longer seen to be impartial. In February, the key town of Kismayu, fought over so bitterly in 1991 and 1992 by the pro-Barre forces of General 'Morgan' and General Aidid's ally, Omer Jess, was the scene of a characteristic débâcle in which, when the supporters of Jess had agreed to disarmament by UNITAF, the forces of Morgan took the opportunity to seize control, under the noses of US and Belgian troops. UNITAF operated in only 40 per cent of the country, which led to increased insecurity in the rest. The complex security arrangements struck by the aid agencies were disrupted as US forces disarmed NGO-paid Somali guards but failed to disarm the warring militias generally: 'During the first three months of foreign troop occupation, three expatriate aid workers were killed, compared to only two during the preceding two years' (Stevenson, 1993, 139). As the US and UN became increasingly unpopular, this reflected back on the aid workers, who came to be identified with them. Finally, it is argued, the UN–US invasion came at exactly the wrong moment for economic recovery prospects. Although little had been planted in the Juba valley and Bay region, farmers in the Shebelle valley had produced a surplus from the short rains. Having 'flooded the country with food' during the worst of the famine, now was the moment to reduce aid so that local prices, now nearly normal in Mogadishu, could sustain a profitable return for normal farming. Instead, the indiscriminate further flood of relief food that accompanied UNITAF filled the shops of Mogadishu and impressed visitors, but drove cereal prices down and removed the profitability from farming. This had the further knock-on effect of undermining seasonal employment for migrant Bay region labourers in the farming regions. The beginnings of recovery were replaced by renewed aid dependency (de Waal, 1994, 157).

2.4 May 1993–March 1995: UNOSOM II

The US government had been determined not to be drawn into a full-scale operation of disarming the militias and impounding heavy weapons, as the UN Secretary-General and probably most war-weary Somalis wanted. Nor did the US want to become responsible for the intricacies of political settlement and long-term reconstruction. In response to those who said that UNITAF thus had no clear mission, Defense Secretary Dick Cheney replied: 'I would take strong exception to that notion. The mission is very clear indeed. It is a humanitarian mission' (4 December 1992, quoted in Roberts 1993a, 441). Despite pressure from the UN, the new US President, Bill Clinton, was determined to hand over as soon as possible to the United Nations.

The result was the most ambitious collective humanitarian and rehabilitation enforcement enterprise so far mounted by the UN. On 3 March 1993, the UN Secretary-General, in fulfilment of plans for 'peace enforcement' first aired in his *Agenda for Peace* a few months before, submitted a report to the Security Council recommending powers under Chapter VII of the UN Charter going beyond those mandated for UNITAF. Unlike UNITAF, UNOSOM II's writ would cover the whole of Somalia. It would have an extraordinarily comprehensive brief, which in the eyes of some amounted to a revived international trusteeship for Somalia as in 1950–60. UNOSOM's mandate was to complete the task of restoration of peace, stability, law and order; provide assistance to the Somalis in rebuilding economic, social and political life, re-establishing the country's institutional structure, achieving national reconciliation and recreating a Somali state based on democratic governance; and rehabilitating the country's economy and infrastructure. With hindsight, this programme is full of hubris. Nevertheless, promising progress was made (a) on economic rehabilitation at a UN Conference on Humanitarian Assistance to Somalia attended by 190 Somali representatives on 11–13 March and (b) on political settlement at a series of meetings in Cairo, Nairobi and Addis Ababa, culminating in a Conference on National Reconciliation and agreement among the 15 factions on the formation of a transitional National Council on 19 March 1993. Finally, on 26 March, by SCR 814, UNOSOM II was authorized to take over from UNITAF with a force level of 20,000, together with 8,000 logistical support and 2,800 civilian personnel, backed up by a US tactical quick reaction force. Twenty-nine countries initially contributed forces. Remaining US troops would for the first time (apart from those with UNPROFOR III in Macedonia) serve under UN command, although overall leadership of UNOSOM II was assumed by the American retired admiral Jonathan Howe, who replaced Ismat Kittani as special representative on 9 March.

The official hand-over from UNITAF to UNOSOM II took place on 4 May. A month later disaster struck, the four-month period of 'humanitarian war' between UNOSOM II and General Aidid beginning with what became known as the '5 June 1993 incident'. UNOSOM's determination to disarm the militias aroused fears of differential advantage and loss of power. On 5 June UN Pakistani troops were ambushed in southern Mogadishu as some of them were inspecting an arms depot belonging to General Aidid's USC/SNA and others were helping unload food at a feeding station. Twenty-five UN soldiers were killed, 10 were missing, and 54 were wounded. The victims' bodies were mutilated. Aidid's supporters said that the UN was trying to close down 'Radio Mogadishu', which had been broadcasting anti-UN messages. The UN Secretary-General reacted with emotion, on 6 June condemning the 'treacherous attack' on those who 'were on a mission of peace, reconciliation and reconstruction' by 'cowards who placed women and children in front of armed men'. This is a graphic illustration of the confusion that results from combining humanitarian with military-political action. On 6 June, SCR 837 authorized strong counter-measures, which were also approved by 11 of the Somali political movements – needless to say, opponents of Aidid. On 12 June, UNOSOM II launched its attack on USC/SNA forces in southern Mogadishu, announcing as it did so that the objective of the action was 'so that the political reconciliation, rehabilitation and disarmament process can continue to move forward'. According to some estimates, about 100 Somalis, including women and children, were killed in three nights of bombardment (Makinda, 1993a, 81). An MSF hospital was hit. Although the Security Council regretted the civilian casualties, on 18 June it put the blame on the fact that 'some Somali factions and movements' had used 'women and children as human shields to perpetrate their attacks against UNOSOM', deploring the deaths 'despite the timely measures adopted to prevent this from happening'. It was painfully evident that, because the UN itself is not party to the 1949 Geneva Conventions and 1977 Additional Protocols and has no court martial procedure for UN forces, there was no independent appeal when the humanitarian enforcers acquitted themselves of violating the *jus in bello* provisions of international humanitarian law. When General Aidid was accused of war crimes and branded an international outlaw, he accused the UNOSOM commander of the same offences. Over the next few weeks, the man-hunt for Aidid, spear-headed by US Rangers and Delta Force commandos, failed. On 3 October, in a US Rangers operation to seize key Aidid aides, two US helicopters were shot down, 18 US soldiers were killed, and 75 were wounded. The bodies were paraded and mutilated in full view of TV cameras. The effect in the United States was devastating. Senators demanded to know why young American lives were being sacrificed in an incompetently managed UN operation which had been side-tracked by the UN Secretary-General's personal vendetta against Aidid. President Clinton's response was (a) to reinforce the Quick Reaction Force with M1A1 tanks and Bradley fighting vehicles and (b) to announce that US troops would be pulled out of Somalia by 31 March 1994. There was no doubt which of these two contradictory signals conveyed the main message. Robert Oakley, former US ambassador to Somalia, who had ably overseen the political side of the UNITAF operation between December 1992 and February 1993, returned to negotiate with the erstwhile war criminal General Aidid, who was now widely admired in Somalia as a hero who had defied the foreign oppressor. On 9 October the USC/SNA declared a unilateral cessation of hostilities against UNOSOM II. One war-lord, with vastly inferior forces in what had been thought to be an 'easy' military operation, had done what Saddam Hussein with all his armies had failed to do. He had single-handedly destroyed the will to engage of the only superpower, encouraging similar defiance in Haiti. He provided the catalyst in a reversal of US policy on UN peacekeeping which may have far-reaching consequences. The fruits were immediately seen in the announcement of plans to rein back US contributions to UN peacekeeping in Presidential Decision Directive 25 of May 1994 and in the even more severe anti-UN backlash that followed the Republican triumph in the autumn congressional elections. Belgium, France and Sweden pulled out their troops from UNOSOM II by the end of 1993; Germany, Italy, Norway and Turkey did the same by March 1994. The final UNOSOM II withdrawal came in March 1995.

3 Conclusion

What went wrong? Although not directly part of our subject, we should note the dispute between those (particularly in the US) who blame the United Nations for the débâcle and those who blame the politico-military culture of the United States.

For US Republican Senator John McCain, '[t]he lesson of Somalia is simple: it is clearly not in the interest of the US to subject US decision-making on grave matters of state or the lives of American soldiers to the frequently vacillating, frequently contradictory, and frequently reckless collective impulses of the United Nations' (1994, 67). Whereas 'to Americans, peacemaking in Somalia meant feeding starving people, to the UN Secretary-General it also included warlord hunting'. After the 3 October 1993 débâcle the Senator received a letter from a distraught father: 'in his grief he asked for answers as to why his son had to die. American soldiers have always been prepared to give their lives for the safety and security of this nation; without a higher purpose for such sacrifice, their deaths would be pointless and hollow.'

Others, by contrast, attribute UNOSOM II's aggressive strategy to the United States military culture which, no matter how clearly the distinction between peacekeeping and peace enforcement is spelled out in the US Army Field Manual (100–23), cannot envisage subordination to a mission which does not rely on the Weinberger–Powell doctrine of overwhelming use of force (Mackinlay, 1994, 156). Europeans, inured to overseas garrison duty in counter-insurgency operations, to operating in semi-consensual conditions during the long process of withdrawal from empire, and to subordination to civilian command, were more accustomed to the minimum force and highly politicized peacekeeping environment. The result was a disabling tension between the US-dominated headquarters of UNOSOM, which tried to force co-operation and thought that UNOSOM's mandate allowed forcible disarming of militias, and European and Commonwealth commanders who relied on persuasion (Dobbie, 1994, 127). A comparison to this effect is made between the forcible approach of US Delta Force commander Major-General William Garrison in Mogadishu and the non-forcible approach of Australian operations officer Lieutenant-Colonel Hurley in Baidoa. The commander of the Italian contingent in Mogadishu was also reluctant to participate in US attempts to hunt down General Aidid (Mackinlay, 1994, 156). From this perspective, the use of local force against petty criminals and small gangs of bandits is quite compatible with an overall consensual peacekeeping option (c) approach, but the inability of the US Army to operate this way and the excessive, indiscriminate use of force jeopardized, rather than assisted, relief efforts. Oxfam had to evacuate Mogadishu as a result (Oxfam, 1993, cited in Mackinlay, 1994). When John Mackinlay visited Somalia in May–June 1993, he found near unanimity at battalion level that 'overwhelming use of force' did not work in these conditions, and that the success of the humanitarian enterprise depended upon fostering local co-operation. Despite US disclaimers of responsibility for overall UNOSOM II strategy, critics point out that Admiral Howe was the senior UN representative in charge, that the UNOSOM II commander, Turkish Lieutenant-General Cevik Bir, was a former NATO commander who was well known to and trusted by the US, and that US Army Major-General Thomas M. Montgomery was his deputy. The 750 US Army Rangers had a separate chain of command, over which Montgomery had a veto.

Mutual buck-passing of this kind has been as typical a response to perceived failure, as has mutual claiming of credit when things seem to have gone right. The overall conclusion from the Bosnia and Somalia case-studies taken together is that, faced with the violence, confusion and complexity of international-social conflict, the international community is only beginning to learn how best to respond. The case-studies show that none of the three options is either ethically or politically free of grave problems and dilemmas. This is also true of non-intervention, which the Bosnia example shows to be a highly problematic concept in any case. Bosnia through to the end of 1994 offers an example of an attempt at option (c). Somalia shows, first, an example of option (d/e); second, an example of option (a). The importance of such comparison, and hence of the reconceptualization which makes it possible, is that it gives the lie to those who present the issue as a simple either/or: intervention or non-intervention. Sweeping condemnations are easy to make, implying as they often do that there are clear-cut, manifestly superior alternatives. The danger here is that moods are likely to swing violently under the impulse of the most recent experience. After the 3 October set-back, which had a devastating impact in the United States, a revulsion against all involvement with United Nations missions set in, together with a general backlash against the very concept of humanitarian relief. The result was that when the Rwanda crisis erupted six months later, United States policy was to prevent vigorous, timely UN response and to instruct officials to use the phrase 'acts of genocide' rather than acknowledge that this was a genuine case of deliberately planned genocide that required energetic response in international law (*International Herald Tribune*, 16 June 1994, cited by Vassall-Adams, 1994, 43). The OAU and African countries such as Tanzania called for a UN option (a) response: 'Where the very survival of humanity is at stake, where the outbreak and level of violence reaches enormous proportions to threaten the very fabric of human civilisation and where ethnic conflicts might threaten international peace, the United Nations must be able to act promptly and decisively' (President Ali Hassan Mwinyi, 1 May 1994, quoted in Vassall-Adams, 1994, 41–2). This shows once again that the idea that Third World countries are always opposed to forcible humanitarian intervention is misconceived. Aid organizations such as Oxfam also urged forcible action. On 13 May 1994, the UN Secretary-General recommended the immediate dispatch of 5,500 troops, full deployment to be completed within 31 days, but the Security Council turned him down.

Taken as a whole, this demonstrates the scale of the challenge posed by international-social conflict to the international community. It is a challenge that it is only beginning to learn how to address. It is all too easy to criticize every option that has been tried, blaming the use of too little force in Bosnia and Rwanda and too much in Somalia for what happened in those places. Both the United Nations and the United States in particular suffer in this way. Nothing they do is thought right. That is not our response in this book. We suggest, rather, that, instead of buck-passing and *post hoc* recrimination, it is better to maintain a clear conceptual grasp of what the main options are, to keep all options open for maximum flexibility, and to learn from past difficulties and mistakes what works, what does not work, and why. The main aim is to learn how to improve international response in future.

Suggested reading

Two books by Ioan Lewis (1993, 1994) are highly recommended for background reading. We are indebted to Professor Lewis for insight into the roots of the Somali conflict. On the 1991–4 interventions, Clark, 1993; de Waal, 1994; Makinda, 1993a,b; and Stevenson, 1993, give good overviews from varying perspectives.

Conclusion

In the *Just So Stories* Rudyard Kipling tells how King Solomon, determined to alleviate the suffering of all living things, collected a huge quantity of food by the quayside to feed the animals. Suddenly, a colossal creature, hitherto unknown, emerged from the depths of the ocean and swallowed it all in three mouthfuls. It said that it was the smallest of 30,000 brothers and had been sent to ask when dinner was ready (Kipling, 1987/1902, 153). Solomon was suitably chastened.

Heartened by events in Afghanistan, Namibia, Cambodia, Angola, El Salvador and Nicaragua, world leaders, including the President of the Soviet Union, the President of the United States, and the Secretary-General of the United Nations proclaimed a new world order in which the strong would respect the rights of the weak and the international community would take a more active, shared responsibility for the welfare of humanity (Gorbachev, 1988; Bush, 1990; Boutros-Ghali, 1992). Since then, as described in chapter 3, patterns of ancient conflict, hitherto more or less concealed beneath the cold war waves, have re-emerged with unexpected force to challenge this programme. Civil war, genocide and state collapse have caused unimaginable suffering to millions, and have confronted would-be interveners with apparently insurmountable difficulties when they have tried to do something about it. Euphoria has been succeeded in some quarters by disillusionment, if not despair. If we cannot do everything, the argument seems to go, then it would be better to do nothing. That is not our conclusion. The reconceptualization offered here suggests that these are false alternatives. As the case-studies show, in the face of actual or threatened mass suffering in other countries, outsiders are presented with a range of intervention and non-intervention options from among which they must choose. There is rarely an 'all-or-nothing' solution. The revised concept of humanitarian intervention, therefore, may be said to open the way for analysis of the much maligned idea of 'doing something' – not in the rightly criticized sense of 'doing anything', but in the sense of weighing up the realistic alternatives and learning from past experience how to do better in future.

1 Doing nothing, doing everything and doing something

Chapter 4 listed the following humanitarian intervention options: (a) forcible humanitarian intervention, (b) coercive non-military humanitarian intervention, (c) non-forcible military humanitarian intervention, (d) non-coercive, non-military governmental humanitarian intervention, and (e) transnational and non-governmental humanitarian intervention. *Doing nothing* has been shown to be a highly questionable concept in this context. What we call 'pure non-intervention' – that is, for outsiders to take up none of options (a) to (e) in the face of gross denial or violation of human rights or needs in other countries – whatever judgement may be made of it, is not 'doing nothing'. It is yet a further option, and has consequences like all the others. In the international society of states, both to impose a weapons embargo and not to impose a weapons embargo, both to recognize or not to recognize a state, materially affects the situation. So does the refusal to make diplomatic representations or contribute aid or support peacekeeping operations. If those who can do something choose not to do so, they are rightly seen to be implicated for better or worse in the consequences of that decision. Beyond this lies structural or historical prior responsibility for many of the features which may have generated the crisis in the first place. In the cauldron of international-social conflict, responsibility is in any case imputed to outsiders, whether they think that they are involved or not.

Doing everything is equally chimerical. Whatever may have been the case in classic instances of forcible humanitarian intervention (where a normal stipulation was that these should be brief, limited operations minimally affecting target authority structures), in the context of international-social conflict, it is usually difficult to determine what 'doing everything' – in the sense of finally ending the danger to those threatened – might imply. Certainly, in all the cases of severe conflict considered here, there is no 'quick military fix'.

We are left, then, with a cluster of options best described as *doing something*. This book is an attempt to specify what these options are and to map out some of the relations between them. The argument has been for conceptual clarity, however complex and ambivalent the situation on the ground may be. The Bosnian case-study through to the end of 1994 shows how damaging lack of clarity can be. Decision-makers in national capitals and in New York would have done better had they faced up to the choice between options (a), (c) and (d/e) more coherently from the start, and then been lucid and consistent in following through on their decisions and explaining the implications to their general publics. As it was, the gap between forcible rhetoric and non-forcible deployment, accentuated by unplanned accretion of mandates and 'mission creep', was matched by an equally wide gap between public expectations and operational realities. The danger of perceived failure of this kind is that international action becomes indiscriminately discredited in the ensuing confusion, and options which in other circumstances might have played a constructive and crucial role are over-hastily and unnecessarily foreclosed. The failure of collective forcible intervention in Somalia, for example, does not mean that collective forcible intervention in Rwanda, properly conducted, might not have succeeded. Nor should the difficulties encountered by the exceptional non-forcible military intervention in Bosnia through to the end of 1994 entirely discredit this option. A large number of other UN peacekeeping missions with important humanitarian dimensions need also to be weighed in the balance, as do non-forcible military contributions to other disaster areas, as well as suggestions for some kind of specialized, lightly armed military units specifically trained for humanitarian missions. The same applies to the other intervention and non-intervention options analysed in chapters 4 and 5.

Above all, we suggest that the humanitarian problems posed by international-social conflict, far from being underplayed, should be widely and carefully expounded, in order to dampen unreasonable expectations. Chapter 3 shows why the challenge is so great. There are no easy solutions, and all options, including various forms of non-intervention, are likely in one way or another to prove unsatisfactory and risky. This should be stressed constantly. Engagement must be patient, informed, flexible and determined. It is a question of finding the best combinations of options over the long term. We have seen how in these circumstances humanitarianism is unavoidably *politicized* and, more often than not, *militarized*.

Politicization follows from a combination of factors analysed earlier in the book. Among them are the following: (i) that humanitarian aims will often run counter to the deliberate policy goals of belligerent parties, such as reduction of civilian centres by starvation or ethnic cleansing; (ii) that conflict parties will use both aid and aid workers as political pawns in their struggle, and that, once involved, interveners will be caught up in a complex web of interest in which antagonists will have reasons for both wanting them to stay and wanting them to leave; (iii) that humanitarian interveners come with their own agendas, and humanitarian action is bound in some way or other to have a political effect on the conflict; (iv) that whatever interveners may genuinely believe, conflict parties will perceive them to be partisan, often in mutually incompatible ways, there being no room for neutrality in international-social conflict; (v) that these problems are compounded as we move from NGO/ICRC to UN agency intervention, in so far as the latter is implicated in political action by the UN Security Council (option (e)), from IGO/NGO to non-military governmental intervention (option (d)), from non-military to non-forcible military governmental intervention (option (c)), from non-coercive to coercive governmental intervention (option (b)), and from non-forcible to forcible governmental intervention (option (a)).

How much of the key principle of 'neutrality' (non-political involvement) is left at each stage is a deep question. On the one hand, there is the argument that as we move to the coercive options (b) and (a), intervention can no longer be seen as 'humanitarian'. 'Forcible humanitarian intervention' or 'humanitarian war', from this perspective, is an oxymoron. On the other hand, there is the equally powerful argument that, faced with atrocities perpetrated by one party to a conflict, neutrality is a false principle. From this perspective, the international community should use force against the guilty party in order to protect the innocent. If it does not, humanitarianism is betrayed. For this reason, the somewhat bold step is taken of omitting neutrality from the framework principles for humanitarian intervention outlined below. Since the framework principles cover forcible as well as non-forcible intervention, neutrality in its usual sense cannot be a general requirement. Neutrality is a central value for non-coercive humanitarian intervention, but not for coercive or forcible humanitarian intervention, which may have to 'take sides', not directly in the political conflict but in order to protect the innocent. Having conceded this, however, the fact that force is not used for direct political purposes does preserve something of the non-political quality of neutrality. Further, the principle of impartiality, in the sense of non-discrimination, remains central for all types of humanitarian intervention. Forcible UN Security Council humanitarian mandates can still be carried out impartially. If one side is guilty, to punish it is quite compatible with impartially administered justice. Needless to say, in the crucible of international-social conflict, where all parties, including those responsible for the atrocities, are passionately convinced that it is they who are the beleaguered victims of injustice, the protagonists are unlikely to accept that those who thwart them are administering justice impartially. Interveners' actions will be interpreted not as humanitarian, but as political through and through. Neither neutrality nor impartiality – nor disinterestedness – are uncontested concepts. There is no escape from the politicization of humanitarianism in contemporary international-social conflict. It is as well for all those concerned, governments and the general public alike, to recognize as much.

A second critical aspect is the fact of militarization, which works in two directions. First, there is the almost unavoidable *militarization of humanitarianism* in international-social conflict. As we have seen, in the worst cases of breakdown the conflict disintegrates into a chaos of indiscriminate violence in which warring factions prey on the civilian population and humanitarian aid, like all other assets, fuels continuing war. All resources are seen simply as means to sustain power, and fighting becomes endemic, a way of life for a whole generation of young belligerents without other sources of employment. 'The Liberian civil war reached such maniacal and psychotic proportions that the ICRC withdrew and several delegates required psychiatric hospitalisation. These conditions have caused fewer young Swiss to volunteer, leading the ICRC to recruit some staff from outside Switzerland. It is an indication of the chaos spreading through the world that for the first time in its 150-year history the ICRC has been forced to hire non-Swiss staff' (Natsios, 1995, 74). How are humanitarian interveners to gain access and security in these circumstances? Evidently, military forces can offer logistical support, as well as a measure of protection, without which the scope for humanitarian relief will be diminished. On the other hand, humanitarian agencies stand to lose political independence and to become associated in the eyes of conflict parties with the interests of the protecting powers. We have seen that the alternatives are to rely on recruiting indigenous guards (option (d/e)), to rely on non-forcible external peacekeepers (option (c)), or to work under an enforcement umbrella (option (a)). Again, it is indicative that the ICRC has for the first time accepted the necessity for defensive protection, choosing the first of these three options:

> In principle, the ICRC will not use armed escorts. It will consider doing so only if the situation leaves no alternative, i.e. if the escort is the sole means of carrying out its mission with complete independence. Should such a situation arise, the ICRC will take the following steps: (i) seek the opinion of the party controlling the territory in which the escort is to operate – if that party is opposed to the escort, the ICRC will abandon the idea; (ii) ensure that the sole purpose of the escort is protection against bandits and irregular armed groups, never against the warring parties themselves. (ICRC document DDM/DRM 93/518B, 13 September 1993, quoted in Sandoz, 1993, 32)

Conversely, there is also the fact of the *humanitarianization of the military*. Here we touch on another crucial element in this book. The role of military forces in humanitarian intervention, both forcible and non-forcible, is to create humanitarian space for non-military relief. This goes against the normal military ethos: 'soldiers trained for warfare and national security have little in common with relief personnel seeking the goal of humanitarianism' (Dedring, 1994, 15). Doctrine, training, experience and recruitment do nothing to prepare military forces for this task or for subordination to essentially civilian purposes (Brady and Daws, 1994). According to Richard Rinaldo of the US Army's Training and Doctrine Command at Fort Monroe, Virginia, where the new US Army manual *FM 100-23: Peace Operations* was prepared: 'The goal of peace support operations is not military victory. The conflict is the enemy, rather than specific enemy forces' (Rinaldo, 1994, 8). This is unfamiliar territory for combat troops. We have seen how some national forces are better resourced for adapting to this transformed role than others. Here again there is a major task to be performed in making all this familiar to political leaders and to the general public in donor countries.

In addition to the politicization and militarization of humanitarianism, humanitarian intervention in contemporary conflict involves all the further considerations outlined in chapter 5, which need not be repeated here. How do immediate humanitarian goals relate to the wider social, cultural, political and economic dimensions of the long-term stability and sustainable development needed if the conditions which prompted the intervention are not to recur? Involvement will inescapably be complex, controversial and prolonged. We should learn to expect this. Behind this lie all the logistical, organizational and financial aspects and other factors relevant to questions of prudence and 'do-ability'. The aim of this book has been to offer a thorough review of the *concept* of humanitarian intervention, so there has not been space to do more than map out these issues. Beyond this again lie questions of agency and political will and the overriding requirement to reconcile effectiveness and capability, on the one hand, with international acceptability and legitimacy, on the other.

We end the book by relating the reconceptualization outlined in Parts II and III to the analysis in Part I. First, we relate the discussion in chapters 3–7 to the concept of international community as developed in chapters 1 and 2. Then, as an epilogue, we draw on the idea of humanitarianism expounded in chapter 1 to formulate framework principles for humanitarian intervention to cover all kinds of humanitarian intervention, forcible and non-forcible. These principles are deduced from the many sets of criteria suggested in the literature on humanitarian intervention listed in the references at the end of the book. We recommend that due note be taken of these principles by all who aspire to intervene across borders in response to human suffering in contemporary conflicts.

2 Humanitarian intervention and the concept of international community

In chapters 1 and 2 we introduced the idea that the informal term 'international community' might best be located at the 'upper' or 'solidarist' end of the international society spectrum, what we called level 3 (see diagrams 1 and 2, pages 30 and 31).

> Level 1: International anarchy: realist
> Level 2: International society (i): pluralist
> Level 3: International society (ii): solidarist
> INTERNATIONAL COMMUNITY
> Level 4: World Community: universalist

We suggested that international community represented the 'sub-set of international society which embodies the minimum solidarity needed for the question of humanitarian intervention to be raised in the first place'. We contrasted this with the 'pluralist' end of the international society spectrum, which we called level 2, where the predominant value was cultural autonomy and international order protected by the non-intervention norm. 'Above' and 'below' the international society of states we recognized the universalism of world community, level 4, and the realism (in its technical sense) of international anarchy, level 1, respectively. This is the model that we carried through the rest of the book to help analyse the conceptual framework within which the humanitarian intervention debate has been argued out. A central theme has been that all these levels have their own authenticity and coexist as recognizable aspects of the international collectivity, without any one having a monopoly of the whole. We used this idea to unpack the intervention/non-intervention/ humanitarian intervention debate (diagram 4, page 58), suggesting that these three alternatives could usefully be located at levels 1, 2 and 3 respectively. We used it again to show how international law, a characteristic product of international society, partakes ambivalently of both level 2 and level 3, and how the humanitarian intervention debate is thus a debate both within international law and about its nature (diagram 5, page 65). We also used the model to suggest that the United Nations, the prime institutional expression of the international collectivity, exhibits all four levels, and that the role of the UN in collective humanitarian intervention cannot be properly understood unless this is recognized (diagram 8, page 159).

Using the model one final time, we can briefly sum up the implications of the challenge of humanitarian intervention for the international community. The horrors of international-social conflict represent forces that lie even beneath level 1, which is the level of the relatively organized international 'anarchy' of states. In their most virulent form, they epitomize the Hobbesian pre-state 'war of all against all', in which human life is, literally, 'nasty, brutish and short' (Hobbes, 1962/1651, 65). Against this, the international community in its current form is hardly as yet a match. Borrowing Richard Rinaldo's phrase, if it is the most violent manifestation of conflict itself which is the enemy of collective humanitarian intervention, then, at the moment, the struggle is decidedly unequal. Humanitarian need is at its most intense where the international community is as yet least able to respond. Whereas the challenge emanates from depths below level 1, the response is best understood as representing an uneasy combination of all four levels of the international collectivity. If it comes to mobilizing force to meet force, this can only be done at level 1 through the coercive, military capabilities of regional or global great powers. International co-operation underpinned by coincidence of interest and shared perceptions of danger and mutual advantage is found at level 2. This makes co-ordinated mobilization through international organizations possible, while nevertheless safeguarding principles of cultural pluralism and non-intervention. But the humanitarian values themselves, which should imbue humanitarian intervention if it is to be worthy of that name, come from the solidarist level 3, which includes international humanitarian law, if not, ultimately, from the barely glimpsed universalism of the world community at level 4, possibly represented by genuinely non-political humanitarian agencies. Capability and international legitimacy represent two poles of this overall spectrum. Each is needed if collective humanitarian intervention is to be both effective and universally endorsed.

In short, the international community, struggling into existence within the nexus of the international society of states, summoned to act in accordance with humanitarian values derived from the possibility of a world community of humankind, but at the same time having to rely on means provided by the most powerful states within the international anarchy, confronts the most vicious atavistic forces unleashed by the eruption of international-social conflict.

Such is the challenge of humanitarian intervention in contemporary conflict. Much depends upon the outcome.

Epilogue:
Framework Principles
for Humanitarian
Intervention

What follow are framework principles which apply to all kinds of humanitarian intervention, military and non-military (see box 23). They have been derived from the large numbers of sets of criteria for humanitarian intervention to be found in the cold war and post-cold war literature. They were first formulated in Lewer and Ramsbotham, 1993, and have since been adapted in Ramsbotham (forthcoming), where a fuller derivation and commentary can be found. The ambitious claim is that they have been selected to represent a general consensus among not only those who advocate various forms of humanitarian intervention, but also those who oppose such intervention, the latter appealing to the same principles in ruling it out. It was encouraging subsequently to find a close overlap with Larry Minear's and Thomas Weiss's eight 'Providence Principles of Humanitarian Action in Armed Conflict', part of their splendid work on the Brown University and Refugee Policy Group's *Humanitarianism and War Project* (Minear and Weiss, 1993, 19), and with the 'Mohonk criteria for humanitarian assistance in complex emergencies', produced by the World Conference on Religion and Peace (World Conference on Religion and Peace, 1994, 4), although both of these apply only to non-military intervention.

Although it is clearly possible to order the criteria differently, and to produce a larger or smaller number by amalgamation or subdivision, there is a further logic to the arrangement given here (see diagram 10). Principles 1–5 go together, and are already familiar from earlier chapters. They are the principles of (1) humanitarian cause, (2) humanitarian end, (3) humanitarian approach, (4) humanitarian means and (5)

Box 23: Framework Principles for Humanitarian Intervention

1. **The principle of humanitarian cause:** Where there is unacceptable denial or violation of fundamental human needs or rights, actual or threatened, the international community has a duty to attempt redress and a prima facie right to intervene, subject to the condition laid down in principle (11).

2. **The principle of humanitarian end:** The aim of the intervention should be effective redress throughout the affected region.

3. **The principle of humanitarian approach:** The intervention should be impartially conducted.

4. **The principle of humanitarian means:** The means employed should be appropriate – that is, they should be (a) necessary, (b) sufficient, (c) proportional and (d) discriminate.

5. **The principle of humanitarian outcome:** The outcome of the intervention should be to the overall advantage of those in whose name it is carried out.

6. **The principle of mutuality:** The intervention should be conducted in terms understood and accepted within the affected region and in such a way as to preserve autonomy and support those working locally to resolve conflict and alleviate suffering.

7. **The principle of reflexivity:** Interveners' interests, motives and previous behaviour should be compatible with the professed purpose of their intervention.

8. **The principle of complementarity:** Interveners' actions should be mutually complementary.

9. **The principle of consistency:** Interventions should be consistent across different crisis situations, and relevant experience should be cumulatively transferred.

10. **The principle of legitimacy:** Interveners should hold themselves accountable to the international community for their intervention, since it is from the international community that they derive the authority to intervene.

11. **The principle of contingency and graduated response:** Where possible, intervention should be preventive, non-violent and with the consent of all parties. Where this is not possible, additional criteria should be met as appropriate at the relevant decision points, without prejudice as to the outcome.

12. **The principle of universality:** The principles which govern just humanitarian intervention should be endorsed by the international community.

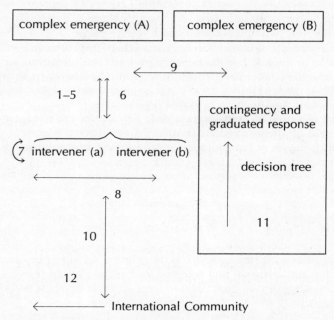

Diagram 10: *Framework Principles and Intervention Relations*

humanitarian outcome. These principles govern the primary intervention relations. Principles 6–10 are generated by five reciprocal intervention relations, namely: (6) relations between interveners and those subject to the intervention (the principle of mutuality), (7) relations between interveners and their interventions (the principle of reflexivity), (8) relations between different interveners (the principle of complementarity), (9) relations between different interventions (the principle of consistency), (10) relations between interveners and the international community (the principle of legitimacy). Principle (11) is a linking principle, which relates the Framework Principles in turn to the various sets of special criteria for particular types of intervention at the appropriate decision points. It is also an ordering principle. It is the principle of contingency and graduated response. Principle (12) acknowledges the fundamental constitutive relation which generates both the justification for humanitarian intervention in the first place and the Framework Principles under which it is subsequently legitimately conducted. This is the principle of universality.

These are framework principles covering all types of intervention which purport to be humanitarian. In order to apply them to particular categories of humanitarian intervention, additional specific criteria must be invoked. There are specific criteria for each of the options (a) to (e) described in chapter 4. For example, there have been attempts to adapt just war thinking to cover forcible humanitarian intervention (Beach, 1993; Fisher, 1994; Himes, 1993). As explained more fully elsewhere, however, when forcible humanitarian intervention is brought under the framework principles, traditional just war criteria have to be significantly adapted (Ramsbotham, forthcoming).

Comparison with the representative sample of just war criteria given in box 24 shows that, although framework principles (1), (2), (4), (7), (10)

Box 24: Traditional Just War Criteria

There is no definitive list of just war criteria. However, in this tradition (which goes back as far as Cicero, received its characteristic form in the Middle Ages, and has been vigorously revived in the twentieth century), there is a core of generally agreed stipulations.

War decision criteria (jus ad bellum)

War must be
1 publicly declared,
2 conducted by a competent authority,
3 fought for a just cause,
4 fought with a right intention,
5 fought with a view to a just peace,
6 fought with a reasonable prospect of success,
7 fought for a proportionate reason,
8 fought as a last resort.

War conduct criteria (jus in bello)

In fighting a war,
9 the harm judged likely to result from a particular military action should not be disproportionate to the good aimed at (the principle of proportion),
10 non-combatants should be immune from direct attack (the principle of discrimination).

Sources: Johnson, 1981; O'Brien, 1981.

and (11) more or less coincide with them, principles (3), (5), (6), (8), (9) and (12) do not. The latter are a measure of the difference that a humanitarian brief makes to traditional military values. Even where the criteria and framework principles do coincide, the fact that the criteria now come under the principles also makes a difference. *Just cause*, for example (just war criterion 3; framework principle 1), now revives the medieval category 'defence of the innocent', which goes back more than 1,000 years and encompasses the Germanic chivalric codes (Keen, 1965; Johnson, 1981). This goes beyond restrictionist interpretations of the UN Charter as outlined in chapter 2, section 1.3.3. Forcible humanitarian interveners are in this sense 'knights of humanity'. This adds a further layer to Reinhold Niebuhr's 'ethical paradox of patriotism', which 'transmutes individual selfishness into national egoism' (1932, 19). Here, national egoism is in turn transmuted into solidarist unselfishness, and individual soldiers are asked to risk their lives, not for their countries, but for humanity. We have arrived at the most sensitive point in the tension between statist and solidarist sentiments which lies at the heart of the forcible humanitarian intervention debate. Whether the idea of knights of humanity seems absurd and ethically wrong (McCain, 1994) or uplifting and an essential transformation of unethical exclusive statism (Parekh, 1995) serves as a measure of where we stand in this regard.

There is no space to comment further on the framework principles. But emphasis must be placed on principle (12), the principle of universality. The whole of this book is predicated on the assumption that there are shared cross-cultural norms sufficient to underpin some idea of basic human needs or rights and the possibility of collective action to realize them. If there is not at least this measure of human solidarity, then, in our view, the entire enterprise of humanitarian intervention collapses. The principle of universality underlies the rest. For example, it is possible that the revival of older Western just war concepts of 'defence of the innocent' in the criteria for forcible humanitarian intervention may open the way to dialogue with other cultures, such as Islam, which also recognize these values (see box 25).

The framework principles for humanitarian intervention can be seen to impose strict criteria, albeit in each case widely endorsed in the literature. It may be thought that they are unlikely to prove useful to hard-pressed decision-makers in fraught political situations. Nevertheless, they show what the most thoughtful and experienced theorists and practitioners mean by the humanitarian values in whose name humanitarian intervention is being carried out. The framework principles do not on their own make choices or decide actions. But, if borne in mind, they may help to leaven the debate and slowly begin to transform the value system

Box 25: Islam and Forcible Humanitarian Intervention

'The crisis in Bosnia, as well as the many other humanitarian crises in other parts of the Muslim world, have created a popular climate that not only permits but demands consideration of principles of intervention. Indeed, in all the crises to date, the Organization of the Islamic Conference (OIC) member-states have been moved to whatever belated action they have taken by strong internal pressures' (Hashmi, 1993, 72).

Seven of the 10 'most pressing humanitarian crises of the 1990s' listed by MSF in 1993 involved Muslim populations. The OIC, founded in 1972, has 47 member states, a quarter of the UN membership and a fifth of humanity. What does Islam say about forcible humanitarian intervention? At the outset, Islam has less trouble with the problem of state sovereignty than do Western theorists, to the extent that Islam recognizes the primacy of the *umma wahida* (original oneness of humankind) over the subsequent divisions into states. Muslim theorists differ in how they regard the relationship between Islam and the state. Three approaches may be distinguished: a modernist secular school, which plays down ideas of the Muslim *umma* (community); a revisionist school, which tries to reconcile the two; and a pan-Islamic school, which rejects the nation-state system as a relic of European colonialism, the product of the 'deficient human mind', as Ayatollah Ruhollah Khomeini put it. Muhammad Iqbal, a representative of the revisionist school, argued that '[t]ribal or national organizations on the lines of race or territory are only temporary phases in the [evolution] of collective life, and [as such] I have no quarrel with them; but I condemn them in the strongest possible terms when they are regarded as the ultimate expression of the life of mankind' (quoted in Hashmi, 1993, 61).

Sohail Hashmi argues that '[i]t is vital . . . that during this period of development, principles of humanitarian intervention be based on as truly a universal and cross-cultural consensus of fundamental human rights, and the legitimate means to enforce them, as possible' (p. 56). Islam certainly shares broad humanitarian principles with other cultures, as well as a universalist ethic. In response to the question 'Can Muslim states ally themselves with non-Muslim powers to fight another Muslim state that may be committing massive human rights violations against its own people?', Hashmi answers, 'of course Muslim states should be foremost in undertaking humanitarian intervention and conflict resolution within the Muslim world. This is unambiguously demanded by Qur'anic ethical principles' (p. 68).

within which it is subsequently argued out. Those who claim to intervene in contemporary conflict on humanitarian grounds, whatever the nature of their intervention, should make their decisions accordingly. If they do not, they should not call their intervention 'humanitarian'.

Appendix 1: United Nations Peacekeeping and Observer Missions Operating 1991–4

UNTSO	United Nations Truce Supervision Organization
UNMOGIP	United Nations Military Observer Group in India and Pakistan
UNFICYP	United Nations Peacekeeping Force in Cyprus
UNDOF	United Nations Disengagement Force
UNIFIL	United Nations Interim Force in Lebanon
UNIKOM	United Nations Iraq–Kuwait Observation Mission
UNAVEM II	United Nations Angola Verification Mission II
ONUSAL	United Nations Mission in El Salvador
MINURSO	United Nations Mission for the Referendum in Western Sahara
UNAMIC	United Nations Advance Mission in Cambodia
UNTAC	United Nations Transitional Authority in Cambodia
UNPROFOR	United Nations Protection Force
UNOSOM I	United Nations Operation in Somalia I
ONUMOZ	United Nations Operation in Mozambique
UNOSOM II	United Nations Operation in Somalia II
UNOMUR	United Nations Observer Mission in Uganda–Rwanda
UNOMIG	United Nations Observer Mission in Georgia
UNOMIL	United Nations Observer Mission in Liberia
UNMIH	United Nations Mission in Haiti
UNAMIR	United Nations Assistance Mission for Rwanda
UNASOG	United Nations Aouzou Strip Observer Group
UNMOT	United Nations Mission of Observers in Tajikistan

Appendix 2: Other Acronyms

ASEAN	Association of Southeast Asian Nations
CERF	Central Emergency Revolving Fund
CRB	Committee for Relief in Belgium
CRS	Catholic Relief Service
CSCE	Conference on Security and Co-operation in Europe
DAM	Department of Administration and Management
DHA	Department of Humanitarian Affairs
DPA	Department of Political Affairs
DPKO	Department of Peacekeeping Operations
EC	European Community
ECHO	EC Humanitarian Office
ECOMOG	ECOWAS Ceasefire Monitoring Group
ECOSOC	Economic and Social Council
ECOWAS	Economic Community of West African States
EDF	European Development Fund
EU	European Union
FAO	Food and Agriculture Organization
GAR	General Assembly Resolution
HDZ	Croatian Democratic Union
ICJ	International Court of Justice
ICRC	International Committee of the Red Cross
IMF	International Monetary Fund
IOM	International Office for Migration
JNA	Yugoslav National Army
MSF	Médecins Sans Frontières
NPFL	National Patriotic Front of Liberia
OAS	Organization of American States

OAU	Organization of African Unity
ODA	Overseas Development Administration
OFDA	Office of Foreign Disaster Assistance
OIC	Organization of the Islamic Conference
OSCE	Organization for Security and Co-operation in Europe
PDD	Presidential Decision Directive
RPF	Rwanda Patriotic Front
SCF	Save the Children Fund
SCR	Security Council Resolution
SDA	Somali Democratic Alliance
SDM	Somali Democratic Movement
SNA	Somali National Alliance
SNF	Somali National Front
SNM	Somali National Movement
SPLA	Sudanese People's Liberation Army
SPM	Somali Patriotic Movement
SRCS	Somali Red Crescent Society
SSDF	Somali Salvation Democratic Front
UN	United Nations
UNDP	UN Development Programme
UNGAR	UN General Assembly Resolution
UNHCR	Office of the UN High Commissioner for Refugees
UNICEF	UN International Children's Emergency Fund
UNITA	National Union for the Total Independence of Angola
UNITAF	Unified Task Force
UNRRA	UN Relief and Rehabilitation Administration
UNSGSR	UN Secretary-General's Special Representative
USAID	US Agency for International Development
USC	United Somali Congress
USF	United Somali Front
USP	United Somali Party
WFP	World Food Programme
WHO	World Health Organization
WTO	Warsaw Treaty Organization

References

Adelman, H. 1992a: The ethics of humanitarian intervention: the case of the Kurdish refugees. *Public Affairs Quarterly*, 6(1), 61–87.
——1992b: Humanitarian intervention: the case of the Kurds. *International Journal of Refugee Law*, 4(1), 4–38.
Aga Khan, S. 1988: Forty years on: and so much left to do. In Davies (ed.), 155–63.
Akehurst, M. 1984: Humanitarian intervention. In Bull (ed.), 95–118.
Alston, P. (ed.) 1992: *The United Nations and Human Rights: A Critical Appraisal*. Oxford: Clarendon Press.
Amnesty International 1983: Extra-legal executions in Uganda. In *Political Killings by Governments*. London: Amnesty International, 34–43.
Anderson, B. 1983: *Imagined Communities*. London: Verso.
Anderson, M. 1993: Development and the prevention of humanitarian emergencies. In Weiss and Minear (eds), 23–38.
——and Woodrow, P. 1989: *Rising from the Ashes: Development Strategies in Times of Disaster*. Boulder, Colo.: Westview.
An-Naim, A. and Deng, F. (eds) 1990: *Human Rights in Africa: Cross-Cultural Perspectives*. Washington, DC: The Brookings Institution.
Arend, A. and Beck, R. 1993: *International Law and the Use of Force*. London: Routledge.
Austin, J. 1954 (1832): *The Province of Jurisprudence Determined*. London: Weidenfeld and Nicolson.
Awoonor, K. 1993: The concerns of recipient nations. In Cahill (ed.), 63–81.
Azar, E. 1990: *The Management of Protracted Social Conflict: Theory and Cases*. Aldershot: Dartmouth.
——1991: The analysis and management of protracted social conflict. In Volkan et al., 93–120.

—and Burton, J. 1986: *International Conflict Resolution: Theory and Practice*. Brighton: Wheatsheaf.

Bailey, S. 1987: *War and Conscience in the Nuclear Age*. Basingstoke: Macmillan.

Barzani, M. 1993: Hope restored: benefits of humanitarian intervention [interview]. *Harvard International Review*, 16(1), 18–19, 63.

BASIC 1994: *NATO, Peacekeeping, and the United Nations*. Washington, DC: British American Security Information Council.

Bazyler, M. 1987: Re-examining the doctrine of humanitarian intervention in light of the atrocities in Kampuchea and Ethiopia. *Stanford Journal of International Law*, 23, 547– 619.

Beach, H. 1993: Do we need a doctrine of just intervention? *Council for Arms Control*. London: Centre for Defence Studies.

Behuniak, T. 1978: The law of unilateral intervention by armed force: a legal survey. *Military Law Review*, 79, 157–91.

Beigbeder, Y. 1991: *The Role and Status of International Volunteers and Organizations*. Dordrecht: Martinus Nijhoff.

Beitz, C. 1975: Justice and international relations. Reprinted in Beitz et al., 1985, 282–311.

—1979: *Political Theory and International Relations*. Princeton: Princeton University Press.

—1980a: Bounded morality: justice and the state in world politics. *International Organization*, 33, 405–24.

—1980b: Nonintervention and communal integrity. *Philosophy and Public Affairs*, 9(4), 385–91.

—et al. 1985: *International Ethics*. Princeton: Princeton University Press.

Benjamin, B. 1992–3: Note – unilateral humanitarian intervention: legalising the use of force to prevent human rights atrocities. *Fordham International Law Journal*, 16, 120–58.

Benthall, J. 1993: *Disasters, Relief and the Media*. London: Tauris.

Berdal, M. 1993: *Whither UN Peacekeeping?*. Adelphi Paper, 281. London: Brassey's, for the International Institute for Strategic Studies.

—1994: Fateful encounter: the United States and UN peacekeeping. *Survival*, 36(1), 30–50.

Bermant, G. and Warwick, D. 1978: *The Ethics of Social Intervention*. New York: Wiley.

Best, G. 1983: *Humanity in Warfare: The Modern History of the International Law of Armed Conflicts*. London: Methuen.

—1994: *War and Law Since 1945*. Oxford: Clarendon Press.

Bettati, M. 1991: Un droit d'ingérence? *Revue générale de droit international publique*, 95, 639–70.

—and Kouchner, B. 1987: *Le Devoir d'ingérence*. Paris: Denöel.

Betts, R. 1994: The delusion of impartial intervention. *Foreign Affairs*, 73(6), 20–33.

Beyerlin, U. 1982: Humanitarian intervention. In Bernhardt (ed.), *Encyclopedia of Public International Law*. Amsterdam: North Holland Publishing Co., 3, 211–15.

Blackburn, R. and Taylor, J. (eds) 1991: *Human Rights for the 1990s: Legal, Political and Ethical Issues*. London: Mansell.

Bodin, J. 1967 (1576): *Six Books of the Commonwealth*. Oxford: Blackwell.

Bogen, D. 1966: The law of humanitarian intervention by armed force: US policy in Cuba (1898) and in the Dominican Republic (1965). *Harvard International Law Journal*, 7, 296–317.

Boissier, P. 1985: *From Solferino to Tsushima: History of the International Committee of the Red Cross*. Geneva: Henry Dunant Institute.

Booth, K. 1994: Military intervention: duty and prudence. In Freedman (ed.), 56–75.

——and Smith S. (eds) 1995: *International Relations Theory Today*. Cambridge: Polity.

Boutros-Ghali, B. 1992: *An Agenda for Peace*. New York: United Nations.

——1992–3: Empowering the United Nations: historic opportunities to strengthen the world body. *Foreign Affairs*, Winter, 71(2), 89–93.

Bowett, D. 1986: The use of force for the protection of nationals abroad. In Cassese (ed.), 39–56.

Boyle, J. 1992: Natural law and international ethics. In Nardin and Mapel (eds), 112–35.

Brady, C. and Daws, S. 1994: UN operations: the political-military interface. *International Peacekeeping*, 1(1), 59–78.

Brauman, R. 1993: The Médecins Sans Frontières experience. In Cahill (ed.), 202–20.

Brown, M. (ed.) 1993: *Ethnic Conflict and International Security*. Princeton: Princeton University Press.

Brown, P. and MacLean, D. (eds) 1979: *Human Rights and US Foreign Policy: Principles and Applications*. Lexington, Mass.: Lexington Books.

Brownlie, I. 1963: *International Law and the Use of Force by States*. Oxford: Clarendon Press.

——1973: Thoughts on kind-hearted gunmen. In Lillich (ed.), 139–48.

——1974: Humanitarian intervention. In Moore (ed.), 217–52.

——1990: *Principles of Public International Law*, 4th edn. Oxford: Clarendon Press.

——(ed.) 1992: *Basic Documents on Human Rights*, 3rd edn. Oxford: Clarendon Press.

Bull, H. 1995 (1977): *The Anarchical Society*, 2nd edn. London: Macmillan.

——(ed.) 1984: *Intervention in World Politics*. Oxford: Clarendon Press.

——and Watson, A. 1984: *The Expansion of International Society*. Oxford: Clarendon Press.

——Kingsbury, B. and Roberts, A. (eds) 1990: *Hugo Grotius and International Relations*. Oxford: Clarendon Press.

Bulletin of the Atomic Scientists 1993: Sanctions: do they work?, special issue, 49(9).

——1995: Peacekeeping's uncertain future, special issue, 51(2).

Burton, J. 1987: *Resolving Deep-Rooted Conflict: A Handbook*. Lanham, Md.: University Press of America.

Bush, G. 1990: *Toward a New World Order*, address to Congress, 11 Sept. US Department of State Current Policy, no. 1298.

Cahill, K. (ed.) 1993: *A Framework for Survival: Health, Human Rights, and Humanitarian Assistance in Conflicts and Disasters*. New York: Basic Books.

Caratsch, C. 1993: Humanitarian design and political interference: Red Cross work in the post-cold war period. *International Affairs*, 11, Apr., 301–13.

Carpentier, C. 1992: La résolution 688 du Conseil de Sécurité: quel devoir d'ingérence? *Etudes internationales*, 23 June, 279–317.

Cassese, A. 1990: *Human Rights in a Changing World*. Cambridge: Polity.

——(ed.) 1986: *The Current Legal Regulation of the Use of Force*. Dordrecht: Martinus Nijhoff.

Chalk, F. and Jonassohn, K. 1990: *The History and Sociology of Genocide*. New Haven: Yale University Press.

Chatterjee, S. 1981: Some legal problems of support role in international law: Tanzania and Uganda. *International and Comparative Law Quarterly*, 30, 755–68.

Childers, E. 1992: UN mechanisms and capacities for intervention. In Ferris (ed.), 39–66.

——with Urquhart, B. 1994: *Renewing the United Nations System*. Uppsala: Hammarskjöld Foundation (also in *Development Dialogue*, 1, 1–214).

Chilstrom, R. 1974: Humanitarian intervention under contemporary international law. *Yale Studies in World Public Order*, 1, 93–111.

Chimni, B. 1980: Towards a third world approach to non-intervention: through the labyrinth of Western doctrine. *Indian Journal of International Law*, 20, 243–64.

Chopra, J. and Weiss, T. 1992: Sovereignty is no longer sacrosanct: codifying humanitarian intervention. *Ethics and International Affairs*, 6, 95–117.

Clark, J. 1993: Debacle in Somalia: failure of the collective response. In Damrosch (ed.), 205–40.

Claude, R. and Weston, B. (eds) 1992: *Human Rights in the World Community*, 2nd edn. Philadelphia: University of Pennsylvania Press.

Coste, R. 1993: The moral dimensions of intervention. *Harvard International Review*, Fall, 28–9, 67–8.

Cranna, M. (ed.) 1994: *The True Cost of Conflict*. London: Earthscan.

Crawford, N. 1993: Decolonization as an international norm: the evolution of practices, arguments and beliefs. In Reed and Kaysen (eds), 37–62.

Cutler, L. 1985: The right to intervene. *Foreign Affairs*, 64, 96–112.

D'Amato, A. 1987: *International law: Process and Prospect*. Dobbs Ferry, NY: Transnational Publishers.

Damrosch, L. 1989: Politics across borders: nonintervention and nonforcible influence over domestic affairs. *American Journal of International Law*, 83, 1–50.

——1993: Changing conceptions of intervention in international law. In Reed and Kaysen (eds), 91–110.

Damrosch, L. (ed.) 1993: *Enforcing Restraint: Collective Intervention in Internal Conflicts.* New York: Council on Foreign Relations Press.

——and Scheffer, J. (eds) 1991: *Law and Force in the New International Order.* Boulder, Colo.: Westview.

Davidson, S. 1993: *Human Rights.* Buckingham: Open University Press.

Davies, P. (ed.) 1988: *Human Rights.* London: Routledge.

De Cuéllar, J. P. 1991: *Report of the Secretary-General of the United Nations.* New York: United Nations.

De Nevers, R. 1993: Democratization and ethnic conflict. In M. Brown (ed.), 61–78.

De Waal, A. 1994: Dangerous precedents? Famine relief in Somalia 1991–93. In MacCrae and Zwi (eds), 139–59.

Dedring, J. 1994: *Humanitarian Interventions by the United Nations.* New York: DHA, United Nations.

Deibel, T. 1993: Internal affairs and international relations in the post-cold war world. *Washington Quarterly,* 16(3), 13–33.

Delbrück, J. 1992: A fresh look at humanitarian intervention under the authority of the United Nations. *Indiana Law Journal,* 67(4), 887–901.

Deng, F. 1993: *Protecting the Dispossessed: A Challenge for the International Community.* Washington, DC: Brookings Institution.

——and Minear L. 1992: *The Challenges of Famine Relief: Emergency Operations in the Sudan.* Washington, DC: Brookings Institution.

Development Studies Association 1992: *The United Nations – Humanitarian Response.* London: Development Studies Association, Nov.

Dewar, M. 1993: Intervention in Bosnia – the case against. *World Today,* 49(2), 32–4.

Dobbie, C. 1994: A concept for post-cold war peacekeeping. *Survival,* 36(3), 121–48.

Donagan, A. 1977: *The Theory of Morality.* Chicago: University of Chicago Press.

Donnelly, J. 1984: Human rights, humanitarian intervention and American foreign policy: law, morality and politics. *Journal of International Affairs,* 37, 311–28.

——1985: *The Concept of Human Rights.* London: Croom Helm.

——1989: *Universal Human Rights in Theory and Practice.* Ithaca, NY: Cornell University Press.

——1993a: Human rights, humanitarian crisis and humanitarian intervention. *International Journal,* 48(4), 607–40.

——1993b: *International Human Rights.* Boulder, Colo.: Westview.

Doppelt, G. 1978: Walzer's theory of morality in international relations. *Philosophy and Public Affairs,* 8(1), 3–26.

Downes, C. 1993: Challenges for small nations in the new era of UN and multinational operations. In H. Smith (ed.), 13–32.

Dreze, J. and Sen, A. 1984: *Hunger and Public Action.* Oxford: Clarendon Press.

Duffield, M. 1994: The political economy of internal war: asset transfer, complex emergencies and international aid. In Macrae and Zwi (eds), 50–69.

Dunant, H. 1986 (1862): *A Memory of Solferino*. Geneva: ICRC.

Dunn, J. 1994: Introduction: crisis of the nation state? *Political Studies*, 42, 3–15.

Durch, W. (ed.) 1993: *The Evolution of UN Peacekeeping: Case Studies and Comparative Analysis*. New York: St Martin's Press.

Dworkin, R. 1977: *Taking Rights Seriously*. London: Duckworth.

Elfstrom, G. 1983: On dilemmas of intervention. *Ethics*, 93, 710–25.

Eliasson, J. 1993a: Confronting reality: the UN prepares for expanded duties. *Harvard International Review*, 16(1), 20–1, 64.

——1993b: The world response to humanitarian emergencies. In Cahill (ed.), 308–18.

Ellis, A. (ed.) 1986: *Ethics and International Relations*. Manchester: Manchester University Press.

European Community Humanitarian Office 1995: *ECHO Annual Report 1994: The Year of the Rwanda Tragedy*. Brussels: ECHO.

Fairley, H. 1980: State actors, humanitarian intervention and international law: reopening Pandora's box. *Georgia Journal of International and Comparative Law*, 10(1), 29–63.

Falk, R. 1981: *Human Rights and State Sovereignty*. New York: Holmes and Meier.

——1985: A new paradigm for international legal studies: prospects and proposals. In Falk et al. (eds), *International Law: A Contemporary Perspective*. Boulder, Colo.: Westview, 651–702.

——1992: *Explorations at the Edge of Time; The Prospects for World Order*. Philadelphia: Temple University Press.

——1993: Intervention revisited – hard choices and tragic dilemmas. *The Nation*, 20, Dec., 755–64.

Farer, T. 1973: Humanitarian intervention: the view from Charlottesville. In Lillich (ed.), 149–66.

——1987: The United Nations and human rights: more than a whimper, less than a roar. *Human Rights Quarterly*, 9, 550–86.

——1991: An enquiry into the legality of humanitarian intervention. In Damrosch and Scheffer (eds), 185–201.

——1993: A paradigm of legitimate intervention. In Damrosch (ed.), 316–47.

Ferris, E. 1992: NGO humanitarian intervention: ethics and pragmatics. *Life and Peace Review*, 6(4), 4–5.

——(ed.) 1992: *The Challenge to Intervene: A New Role for the United Nations?* Uppsala: Life and Peace Institute.

Fetherston, A. B. 1994: *Towards a Theory of United Nations Peacekeeping*. London and New York: Macmillan.

——Ramsbotham, O. and Woodhouse, T. 1994: UNPROFOR: some observations from a conflict resolution perspective. *International Peacekeeping*, 1(2), 179–203.

Fifoot, P. 1992: Functions and powers and inventions: UN action in respect of human rights and humanitarian intervention. In Rodley (ed.), 133–65.

Finnis, J. 1980: *Natural Law and Natural Rights*. Oxford: Oxford University Press.

Finucane, A. 1993: The changing roles of voluntary organisations. In Cahill (ed.), 175–90.

Fisher, D. 1994: The ethics of intervention. *Survival*, 36(1), 51–9.

Fonteyne, J-P. 1973: Forcible self-help by states to protect human rights: recent views from the United Nations. In Lillich (ed.), 197–222.

—— 1974: The customary international law doctrine of humanitarian intervention: its current validity under the United Nations Charter. *California Western International Law Journal*, 4(2), 203–70.

Forbes, I. and Hoffman, M. (eds) 1993: *Political Theory, International Relations and the Ethics of Intervention*. London: Macmillan.

Forsythe, D. 1977: *Humanitarian Politics: The International Committee of the Red Cross*. Baltimore: Johns Hopkins University Press.

—— 1988: *Human Rights and World Politics*, 2nd edn. Lincoln: University of Nebraska Press.

—— 1991: *The Internationalization of Human Rights*. Lexington, Mass.: Lexington Books.

Franck, T. and Rodley, N. 1973: After Bangladesh: the law of humanitarian intervention by military force. *American Journal of International Law*, 67, 275–305.

Freedman, L. (ed.) 1994: *Military Intervention in European Conflicts*. Oxford: Blackwell.

—— and Boren, D. 1992: 'Safe havens' for Kurds in post-war Iraq. In Rodley (ed.), 43–92.

Gallant, J. 1992: Humanitarian intervention and Security Council Resolution 688: a reappraisal in light of a changing world order. *American University Journal of International Law and Policy*, 7, 881–920.

Gardner, R. 1991–2: International law and the use of force. *New Dimensions in International Security*, Adelphi Paper, 266. London: IISS.

—— 1992: International law and the use of force. In Scheffer et al., 15–30.

Garigue, P. 1993: Intervention-sanction and 'droit d'ingérence' in international humanitarian law. *International Journal*, 48(4), 668–86.

Gentili, A. 1964 (1598): *De Jure Belli Libri Tres*. New York: Oceana.

Gewirth, A. 1982: *Human Rights: Essays on Justification and Application*. Chicago: University of Chicago Press.

Girardet, E. 1993: Public opinion, the media and humanitarianism. In Weiss and Minear (eds), 39–55.

Glazer, N. 1983: *Ethnic Dilemmas 1964–1982*. Cambridge, Mass.: Harvard University Press.

Glenny, M. 1992: *The Fall of Yugoslavia: The Third Balkan War*. Harmondsworth: Penguin.

Gorbachev, M. 1988: Address to the United Nations General Assembly, 7 Dec. *Soviet News*, 10 Dec.

Gordenker, L. and Weiss, T. 1991: *Soldiers, Peacekeepers and Disasters*. New York: St Martin's Press.

Grant, J. 1992: *The State of the World's Children*. New York: UNICEF.

Green, L. 1993: *The Contemporary Law of Armed Conflict.* Manchester: Manchester University Press.

Green, R. 1994: The course of the four horsemen: costs of war and its aftermath in sub-Saharan Africa. In Macrae and Zwi (eds), 37–49.

Greenwood, C. 1993: Is there a right of humanitarian intervention? *World Today*, 49(2), 34–40.

Griffiths, M., Levine, I. and Weller, M. 1993: *Sovereignty and Suffering.* London: Action Aid.

Griffiths, S. 1993: *Nationalism and Ethnic Conflict.* Oxford: Oxford University Press.

Grotius, H. 1925 (1625): *The Law of War and Peace*, tr. F. W. Kelsey. Oxford: Clarendon Press.

Guillot, P. 1994: France, peacekeeping and humanitarian intervention. *International Peacekeeping*, 1(1), 30–43.

Gurr, T. and Harff, B. 1994: *Ethnic Conflict in World Politics.* Boulder, Colo.: Westview Press.

Gutman, R. 1993: *A Witness to Genocide.* Shaftesbury: Element.

Haas, E. 1993: Beware the slippery slope: notes toward the definition of justifiable intervention. In Reed and Kaysen (eds), 63–87.

Haas, M. 1989: *The Asian Way to Peace: A Story of Regional Cooperation.* New York: Praeger.

Halliday, F. 1995: The end of the cold war and international relations: some analytic and theoretical conclusions. In Booth and Smith (eds), 38–61.

Halperin, M. and Scheffer, D. 1992: *Self-Determination in the New World Order.* Washington, DC: Carnegie Endowment.

Hampson, F. 1994: Yugoslavia: war crimes fact-finding. *International Law and Armed Conflict Commentary*, 1(1), 29–36.

Hannum, H. 1990: *Autonomy, Sovereignty and Self-Determination: The Accommodation of Conflicting Rights.* Philadelphia: University of Pennsylvania Press.

Harries, R. 1991: Human rights in theological perspective. In Blackburn and Taylor (eds), 1–13.

Hashmi, S. 1993: Is there an Islamic ethic of humanitarian intervention? *Ethics and International Affairs*, 9, 55–73.

Hassan, F. 1981: Realpolitik in international law: after [the] Tanzanian–Ugandan conflict 'humanitarian intervention' re-examined. *Willamette Law Review*, 17, 859–912.

Hawthorn, G. 1994: The crises of southern states. *Political Studies*, 42, 130–45.

Helman, G. and Ratner, S. 1992–3: Saving failed states. *Foreign Policy*, 89 (Winter), 3–30.

Henkin, L. et al. 1991: *Right v. Might: International Law and the Use of Force.* New York: Council on Foreign Relations Press.

Heraklides, A. 1991: *The Self-Determination of Minorities in International Politics.* London: Frank Cass.

Higgins, R. 1984: Intervention and international law. In Bull (ed.), 29–44.

Higgins, R. 1991: United Nations Human Rights Committee. In Blackburn and Taylor (eds), 67–74.

——1993: The new United Nations and former Yugoslavia. *International Affairs*, 69(3), 465–83.

Himes, K. 1993: Just war, pacifism and humanitarian intervention. *America*, 169 (14 Aug.), 10–15, 28–31.

Hobbes, T. 1962 (1651): *Leviathan*. London: Dent.

Hoffmann, S. 1977: *Duties beyond Borders: On the Limits and Possibilities of Ethical International Politics*. Syracuse, NY: Syracuse University Press.

——1978: *Primacy or World Order: American Foreign Policy since the Cold War*. New York: McGraw-Hill.

——1983: Reaching for the most difficult: human rights as a foreign policy goal. *Daedalus*, 112, 19–49.

——1993: Out of the cold: humanitarian intervention in the 1990s. *Harvard International Review*, Fall, 16(1), 8–9, 62–3.

Hohfeld, W. 1919: *Fundamental Legal Conceptions*. New Haven: Yale University Press.

Holsti, K. 1991: *Peace and War: Armed Conflicts and International Order 1648–1989*. Cambridge: Cambridge University Press.

Horowitz, D. 1985: *Ethnic Groups in Conflict*. Berkeley: University of California Press.

House of Commons Defence Committee, Fourth Report, Session 1992–1993: *United Kingdom Peacekeeping and Intervention Forces*. London: HMSO.

Hurd, D. 1992: Speech at Royal United Services Institute, 13 Oct. *Arms Control and Disarmament Quarterly Review*, 27, 34–5.

International Commission of Jurists 1974: *Violations of Human Rights and the Rule of Law in Uganda*. Geneva: ICJ.

——1977: *Uganda and Human Rights: Reports to the United Nations*. Geneva: ICJ.

International Committee of the Red Cross 1993: *Guiding Principles on the Right to Humanitarian Assitance*. Geneva: ICRC.

International Federation of Red Cross and Red Crescent Societies 1994: *Code of Conduct for the International Red Cross Movement and Red Crescent Movement and Non-Governmental Organizations in Disaster Relief*. Geneva: IFRCRCS.

International Journal 1993: special issue on humane intervention, 48(4), Autumn.

International Peacekeeping 1994: Peacekeeping News Digest, 1(3), 349–56.

Isaac, E. 1993: Humanitarianism across regions and cultures. In Weiss and Minear (eds), 13–22.

Ispahani, M. 1992: India's role in Sri Lanka's ethnic conflict. In Levite et al. (eds), 209–39.

Jackson, R. 1990: *Quasi-States, Sovereignty, International Relations and the Third World*. Cambridge: Cambridge University Press.

——1992: Is there an international community: intervention or isolationism? Paper presented at Dartmouth College, UN conference on 'national sovereignty and collective intervention,' 18–20, May.

——1993: Armed humanitarianism. *International Journal*, 48(4), 579–606.

James, A. 1990: *Peacekeeping in International Politics*. London: Macmillan for the International Institute for Strategic Studies.

——1993a: Internal peace-keeping: a dead end for the UN? *Security Dialogue*, 24(4), 359–68.

——1993b: System or society? *Review of International Studies*, 19(3), 259–88.

——1994: UN peacekeeping: recent developments and current problems. *Paradigms*, 8(2), 18–34.

Jansson, K., Harris, M., and Penrose, A. 1987: *The Ethiopian Famine: The Story of an Emergency Relief Operation*. London: Zed Books.

Jean, F. (ed.) 1993: *Life, Death and Aid: The Médecins Sans Frontières Report on World Crisis Intervention*. London: Routledge.

Jennings, R. and Watts, A. (eds) 1992: *Oppenheim's International Law*, 9th edn. London: Routledge, vol. 1.

Jhabvala, F. 1981: Unilateral humanitarian intervention and international law. *Indian Journal of International Law*, 21, 208–30.

Johnson, J. 1981: *Just War Tradition and the Restraint of War*. Princeton: Princeton University Press.

Jonah, J. 1993: Humanitarian intervention. In Weiss and Minear (eds), 69–84.

Jones, B. 1995: 'Intervention without borders': humanitarian intervention in Rwanda, 1990–94. *Millennium*, 24(2), 225–50.

Jones, D. 1992: The declaratory tradition in modern international law. In Nardin and Mapel (eds), 42–61.

Kalshoven, F. (ed.) 1989: *Assisting the Victims of Armed Conflicts and Other Disasters*. Dordrecht: Martinus Nijhoff.

Kampelmann, M. 1993: Secession and the right of self-determination: an urgent need to harmonize principle with pragmatism. *Washington Quarterly*, 16(3), 5–12.

Kant, I. 1991 (1793): Perpetual peace: a philosophical sketch. In H. Reiss (ed.), *Kant's Political Writings*, 2nd edn. Cambridge: Cambridge University Press, 93–130.

Kartashkin, V. 1991: Human rights and humanitarian intervention. In Damrosch and Scheffer (eds), 202–11.

Keen, D. and Wilson, J. 1994: Engaging with violence: a reassessment of relief in wartime. In Macrae and Zwi (eds), 209–21.

Keen, M. 1965: *The Laws of War in the Late Middle Ages*. London: Routledge and Kegan Paul.

Kennan, G. 1985–6: Morality and foreign policy. *Foreign Affairs*, 64, 205–18.

Kennedy, P. 1993: *Preparing for the Twenty First Century*. London: Harper Collins.

Keohane, R. and Nye, J. 1977: *Power and Interdependence: World Politics in Transition*. Boston: Little, Brown and Co.

Kirkpatrick, J. and Gerson, A. 1991: The Reagan doctrine, human rights and international law. In Henkin et al., 19–34.

Klare, M. 1995: Flawed but vital. *Bulletin of the Atomic Scientists*, 51(2), 62–5.

Klintworth, G. 1989: *Vietnam's Intervention in Cambodia in International Law*. Canberra: AGPS Press.

——1991: The 'right to intervene' in the domestic affairs of states. *Australian Journal of International Affairs*, 46 (Nov.), 249–66.

Kouchner, B. 1992: A call for humanitarian intervention. *Refugees*, 91, 14–15.

Krasner, S. 1985: *Structural Conflict: The Third World versus Global Capitalism*. Berkeley: University of California Press.

——(ed.) 1983: *International Regimes*. Ithaca, NY: Cornell University Press.

Kriesberg, L. et al. (eds) 1989: *Intractable Conflicts and their Transformation*. Syracuse, NY: Syracuse University Press.

Kuper, L. 1981: *Genocide: Its Political Use in the Twentieth Century*. New York: Penguin.

——1985: *The Prevention of Genocide*. New Haven: Yale University Press.

Kyemba, H. 1977: *State of Blood*. London: Transworld Publishers.

Lake, A. (ed.) 1990: *After the Wars: Reconstruction in Afghanistan, Indochina, Central America, Southern Africa, the Horn of Africa*. New Brunswick, NJ: Transaction Publishers.

Lauterpacht, H. 1955 (1906): Oppenheim's *International Law*, 8th edn. London: Longmans, Green.

Levite, A., Jentleson, B. and Berman, L. (eds) 1992: *Foreign Military Intervention: The Dynamics of Protracted Conflict*. New York: Columbia University Press.

Levitin, M. 1986: The law of force and the force of law: Grenada, the Falklands and humanitarian intervention. *Harvard International Law Journal*, 27(2), 621–57.

Lewer, N. and Ramsbotham, O. 1993: *'Something Must be Done': Towards an Ethical Framework for Humanitarian Intervention*. Bradford: Department of Peace Studies.

Lewis, I. 1993: *Understanding Somalia: Guide to Culture, History and Social Institutions*. London: Haan Associates.

——1994: *Blood and Bone: The Call of Kinship in Somali Society*. Lawrenceville, NJ: Red Sea Press.

Lillich, R. 1967: Forcible self-help by states to protect human rights. *Iowa Law Review*, 53, 325–51.

——(ed.) 1973: *Humanitarian Intervention and the United Nations*. Charlottesville: University of Virginia Press.

Little, R. 1975: *Intervention: External Involvement in Internal Wars*. Totowa, NJ: Rowman and Littlefield.

——1993: Recent literature on intervention and non-intervention. In Forbes and Hoffman (eds), 13–31.

Luard, E. 1981: *Human Rights and Foreign Policy*. Oxford: Pergamon Press.

——(ed.) 1992: *Basic Texts in International Relations*. London: Macmillan.

Luban, D. 1980a: Just war and human rights. *Philosophy and Public Affairs*, 9(2), 160–81.
——1980b: The romance of the nation state. *Philosophy and Public Affairs*, 9(4), 392–7.
Macalister-Smith, P. 1985: *International Humanitarian Assistance – Disaster Relief Actions in International Law and Organization*. Dordrecht: Martinus Nijhoff.
MacFarlane, N. and Weiss, T. 1992–3: Regional organisations and regional security. *Security Studies*, 2(3), 6–37.
Mackinlay, J. 1994: Improving multifunctional forces. *Survival*, 36(3), 150–74.
——and Alao, A. 1994: *Liberia 1994: ECOMOG and UNOMIL – Response to a Complex Emergency*. New York: United Nations University Occasional Paper.
——and Chopra, J. 1992: Second generation multinational operations. *Washington Quarterly*, 15(3), 113–31.
Macrae, J. and Zwi, A. (eds) 1994: *War and Hunger: Rethinking International Responses to Complex Emergencies*. London: Zed Books for Save the Children Fund (UK).
Makinda, S. 1993a: *Seeking Peace from Chaos: Humanitarian Intervention in Somalia*, International Peace Academy Occasional Paper. Boulder, Colo.: Lynne Rienner.
——1993b: Somalia: from humanitarian intervention to military offensive. *World Today*, 49 (Feb.) 184–6.
Malanczuk, P. 1993: *Humanitarian Intervention and the Legitimacy of the Use of Force*. Amsterdam: Martinus Nijhoff.
Mandelbaum, M. 1994: The reluctance to intervene. *Foreign Policy*, 95, 3–18.
Mapel, D. 1991: Military intervention and rights. *Millennium: Journal of International Studies*, 20(1), 41–55.
Martin, D. 1974: *General Amin*. London: Faber and Faber.
Mayall, J. 1990: *Nationalism and International Society*. Cambridge: Cambridge University Press.
——1991: Non-intervention, self-determination and the 'New World Order'. *International Affairs*, 67(3), 421–9.
Maynes, C. 1993: Containing ethnic conflict. *Foreign Policy*, 90 (Spring), 3–21.
Mazarr, M. 1993: The military dilemmas of humanitarian intervention. *Security Dialogue*, 24(2), 151–62.
McCain, J. 1994: To intervene or not to intervene? *Armed Forces Journal*, Sep., 67–9.
McCoubrey, H. 1990: *International Humanitarian Law*. Aldershot: Dartmouth.
——and White, N. 1995: *International Organizations and Civil Wars*. Aldershot: Dartmouth.
McGarry, J. and O'Leary, B. (eds) 1993: *The Politics of Ethnic Conflict Regulation*. London: Routledge.

McMahon, J. 1986: The ethics of international intervention. In Ellis (ed.), 24–60.

Mehic, D. 1995: 'Your protection is killing us', *Bulletin of the Atomic Scientists*, 5/(2), 41–4.

Meron, T. 1986: *Human Rights Law-Making in the United Nations: A Critique of Instrument and Process*. Oxford: Clarendon Press.

——1987: *Human Rights in Internal Strife: Their International Protection*. Cambridge: Grotius Publications.

——1991a: Commentary. In Damrosch and Scheffer (eds), 212–14.

——1991b: Common rights of mankind in Gentili, Grotius and Suarez. *American Journal of International Law*, 85, 110–16.

——and Rosas, A. 1991: A declaration of minimum humanitarian standards. *American Journal of International Law*, 85, 375–81.

Metz, H. (ed.) 1990: *Iraq: A Country Study*. Washington, DC: Library of Congress.

Mill, J. S. 1959 (1875): A few words on non-intervention. In *Dissertations and Discussions, Political, Philosophical and Historical*. vol. 3, London: Longman, Green, Reader and Dyer, 147–78.

Minear, L. 1991: *Humanitarianism under Siege: A Critical Review of Operation Lifeline Sudan*. Trenton, NJ: Red Sea Press.

——and Weiss, T. 1993: *Humanitarian Action in Times of War*. Boulder, Colo.: Lynne Rienner.

Montville, J. (ed.) 1990: *Conflict and Peacekeeping in Multiethnic Societies*. Lexington, Mass.: Lexington Books.

Moore, J. 1972: The control of foreign intervention in internal conflict. In *Law and the Indo-China War*. Princeton: Princeton University Press, 115–286.

——1974: Toward an applied theory for the regulation of intervention. In Moore (ed.), 3–37.

——(ed.) 1974: *Law and Civil War in the Modern World*. Baltimore: Johns Hopkins University Press.

Morgenthau, H. 1967: To intervene or not to intervene. *Foreign Affairs*, 45(3), 425–36.

Morris, J. 1991: The concept of humanitarian intervention in international relations. MA dissertation, University of Hull.

Moynihan, D. 1993: *Pandaemonium: Ethnicity in International Politics*. Oxford: Oxford University Press.

Mugabe, R. 1994: Address. Royal Institute of International Affairs, London, 20 May.

Nafziger, J. 1991: Self-determination and humanitarian intervention in a community of power. *Denver Journal of International Law and Policy*, 20(1), 9–39.

Nanda, V. 1992: Humanitarian intervention and international law. In Ferris (ed.), 27–38.

——Farer, T. and D'Amato, A. 1990: Agora: US forces in Panama: defenders, aggressors or human rights activists? *American Journal of International Law*, 84, 494–524.

Nardin, T. and Mapel, D. (eds) 1992: *Traditions of International Ethics*. Cambridge: Cambridge University Press.

Natsios, A. 1993: Food through force: humanitarian intervention and US policy. *Washington Quarterly*, 17(1), 129–44.

——1995: The international humanitarian response system. *Parameters*, 25(1), 68–81.

Nicholls, B. 1987: Rubber band humanitarianism. *Ethics and International Affairs*, 1, 191–210.

Niebuhr, R. 1932: *Moral Man and Immoral Society: A Study in Ethics and Politics*. New York: Scribner.

Northrup, T. 1989: The dynamic of identity in personal and social conflict. In Kriesberg et al., 55–82.

O'Brien, W. 1981: *The Conduct of Just and Limited War*. New York: Praeger.

——1990: *Law and Morality in Israel's War with the PLO*. London: Routledge.

Ofuatey-Kodjoe, W. 1994: Regional organisations and the resolution of internal conflict: the ECOWAS intervention in Liberia. *International Peacekeeping*, 1(3), 261–302.

Ogata, S. 1993: *The State of the World's Refugees: The Challenge of Protection*. New York: Penguin.

O'Halloran, P. 1995: Humanitarian intervention and the genocide in Rwanda. *Conflict Studies*, 277, 1–32.

Onuf, N. 1971: The principle of nonintervention, the United Nations and the international system. *International Organization*, 25, 209–27.

Owen, D. 1993: Obligations and responsibilities of donor nations. In Cahill (ed.), 52–62.

Palwankar, U. (ed.) 1994: *Symposium on Humanitarian Action and Peacekeeping Operations – Report*. Geneva: International Committee of the Red Cross.

Parekh, B. 1995: Beyond humanitarian intervention. Unpublished paper.

Pastor, R. 1993: Forward to the beginning: widening the scope for global collective action. *International Journal*, 48(4), 641–67.

Pease, K. and Forsythe, D. 1993: Human rights, humanitarian intervention and world politics. *Human Rights Quarterly*, 15(2), 290–314.

Pictet, J. 1979: *The Fundamental Principles of the Red Cross: Commentary*. Geneva: Henry Dunant Institute.

——1985: *Development and Principles of International Humanitarian Law*. Dordrecht: Martinus Nijhoff.

——1988: International humanitarian law: definition. In UNESCO 1988, xix–xxii.

Pilger, J. 1994: *Distant Voices*, 2nd edn. London: Vintage.

Plant, R. 1993: The justifications for intervention: needs before contexts. In Forbes and Hoffman (eds), 104–12.

Pogany, I. 1986: Humanitarian intervention in international law: the French intervention in Syria re-examined. *International and Comparative Law Quarterly*, 35, 182–90.

Pollis, A. and Schwab, P. (eds) 1980: *Human Rights: Cultural and Ideological Perspectives.* New York: Praeger.

Posen, B. 1993: The security dilemma and ethnic conflict. In M. Brown (ed.), 103–24.

Powell, S. 1994: American troops – American command. *Airforce Magazine*, Jan., 46–9.

Prasso, S. 1995: Cambodia a three billion dollar boondoggle. *Bulletin of the Atomic Scientists*, 51(2), 36–40.

Presidential Decision Directive 25 1994: *The Clinton Administration's Policy on Reforming Multilateral Peace Operations.* Executive Summary. Washington, DC: Department of State Publication 10161.

Quigley, E. 1983: Humanitarian intervention: a possibility for Northern Ireland. *Denver Journal of International Law and Policy*, 12, 295–306.

Quinn, D. (ed.) 1994: *Peace Support Operations and the US Military.* Washington, DC: National Defense University Press.

Rahman, S. 1993: Disaster in Bangladesh: a multinational relief effort. *Naval War College Review*, 46(1), 58–72.

Ramsbotham, O.: Towards an ethical framework for humanitarian intervention. *Review of International Studies*, forthcoming.

Rapoport, A. 1971: Various conceptions of peace research. *Peace Research Society*, 19, 91–106.

Ramet, S. 1992 (1984): *Nationalism and Federalism in Yugoslavia 1962–1991*, 2nd edn. Indianapolis: Indiana University Press.

Rawls, J. 1972: *A Theory of Justice.* Oxford: Oxford University Press.

Reed, L. and Kaysen, C. (eds) 1993: *Emerging Norms of Justified Intervention.* Cambridge Mass.: American Academy of Arts and Sciences.

Reisman, M. 1990: Sovereignty and human rights in contemporary international law. *American Journal of International Law*, 84, 866–76.

——and McDougal, M. 1973: Humanitarian intervention to protect the Ibos. In Lillich (ed.), 167–96.

Renteln, A. 1990: *International Human Rights: Universalism versus Relativism.* Newbury Park: Sage.

Rieff, D. 1994a: The illusions of peacekeeping. *World Policy Journal*, 11(3), 1–18.

——1994b: The United Nations: accomplice to genocide. *Balkan War Report*, 28 (Sept.), 35–40.

——1995: *Slaughterhouse: Bosnia and the Failure of the West.* London: Vintage.

Rinaldo, R. 1994: Communication. *Defense News*, 21–7 Mar., 8–10.

Rivlin, B. 1992: Regional arrangements and the UN system for collective security and conflict resolution. *International Relations*, 11(2), 95–108.

Roberts, A. 1990: Law, lawyers and nuclear weapons. *Review of International Studies*, 16(1), 75–92.

——1993a: Humanitarian war: military intervention and human rights. *International Affairs*, 69, 429–49.

——1993b: 'The road to hell': a critique of humanitarian intervention. *Harvard International Review*, 16(1), 10–13, 63.

——1994: The crisis in UN peacekeeping. *Survival*, 36(3), 93–120.

Rodley, N. 1989: Human rights and humanitarian intervention: the case law of the World Court. *International and Comparative Law Quarterly*, 38, 321–33.

——1992: Collective intervention to protect human rights and civilian populations: the legal framework. In Rodley (ed.), 14–42.

——(ed.) 1992: *To Loose the Bands of Wickedness. International Intervention in Defence of Human Rights*. London: Brassey's.

Rogers, P. and Dando, M. 1992: *A Violent Peace*. London: Brassey's.

Ronzitti, N. 1985: *Rescuing Nationals Abroad through Military Coercion and Intervention on Grounds of Humanity*. Dordrecht: Martinus Nijhoff.

Rosenau, J. 1969: Intervention as a scientific concept. *Journal of Conflict Resolution*, 13, 149–71.

Ross, M. 1993: *The Culture of Conflict: Interpretations and Interests in Comparative Perspective*. New Haven: Yale University Press.

Rufin, J. 1993: The paradoxes of armed protection. In Jean (ed.), 111–23.

Ruggie, J. 1993: Wandering in the void. *Foreign Affairs*, 72, 26–31.

Rupesinghe, K. (ed.) 1992: *Internal Conflict and Governance*. London: Macmillan.

Ryan, K. 1991: Rights, intervention and self-determination. *Denver Journal of International Law*, 20(1), 55–71.

Ryan, S. 1990: *Ethnic Conflict and International Relations*. Brookfield, Vt.: Dartmouth.

Sahnoun, M. 1994: Prevention in conflict revolution: the case of Somalia. *Irish Studies in International Affairs*, 5, 5–13.

Sandoz, Y. 1992: Droit ou devoir d'ingérence and the right to assistance: the issues involved. *International Review of the Red Cross*, 32(2), 215–27.

——1993: *A Consideration of the Implementation of International Humanitarian Law and the Role of the International Committee of the Red Cross in the Former Yugoslavia*. Geneva: ICRC.

Schachter, O. 1984: The legality of pro-democratic invasion. *American Journal of International Law*, 78, 645–50.

Scheffer, D. 1992: Toward a modern doctrine of humanitarian intervention. *University of Toledo Law Review*, 23, 253–93.

——Gardner, R. and Helman, G. 1992: *Three Views on the Issue of Humanitarian Intervention*. Washington, DC: United States Institute of Peace.

Scoble, H. and Wiseberg, L. (eds) 1985: *Access to Justice: Human Rights Struggles in South-East Asia*. London: Zed Books.

Scott, C. 1993: Humanitarian intervention revisited. Unpublished M.Sc. dissertation. London School of Economics.

Sesay, A. 1995: Humanitarian intervention in Liberia: implications for state and sub-regional security, and international society. Paper delivered at LSE, 13 May, unpublished.

Sharp, J. 1993: Intervention in Bosnia – the case for. *World Today*, 49(2), 29–32.

Shue, H. 1980: *Basic Rights: Subsistence, Affluence and U.S. Foreign Policy*. Princeton: Princeton University Press.

Singer, P. 1993: *Practical Ethics*. Cambridge: Cambridge University Press.

Sivard, R. 1993: *World Military and Social Expenditures*. Washington, DC: World Priorities.

Slater, J. and Nardin, T. 1986: Nonintervention and human rights. *Journal of Politics*, 48, 89–96.

Slim, H. and Penrose, A. 1994: UN reform in a changing world: responding to complex emergencies. In MacCrae and Zwi (eds), 194–208.

Smith, A. 1986: *The Ethnic Origins of Nations*. Oxford: Blackwell.

Smith, H. (ed.) 1993: *Peacekeeping: Challenges for the Future*. Canberra: Australian Defence Studies Center.

Smith, M. 1989: Ethics and intervention. Paper presented at International Studies Association Conference, London, Mar.

Smith, T. 1994: In defence of intervention. *Foreign Affairs*, 73(6), 34–46.

Sornarajah, M. 1981: Internal colonialism and humanitarian intervention. *Georgia Journal of International and Comparative Law*, 11(1), 45–77.

Stedman, S. 1993: The new interventionists. *Foreign Affairs*, 72, 1–16.

Steinberg, J. 1993: International involvement in the Yugoslavia conflict. In Damrosch (ed.), 27–76.

Stevenson, J. 1993: Hope restored in Somalia? *Foreign Policy*, 91, 138–54.

Stromseth, J. 1993: Iraqi repression of its civilian population: collective response and contingency challenges. In Damrosch (ed.), 76–117.

Swidler, A. (ed.) 1982: *Human Rights in Religious Traditions*. New York: Pilgrim.

Taylor, P. 1993: *Options for Reform of the International System for Humanitarian Assistance*. London: Centre for the Study of Global Governance and Save the Children Fund (UK).

Tesón, F. 1988: *Humanitarian Intervention: An Inquiry into Law and Morality*. Dobbs Ferry, NY: Transnational Publishers.

Thomas, A. and Thomas, A. 1956: *Non-Intervention: The Law and its Import in the Americas*. Dallas: Southern Methodist University Press.

Thomas, C. 1985: *New States, Sovereignty and Intervention*. London: Gower.

—— 1993: The pragmatic case against intervention. In Forbes and Hoffman (eds), 91–103.

—— 1994: Human rights and intervention: a case for caution. *Irish Studies in International Affairs*, 5, 15–33.

—— and Saravanamuttu, P. (eds) 1989: *Conflict and Consensus in North/South Security*. Cambridge: Cambridge University Press.

Toland, J. (ed.) 1993: *Ethnicity and the State*. New Brunswick, NJ: Transaction Press.

Tolley, H. 1987: *The United Nations Commission on Human Rights*. Boulder, Colo.: Westview.

Tomasevski, K. 1994: Human rights and wars of starvation. In Macrae and Zwi (eds), 70–90.

Torrelli, M. 1992: From humanitarian assistance to 'intervention on humanitarian grounds'. *International Review of the Red Cross*, 288, 228–48.

Trachtenberg, M. 1993: Intervention in historical perspective. In Reed and Kaysen (eds), 15–36.

UK Ministry of Defence 1995: *Wider Peacekeeping*. London: HMSO.

Umozurike, U. 1982: Tanzanian intervention in Uganda. *Archiv des Volkerrecht*, 20, 301–13.

UNESCO 1988: *International Dimensions of Humanitarian Law*. Dordrecht: Martinus Nijhoff.

United Nations 1994: *United Nations Peacekeeping: Information Notes*. New York: UN Department of Public Information, June.

US Army 1994: *FM 100–23: Peace Operations*. Washington, DC: Headquarters Department of the Army, Dec.

Vasak, K. 1977: A thirty-year struggle. *UNESCO Courier*, 29–32.

——1988: Conclusions. In UNESCO, 297–9.

Vassall-Adams, G. 1994: *Rwanda: An Agenda for International Action*. Oxford: Oxfam.

Vattel, E. de 1964 (1758): *The Law of Nations or the Principles of Natural Law Applied to the Conduct and to the Affairs of Nations and of Sovereigns*. Dobbs Ferry, NY: Oceana Publications.

Verwey, W. 1985: Humanitarian intervention under international law. *Netherlands International Law Review*, 32, 357–418.

——1986: Humanitarian intervention. In Cassese (ed.), 57–78.

——1992: Legality of humanitarian intervention after the cold war. In Ferris (ed.), 113–22.

Vincent, R. 1974: *Nonintervention and International Order*. Princeton: Princeton University Press.

——1986: *Human Rights and International Relations*. Cambridge: Cambridge University Press.

——1990: Grotius, human rights and intervention. In Bull et al. (eds), 241–56.

——1992: The idea of rights in international ethics. In Nardin and Mapel (eds), 250–69.

——(ed.) 1986: *Foreign Policy and Human Rights*. Cambridge: Cambridge University Press.

——and Wilson, P. 1993: Beyond non-intervention. In Forbes and Hoffman (eds), 122–32.

Volkan, V., Julius, D. and Montville, J. (eds) 1991: *The Psychodynamics of International Relationships*. Lexington, Mass.: D.C. Heath.

Von Hippel, K. 1995: Operation Uphold Democracy: a case of successful intervention? Paper delivered at LSE, 13 May, unpublished.

Wallensteen, P. and Axell, K. 1994: Conflict resolution and the end of the cold war 1989–1993. *Journal of Peace Research*, 31(3), 333–49.

Walzer, M. 1980: The moral standing of states: a response to four critics. *Philosophy and Public Affairs*, 9(3), 209–29.

——1983: *Spheres of Justice: A Defence of Pluralism and Equality.* Oxford: Martin Robertson.

Walzer, M. 1992 (1977): *Just and Unjust Wars: A Moral Argument with Historical Illustrations.* 2nd edn. London: Basic Books.

Wasserstrom, R. 1978: Review of Walzer 1992 (1977). *Harvard Law Review,* 92, 536–45.

Weiss, T. 1994a: Intervention: whither the United Nations? *Washington Quarterly,* 17, 109–28.

——1994b: Triage: humanitarian intervention in a new era. *World Policy Journal,* 11(1), 59–68.

——1994c: UN responses in the former Yugoslavia: moral and operational choices. *Ethics and International Affairs,* 8, 1–22.

——and Campbell, K. 1991: Military humanitarianism. *Survival,* 33(5), 451–65.

——and Minear, L. 1991: Do international ethics matter? Humanitarian politics in the Sudan. *Ethics and International Affairs,* 5, 197–214.

————(eds) 1993: *Humanitarianism across Borders: Sustaining Civilians in Times of War.* London: Lynne Rienner.

——Forsythe, D. and Coats, R. 1994: *The United Nations and Changing World Politics.* Boulder, Colo.: Westview Press.

Wheeler, N. 1992: Pluralist or solidarist conceptions of international society: Bull and Vincent on humanitarian intervention. *Millennium,* 21(3), 463–88.

White, N. 1993: *Keeping the Peace: The United Nations and the Maintenance of International Peace and Security.* Milland Schill Monographs in International Law. Manchester and New York: Manchester University Press.

——1994: Humanitarian intervention. *International Law and Armed Conflict Commentary,* 1(1), 13–27.

Wight, M. 1979: *Power Politics.* Harmondsworth: Penguin.

Williams, B. 1985: *Ethics and the Limits of Philosophy.* London: Fontana.

Williams, P. 1989: Intervention in the developing world: a Northern perspective. In C. Thomas and Saravanamuttu (eds), 144–58.

Wippman, D. 1993: Enforcing the peace: ECOWAS and the Liberian civil war. In Damrosch (ed.) 157–204.

Woodward, S. 1994: *Balkan Tragedy: Chaos and Disintegration After the Cold War.* Washington, DC: Brookings Institution.

World Conference on Religion and Peace 1994: *The Mohonk Criteria for Humanitarian Assistance in Complex Emergencies.* New York: Programme on Humanitarian Assistance, World Conference on Religion and Peace.

Wright, R. 1989: A contemporary theory of humanitarian intervention. *Florida International Law Journal,* 4, 435–63.

Zametica, J. 1992: *The Yugoslav Conflict,* Adelphi Paper 270, London: Brassey's for the IISS.

Zartman, W. 1985: *Ripe for Resolution: Conflict and Intervention in Africa.* Oxford: Oxford University Press.

Zimbler, B. 1984: Peacekeeping without the UN: the multinational force in Lebanon and international law. *Yale Journal of International Law*, 10, 222–51.

Zuberi, M. 1989: Intervention in the developing world: a Southern perspective. In C. Thomas and Saravanamuttu (eds), 135–43.

Index